PREHISTORIC
MAN IN EUROPE

PREHISTORIC
MAN IN EUROPE

by Frank C. Hibben

NORMAN
UNIVERSITY OF OKLAHOMA PRESS

By Frank C. Hibben

Hunting American Bears (Philadelphia, 1945)
The Lost Americans (New York, 1946)
Hunting American Lions (New York, 1948)
Treasure in the Dust (Philadelphia, 1951)
Le Livre des Ours (Paris, 1952)
L'Homme Primitif Américain (Paris, 1953)
Prehistoric Man in Europe (Norman, 1958)

The publication of this volume has been aided by a grant from the Ford Foundation.

Library of Congress Catalog Card Number: 58–11608

TO MY FATHER AND MOTHER

Who encouraged me in the pursuit
of Antiquity

Preface

THIS WORK covering prehistoric man in Europe is based upon the notes of the late Vladimir Fewkes, authority on European beginnings and for many years connected with the American School of Prehistoric Research. Professor Fewkes, with his intimate knowledge of European languages and his wide travels, had amassed an extraordinary amount of information concerning the foundations of prehistoric Europe. However, with the exception of a comparatively small amount of material which was published prior to World War II, he had collected all of his work into an extensive set of notes for eventual formation into a book on European prehistory. His untimely death in 1941 prevented his final writing and publication of the proposed volume.

One of Professor Fewkes' students, James Gaul, who had already done extensive work in the region of the lower Danube, took up the unfinished task. However, Gaul, who was a member of the Office of Strategic Services (O.S.S.) during World War II, dropped by parachute behind enemy lines and was killed there in the performance of his duty.

In this way Professor Fewkes' notes and the task of formulating them into a book on European prehistory fell into the present writer's hands. At a distance from the European field and with immediately available library sources of only mediocre caliber, it was difficult to check the original notes. In the summer of 1951, aided by a sabbatical leave from the University of New Mexico, a trip was made to Europe to consult with authorities there and to use library material available only on the Continent.

With the very kind and certainly indispensable aid of these European leaders in the field of prehistory, a number of palaeographic errors and other misconceptions in the original notes were corrected. A special effort was made to modernize Professor Fewkes' concepts in those areas where considerable work has been done since his death. In some portions of the manuscript the present writing bears little resemblance to the original notes. Also, in many cases one or another authority was not followed in exact detail, but rather a composite picture is presented, reconciling, wherever possible, differences in the interpretation of data.

There undoubtedly remain portions of the outline of prehistoric Europe as here presented with which some scholars will not agree. (Any errors which may still be present are undoubtedly those of the writer and not of Professor Fewkes.) However, it is hoped that these differences are minor and will not detract from the story of the fascinating beginnings of Western civilization.

FRANK C. HIBBEN

Albuquerque, N. M.
September 10, 1958

Acknowledgments

IT IS WITH GREAT HUMILITY that the author acknowledges the assistance and inspiration of the following authorities:

Professor C. F. C. Hawkes, of Keble College, Oxford, England, graciously read the manuscript and aided with major corrections and additions from his great store of knowledge of European prehistory.

Professor V. Gordon Childe of the Archaeological Institute, London, England, also read the manuscript and made many valuable suggestions for its improvement. Professor Childe more than any other person, has reconstructed the sequence of events which are the background of Europe.

Professor Vladimir Milojcic of the *Institut für Vor-Und-Frühgeschichte* of München, Germany, contributed largely to the formation of those chapters dealing with the European Neolithic in which field Professor Milojcic is the leading authority.

Professor George Gaylord Simpson of the American Museum of

Natural History of New York kindly read the geological introduction and suggested improvements.

Professor R. O. Hubbe of the Classics Department of the University of New Mexico graciously read the portion of the book which deals with his field and suggested improvements.

Mr. Harper Kelley of the *Musée de l'Homme,* Paris, France, and Abbé Breuil of the same institution gave freely of their time in the examination of charts of chronology and those portions of the manuscript which deal with the Palaeolithic.

In addition to these specific authorities, a host of others at the British Museum, *Musée de l'Homme,* the University of Heidelberg, the University of Erlangen, Harvard University, the American Museum of Natural History, and, not the least, at the University of New Mexico aided with specific portions of the work and gave valuable advice.

This study of man in European prehistory is, then, not the product of a single person but the composite work of many authorities with differing specialties and points of view.

FRANK C. HIBBEN

Contents

Illustrations

Maps and Charts

PREHISTORIC
MAN IN EUROPE

CHAPTER I

Our Culture

Actually, there is no such thing as prehistory. The distinction between history and prehistory is based solely on the presence or absence of written records. Among some ancient cultures, the written story of their beginnings was initiated very early. Other peoples have not, even in the twentieth century, adopted a written form for recording their past.

But every succession of cultural precedent, whether stabilized by some system of glyphs or evolving in an unformalized and seemingly unrecorded state, has left behind abundant evidences of its passing. Anthropologists, drawing lavishly upon all other sciences, have developed techniques for wringing information from the clues which all people have left behind them. In this way, histories have been recorded which were apparently lost because no chronicler had written of their being or progress. Obviously, then, the separation between history and prehistory is a highly artificial one. These two interests are but two ends of the same process.

There are many strains of culture which may be regarded from the point of view of either the historian or the anthropologist. Certain of these are well known and amply documented. Others are only now being rounded out by increasingly refined techniques. From the purely scientific point of view, we might choose for study any one of a dozen such cultural sequences with equal profit. It is peculiarly pertinent, however, that New World scholars, as well as students in general, study European beginnings in preference to any others at the present time.

It is obvious that the cultures of the Latin American countries, the United States, and Canada are founded upon the European. This sequence of events has given rise to the term "Western civilization" to describe this connection and its location in contrast to more oriental evolutions of history. The European is "our" culture, and for this reason alone would be of utmost importance.

By a series of scientific accidents, the backgrounds of Europe have been studied more than prehistories in other parts of the world. More discoveries have been made because of intense European interest. New techniques of dating and correlation have been worked out here. More evidences of the early evolution of man as a physical being have been made in Europe because they were sought for, and not because such fossils were in greater abundance in the substrata of European soils. Prehistory as a science integrated with other sciences was born in Europe.

In addition to the above reasons for making European beginnings a part of our education, there is a present-day phenomenon which intensifies this urgency. European ways are profoundly affecting the formation of most other important cultures of the world. It is true that this process has been long in the making. European countries have penetrated all continents of the globe and most of the islands, leaving the contaminating hallmarks of European ways. But even as the European empires are shrinking beneath the impact of a wave of nationalism and independence, these same peoples who are casting off European domination are adopting, as rapidly as possible, European culture. This manifestation is most obvious in the adoption of European industrial techniques, but there are other indications as well. European dress, philosophy, modes of government, and even

4

language are spreading cultural stains which may in time dye the world all the same color.

With European culture thus established as the most important civilization study of the world today, it is disappointing to find that so much of the work that has been done deals with the period of political history. The sources for the earliest beginnings are varied and not always in agreement. Especially difficult is the transition from the prehistoric to the modern. Most of the confusion stems from the fact that European prehistory was originally divided into "schools."

The first, and for many years the only study of European foundations was the "classic." Scholars following this line of inquiry steeped themselves in Latin and Greek and reveled in exploring the glories of Athens, Rome, Antioch, and Alexandria and speculating upon their contributions to Western civilization. Classicism became a calling that amounted, at its height, to an obsession. Archaeologists, seeking to elucidate obscure details of Greek and Roman history, professed contempt for the "barbarian" cultures which made up the bulk of Europe during these same times. And yet it became increasingly obvious that these crude and unclassic peoples to the north had also contributed greatly to the formation of later Europe.

Another school of scientific inquiry in Europe was that of the typologists, who laid their arguments upon the first crude flint weapons discovered in northern France. With this as a beginning, the typological fraternity evolved a story of human origins based upon successive discoveries of the new kinds of flint tools. Stratigraphy strengthened these arguments, but the primary premise of typological thought was that tool development progressed from "crude to refined." The classicists and the typological students had little in common, and might as well have been studying different parts of the world.

At the end of the nineteenth century and the beginning of the twentieth, a new interest was added to the other schools of thought. This was the study of mankind's beginnings by means of certain fossil bone finds which turned up in Asia, Africa, and Europe. Through these discoveries, a trend in evolution could be traced by which bestial and subhuman types of primates gradually developed into morpholologically modern types of men. Students were fascinated to find that even Palaeoanthropic peoples were essentially human in some in-

5

stances, in spite of the fact that their head and body contours were primitive. Some attempts were made to correlate the various "fossil" types of humans with particular varieties of early tools and thus round out the prehistoric picture. However, such correlations were very unsatisfactory, in the earliest categories especially. In some instances, the evidence was confusing, with modern and primitive types of humans appearing to be contemporaries instead of succeeding one another in a logical evolutionary sequence.

The first decades of scientific interest in European beginnings were thus hampered by schisms of interest and lines of inquiry. It has been only within the last few years that some of the obvious has been accomplished in the form of combining these studies into an understandable whole. Much of this correlation yet remains to be done.

The roles of professions other than history and anthropology cannot be overemphasized in the process of discovering the foundations of European civilization. Biology, anatomy, geology, chemistry, physics, mathematics, the new science of atomic fission, and a host of other lines of research have all contributed to the whole. We may truly say now that all the sciences are aiding in the revelation of the beginnings of man.

CHAPTER 2

The Stage and the Scenery

THE STORY of human origins makes a fascinating drama. For this cosmic play, the continental stage and environmental scenery in the background shift and change as the action progresses. The acts of the drama are the periods of geological time in which the various phases in the evolution of man took place.

The great drama of mankind did not unfold exclusively in Europe. Indeed, many authorities are impressed by the ample indications that major parts of the play occurred in Asia, or even in Africa. From time to time it will be necessary to allude to the other land masses of the Old World in order to explain occurrences in the European peninsula.

In all of these Old World places, the greatest aid to an understanding of the time sequence of the human drama has been geology. Scientists concerning themselves with the age of the earth and the living things on its surface have evolved a comprehensive story, only a small portion of which deals with man. And yet it is in the geolog-

7

TABLE OF GEOLOGICAL TIME

Eras	Periods	Life Forms
Cenozoic 60 million years	Pleistocene—Quaternary	Man
	Pliocene	
	Miocene	Apes and other primates evolve
	Tertiary	
	Oligocene	
	Eocene	Apes appear
	Palaeocene	First placental mammals
Mesozoic 130 million years	Upper Cretaceous	Extinction of dinosaurs Reptiles dominant in sea, on land, and in air
	Lower Cretaceous	Flowering plants
	Jurassic	Birds appear
	Triassic	First dinosaurs Primitive mammals appear
Palaeozoic 360 million years	Permian	Reptiles evolve
	Pennsylvanian	*Amphibians,* ferns and non-flowering plants
	Mississippian	
	Devonian	Age of fishes
	Silurian	Land plants develop
	Ordovician	First fishes
	Cambrian	Age of invertebrates
Proterozoic 900 million years	Precambrian	Shellfish appear
		Primitive plants and animals begin to evolve
		Algaes
Archaeozoic 550 million years	Precambrian	First life

ical picture that we can first fix the relative position of humans in respect to their surroundings.

The geologic time scale shows that our planet has been in a constant state of flux. Geologists have given convenient names to successive series of rocks and strata which are the remaining indications of these planetary vicissitudes. Other branches of the geological sciences, especially concerned with the story of living things in relation to the earth, have supplemented the pure rock studies with fossil sequences which have served to strengthen and supplement the geological time scale. All of these studies have reconstructed a sequence of events which is now accepted in its essentials by all informed scholars.

If we visualize as the acts of our drama these geological periods which have marked off the age of the earth into divisions of time, it is immediately apparent that man is not a major character in the play. Actually, human life did not come on the world stage until the action had almost run out. Evidences of human beginnings, from a geological point of view, occur only in the most recent strata. Even in relative studies, evidences of man occupy only the last fragment of geological time.

Although most geological time sequences dated one event in its relation to others, many of these series have now been placed against a background of absolute chronology by means developed by the physical sciences. One of the most revealing of these is a time scale evolved by close analysis of the "heavier than lead" metals.

It was found that these substances give off radiations at a regular and predictable rate. Many inquiries with regard to substances which behave in this way have, of course, been made in connection with recent atomic developments. Scientists interested in the degeneration of these strange metals in connection with geological and cultural chronologies have utilized the substances thorium and uranium for the most part. In the process of throwing off alpha, beta, and gamma rays, thorium and uranium eventually degenerate into lead. The process of change from thorium to lead is half completed in eighteen hundred million years. Insomuch as this process takes place at a fixed rate, it is possible to measure with mathematical accuracy the degree of degeneration which is present in various strata

9

of the earth's surface. From the thorium-lead ratio, or similar calculations with uranium and uranium derivatives, geologists have derived a very close approximation of the exact age of the various deposits on the earth's surface. From the uranium-lead ratio in some pitchblende from Manitoba, Canada—the oldest deposits yet discovered—the age of pre-Cambrian rocks there are twenty-three hundred million years old. From the same calculations, the age of man has occupied only the last million years of geologic time.

There are many calculations other than those involving the degeneration of thorium and uranium. However, taking all of these observations into account, it appears quite certain that the human segment of the earth's story has taken place in a period no greater than one two-thousandth of cosmic time. If we think of this relationship in terms of a clock, with twelve hours representing the history of the earth, the drama of man is being enacted in the last twenty seconds.

Realization of the smallness of the fragment of cosmic time which covered the span of human origins has profoundly disturbed some fundamentalists. This need not be so. The story of the creation of the earth and man's part in it, as recounted in the Bible, is a literary history in the mode of writing which was usual in those days. The days and nights of creation recorded in biblical lore are units of geological time, and not necessarily the days and nights which we ordinarily think of, with a span of twenty-four hours. After all, geologists can explain the sequence of events and name the periods. Physicists can enumerate with great clarity the millions of years occupied in these same changes. The fact of the changes themselves is the most wonderful part of the whole story.

Even more recent than the chronological studies based on radioactive materials is a series of researches involving astronomical correlations with time implications. Geologists, evolving their sequence of strata and changes in forms of life, had already pointed out that the essence of these differences was climatic variation. Scientists had been baffled regarding the explanation for these climatic changes until studies of the solar system suggested a reason. Careful mathematical calculations, with which astronomers are extraordinarily facile, have shown that the earth's orbit, far from being regular, as previously supposed, is eccentric. The path of the sun during the course of a year is also oblique in relation to its exposure to the earth. These considerations, when combined with results from recent studies of the length of the perihelion, show that the intensity of solar radiation in respect to our planet has undergone a series of changes. These shifts may be calculated into the past with considerable accuracy by projecting the mathematical data backward. Undoubtedly, there are other considerations which must be calculated in the same manner in order to retell accurately the entire climatic story of the earth. Although the astronomic time scale is referable to only the last movements of time in which mankind has played his role, this newly discovered chronology is of incalculable assistance.

With the relative time scale of the geologists, the atomic sequence of the physicists, and the refinements of the astronomists, students of human history are now in a position to state with considerable accuracy the time when human events started and also punctuate the story with significant waymarks of chronology. For these purposes, anthropologists utilize, of course, geological periods for the major outline.

The current major era of geologic time is known as the Cenozoic, a duration of approximately sixty million years during which mammals have become the dominant form of life on the earth. The Cenozoic period is, for convenience, divided into a number of subperiods or epochs, each with a descriptive Greek name. Unfortunately, into this understandable geologic taxonomy, there must be introduced the remnants of an older nomenclature now outmoded. This obsolete system divided all time into four major periods—Primary, Secondary, Tertiary, and Quaternary. Obviously, this sketchy system was inadequate, and it was soon abandoned. However, the terms "Tertiary" and "Quaternary" have been illogically retained and are today constantly used in connection with the new geologic scale. Thus the subperiods of the Cenozoic through the Pliocene are known as the Tertiary period. The Pleistocene and Recent are often referred to as the Quaternary.

The Pleistocene epoch, or last major portion of the Cenozoic era, is, as far as the anthropologists are concerned, the crux of the matter. It is in this epoch that the evidences for man occur. It is in this period that the astronomic time scale is the most refined.

The Pleistocene epoch is not only a time of the dominance of a number of mammal forms, including man, but is also a geologic time marked by some extraordinary changes of a different character. Periodically during the Pleistocene there formed on the continental land masses, especially in the Northern Hemisphere, vast quantities of glacial ice. These frozen masses accumulated and dissipated with periodic rhythm which serves to divide the Pleistocene into convenient subdivisions. By this method the geologists Penck and Brückner first studied the remains of glacial happenings in the region of the Alps. They found evidence that the ice had collected four times in this area and had melted away successively after each major accumulation. They gave the names of four Alpine localities to the succession of glacial epochs. From earliest to latest, they are the Günz, Mindel, Riss, and Würm glaciations, each named for a valley or location where evidences of the glacial moraine were found.

Since completion of the original work of Penck and Brückner in the Alps, evidence of similar glacial variations has been found in the Scandinavian portion of Europe, in Asia, in North America, and in several minor centers in other parts of the world. However, the time periods may not be identical from one area to another. Not only were the periods of glacial maxima of interest, but also the interglacial periods, which were numbered and studied with equal care. As more attention was lavished upon refinements of the ice rhythm that took place during the Pleistocene, more evidence was unearthed that these had not been simple phenomena. Some students professed to recognize five or six major glaciations. Other experts pointed out that the four glacial periods during the Pleistocene had simply oscillated several times and thus had left multiple evidences in some places during the course of a single glacial period.

The fourth and last of the glacial epochs in Europe, the Würmian, shows a special complexity and variation. Several stadia are known from this one glaciation alone, which amounted, in certain parts of Europe, to separate periods. Insomuch as a major part of the story of the development of mankind in Europe took place during the Würmian, these variations of the glacial background are of great significance.

Scandinavia, in northern Europe, was the center of a parallel ice accumulation during Pleistocene times. Glacial phenomena in this area have been carefully correlated with the original work done in the Alpine center. Periods of ice advance have been separately named in the north to parallel those of central Europe. Thus the Elbe glaciation in northern Europe corresponds with Günz, the Elster with the Mindel, the Saale with the Riss, and the Warthe and Weichsel, or Vistula, with the Würm farther south.

For obvious reasons, the Pleistocene is often referred to as the "Age of Ice." The uninformed might conclude that human life could not survive during the cold and stress of continental glaciations. In spite of the fact that the ice masses were thousands of feet thick and covered thousands of square miles of terrain during their greatest extent, the glaciers did not preclude the existence of human life in their vicinity. Quite the contrary. The time of the piling up of the green ice masses over the Alps—and to the north in Scandinavian Europe—was the same period in which most mammals, including man, flourished around the peripheries of these frigid centers.

The formation of the ice seems to have been not so much a product of pure cold as of increased precipitation. So much snow accumulated during the winter months that it failed to melt during the summer. While the snow was packing down into glacial ice at the centers of glaciation, around the periphery the increased precipitation produced a lush vegetation upon which mammals flourished. Indeed, there has seldom been a time in the history of the earth when the forms of life were as varied and interesting as they were during the Pleistocene epoch.

Since ancestral types of man were also mammals, it is logical that they should play their appropriate part in Pleistocene happenings. Man lived with a background of ice which shifted and changed with the weather. During these shifts, the stage upon which man performed was profoundly affected by wind, snow, melting ice, and other repercussions of the glacial happenings farther back toward the glacial centers.

Perhaps the most obvious of Pleistocene variations was the large number of mammals other than man which flourished around the glacial periphery. Since the remains of early human beings are most often found associated with Ice Age mammals, faunal remains are valuable corroborative data. Elephants, rhinoceroses, and bears changed in form and species from the early Pleistocene to late Ice Age times, so that variations in the morphology of animals is significant as an indicator of the climate and terrain existing in a particular millennium. Pleistocene horses are indicative of open grassland country at the time when they flourished. Reindeer are creatures of steppe or tundra terrain. The presence of hippopotamuses indicates an interglacial period when the climate was mild and suited to the needs of this tropical animal. Vertebrate palaeontologists, working with the abundant remains of the Pleistocene, have evolved a delicate time scale of faunal change, and much of the prehistory of man has been arranged sequentially on the basis of the mammal bones found with his remains.

Not all of the Pleistocene story has been told with teeth and bones, however. One of the most interesting variations is that in connection with river terraces. These formations have been studied in several places in Europe, especially in Germany and northern France.

In flowing to the sea, European rivers originating in the glacial highlands, have built up, in most cases, a series of terraces along the sides of their valleys. These successive levels may be seen clearly on certain of the French rivers, where they have been studied in connection with gravel pits deposited there. Generally, the formation of terraces was the result of glacial debris accumulating in a river valley and the subsequent cutting through the fill by the river.

When the glacial ice was melting at the beginning of an interglacial period, tremendous quantities of melt water were released from the ice cliffs. Streams which flowed away from the retreating glaciers became roaring torrents, and carried with them quantities of detritus and debris which the glacier had collected during its previous advance. Gravel, sand, and glacial silt choked these flooding rivers so that they filled their valleys with this material as the currents slowed far downstream.

Subsequently, as these cosmic events reversed themselves and the ice again began to form over the glacial centers, the amount of water in the beds of these streams decreased and the material which they carried was reduced. One important consideration regarding a glacial advance is the fact that the level of the sea was considerably lowered because of the tremendous volume of moisture locked up in the form of glacial ice. The lowering of the sea level caused a steeper gradient in the beds of the streams. This produced a swifter flow, with resultant cutting action, so that a previous river terrace was trenched during this stage of the river's life. Owing to the alternate building and cutting of terraces, the valleys radiating out from the glacial centers have characteristic profiles which show a series of terraces or steps related to the glacial happenings at the heads of these rivers.

Conversely, along many glacial rivers the cutting cycle was represented by the flood stage, when the glacial ice at the headwaters was melting and the resulting volume of water carved out terraces from the materials which remained from the depositions of a former glacial period. This seeming paradox sometimes occurred in the same valley wherein melt water was cutting terraces near the headwaters and building up levels farther down the valley. Whichever the exact sequence, it is important to keep in mind that the higher terraces are the older, whereas the lowermost terraces close to the present streams are the youngest.

River terraces are of great interest because early men lived along these same streams at a time when some present-day terraces were not yet formed. Campsites, the cracked bones of slain animals, and flint tools may be identified with certain terraces which were riverbanks in those far-off times. These terraces may in turn be connected with certain events of the Ice Age and thus have chronological significance. Much of the early European story has been told by these river valley studies.

Another glacial phenomenon of particular interest to the study of man is the formation of loess. This is a fine, silty substance which was laid down in great blankets over much of Europe, Asia, and North America during the Pleistocene period. Loess is usually yellow in color and made up of fine particles which form a claylike deposit in large quantities. Loess was not washed into place or deposited by glacial ice; it was carried by wind.

During the time of glacial retreats, vast denuded areas were left in the wake of the shrinking ice. These outwash plains were covered with piles of detritus, much of it in the form of fine rock dust which had been milled beneath advancing ice snouts.

As the climate ameliorated, causing the ice to melt, the differential between the cold air chilled by the still existent ice masses and the warmer currents which rose over the land not covered by ice, caused violent storms. These winds swept away from the ice cliffs with great intensity. The course of these currents carried them out over the debris-strewn plains of the retreating glaciers, where quantities of rock dust were already dry along the rivers.

The glacial winds thus swept into the air clouds of this dust. The course of the wind currents carried the material, in some instances, hundreds of miles, where it was gradually deposited as the storms lost their intensity. In Europe, most of the loess was dropped as a result of the fourth (Würmian) glaciation, although there may have been loess deposits from the earlier periods which were destroyed by later advances of ice.

Many of the earlier evidences of human beginnings in Europe lie underneath the loess blanket of the Würmian glaciation. Part of the human story is actually incorporated within the yellow loess masses of central Europe. This indicates that there were lulls in these violent dust storms when human beings could occupy the land. Perhaps these intrepid ancestors remained there even during the times that the loess was sifting down through the upper atmosphere. At any rate, after the Würmian ice had melted, the loess area of central Europe was favorable to the advancement of human culture. Indeed, this is still excellent agricultural land today. Loess is widely used in central Europe for the manufacture of bricks and tile. It is, for the prehistorian, a valuable indicator which separates the earlier parts of the Pleistocene from the more recent.

Certain of the materials carried by the glaciers themselves as they pushed inexorably out from their centers of accumulation constitute archaeological guideposts. Usually early man avoided such active glacial areas as those in which moraines or tills were being formed. However, "boulder clays" and sheets of glacial drift formed by ice action are valuable criteria. Often, human evidences of an interglacial period were buried by glacial deposits of a later epoch. The human story is punctuated by such shifting of the products of the Age of Ice.

In certain instances, land surfaces were altered by cold alone, in a process known as solifluction. This action is the alternate freezing and thawing which produces a sludge. This sludge, in some cases of considerable depth, moves in its thawed state down any slope. This process accounts for a considerable amount of geological complexity on river terraces where materials were moved great distances as the oozing sludge crawled over the surface. So powerful was the action of solifluction during the Pleistocene that boulders and flints were often broken by the movement, and human implements rounded and chipped.

During the latter portion of the Pleistocene a series of lakes or seas formed in northern Europe which had much to do with the history of man. The multitude of lakes and ponds which existed throughout Europe in Pleistocene times attests to the abundance of rain. The major evidence of this sort, however, exists in the alternating fresh-water lakes and salt-water seas which were formed in connection with glacial ice dams in the Scandinavian portion of northern Europe.

During the fluctuations of the Würmian glaciation, ice tongues blocked the narrow entrance of the Baltic Sea in the region of Denmark and Sweden. While these ice dams were in place, the Baltic Sea area behind became filled with fresh water melting from the glaciers. The salt character of the water changed to fresh, and an enclosed lake was thus formed which lasted for several thousand years. Then the ice barriers melted away to the north and the brine of the North Sea again flowed into the Baltic, making it saline. As the colossal load of ice was gradually removed by melting, the depressed land resurged, again cutting off the channel to the north and forming another fresh-water lake.

The succession of fresh- and salt-water bodies in northern Europe also is connected with human events in that area. Different shore lines, rising and falling beach lines, variations in the food supply— all resulting from these happenings—directly affected human development in northern Europe during the waning phases of the Pleistocene.

To the successive fresh-water lakes and salt-water seas of these times have been given the names of Baltic Ice Lake, Yoldia Sea, Ancyclus Lake, and, lastly, the Littorina Sea, the designation of the latter three being derived from the names of distinctive shellfish which lived in each.

As the melting glacial ice masses poured their waters into the many lakes and seas of the northern regions, they left another record of the events that occurred during this period, in the form of glacial varves, which were expertly analyzed by the Swedish geologist Baron deGeer.

During the summer melting period the streams running from the glacial cliffs were boisterous with swollen floodwaters. In these torrents, coarse materials were carried and finally deposited. During each succeeding winter season, the flow of the streams was lessened, and they carried only fine sediments which were spread over the coarser materials of the previous summer. In this way, a varve of coarse and fine sediments represented the glacial happenings of one year.

By correlating thick and thin varves, as the record of warm and cold years, Baron deGeer was able to join a series of varves in one locality with those in another area farther north as the Scandinavian glaciers retreated. With these varve counts, the time in actual years of the waning glaciers could be told. Varve calendars provide the most accurate indication of time in reconstructing the chronology of the late Pleistocene regression.

Coincidental with the variations of the last of the Pleistocene and the water bodies which were a concomitant of these variations were corresponding shifts in vegetation. A casual observer might take it for granted that all evidence of such ephemeral materials as wood or leaves might have long ago disappeared. This is indeed true in most cases. However, certain enterprising workers in the regions of Denmark and Sweden found that late glacial bogs in northern Europe had trapped considerable quantities of ancient pollen within their surfaces. Different kinds and concentrations of pollen from the late Pleistocene still lay preserved in the mucks of successive levels of these swamps. Smears of mud taken from these levels could be treated with caustic potash and subsequently with glycerine, to render the pollen grains visible, and then examined beneath the microscope. As the pollen particles of various trees and shrubs are distinctive, these could be readily recognized and the varieties of vegetation existent in those times could thus be calculated. At the same time, the researcher, by the abundance of various species noted in this way, could gain a relative idea of the makeup and dominance of trees and shrubs in a certain era.

On a basis of pollen analysis, several co-workers evolved a vegetation sequence for northern Europe. This chart was especially valuable in the clarification of those difficult times during the transition from the Age of Ice to the recent period. It has, of course, been pointed out quite properly that pollen analysis has its limitations. Pollen grains of plants of the same genus are difficult to differentiate. Much of the pollen was trapped in mud cracks on the surfaces of late glacial bogs. In this way, misleading concentrations of pollen would be effected which would distort the picture of the makeup of the surrounding trees and shrubs. Certain species, growing well back from the ponds and swamps, were probably not represented as well as those trees on the actual peripheries of the moist areas where the pollen collected. In spite of these difficulties, however, pollen analysis is a very real aid in understanding the changing world of ancient Europe during the last part of the glacial period.

Most of the previous changes mentioned in connection with glacial happenings have been in the background of the human drama. We have been pleased to call these the "scenery" which fluxed and varied while the human play was being enacted on the stage. Actually, the stage itself changed in shape and contour from time to time during the Pleistocene. When the ice collected in astronomical quantities, a tremendous amount of moisture was thus locked up in a frozen form. This materially lowered the levels of the ocean waters. Estimates vary regarding exactly how much the sea level was reduced in various parts of the world. However, even a drop in ocean level of only a few meters would profoundly affect the coast lines of Europe and the other Old World continents. A land bridge between Great Britain and the European continent existed all through the Pleistocene period. During much of the Ice Age, the English Channel was a valley with a sluggish river flowing toward the North Sea. A land bridge undoubtedly connected Europe with Africa across the Strait of Gibraltar and also across Italy and Sicily in the Pleistocene. Islands off the coast of Europe were connected with the continent by necks of land. Of course, these land bridges and other coast-line changes varied as the ice waxed and waned during the major continental variations. If maps had been drawn of Europe at different times during the Pleistocene, they would all have differed greatly from modern charts of the same area.

The lowering of the ocean levels by the withdrawing of moisture in the form of ice was not the only factor in coast-line changes. The weight of the ice itself upon the continents depressed these land bodies to a considerable extent, compensating, in some instances, for the lowering of the ocean level. The depression of the land caused by the overload of ice upon it did not immediately cease as the glacial mass melted away. The resurgence of the land was in many cases prolonged. Thus, some parts of Europe were gradually rising thousands of years after the ice load had disappeared.

From all of these various factors, some coast lines were sinking while others were rising. In this way, the stage upon which the human drama was being played was shifting and tilting as the action went on. The changes were so slow and life so short that the human actors probably never recognized that changes were taking place. Nonetheless, in the aggregate, alterations in coast-line elevation, climate, and vegetation are an integral part of the story.

Time and change were the two greatest considerations in prehistoric Europe, just as they have been the major factors of human life ever since. We are especially fortunate that the glacial happenings which marked the European continent during the Pleistocene punctuate so clearly the time of the beginnings of man, and outline so convincingly the changing world of the Pleistocene.

CHAPTER 3

The Origin of the Actors

In 1859, CHARLES DARWIN, fortified by careful natural observations, propounded his theory of evolution in his book *Origin of the Species.* The enthusiastic followers of the Darwinian principle immediately adapted his arguments to their own theories. Many of these enthusiasts, swept away by the spirit of the new discovery, pictured evolution as a simple progression occurring in a straight line from some primate ancestor through a gorilla- or chimpanzee-like stage and thence through intermediate steps to its culmination in man. A multitude of scientific discoveries since Darwin's day has demonstrated conclusively that evolution was neither straightforward nor simple.

Most of the modern theories of evolution dealing with the rise of man are based upon discoveries of fossilized portions of human or near-human skeletons in various corners of Europe, Asia, Africa, and Oceania. These fragments of skull caps, teeth, thigh bones, and other parts of protohuman beings and man were accidentally preserved in out-of-the-way places by the mineralization of the bones.

Obviously, many more speciments of bygone beings have perished utterly than have fallen into scientific hands. Even from these precious scraps, however, anthropologists and palaeontologists are drawing a picture of our early ancestry which is complete in some details, although sketchy in others.

Obviously, the human evolutionists did not scatter their efforts among all mammals. It seemed patent at the onset that man was most closely connected with the primate order of mammals, and that the origin and history of this one strain of evolutionary progression would constitute the root of the matter. Primates were similar to man in enough bodily features to leave no doubt that the two were related in some ancestral connection.

Irrespective of their various opinions regarding the exact course of man's evolutionary history, all anthropologists came to agree that our earliest ancestors differed from lower apes chiefly in the size and complexity of the brain, in facial features, in posture, and in teeth.

All of the fossil finds pointed up the development of the size of the human brain through successive stages, generally from smaller to larger in proportion to the gross bulk of the being who possessed the brain. This development was not only in cubic capacity of the brain case, but also in the complexity of the convolutions on the surface of the brain, as well as in the development of certain lobes and areas of gray matter. The latter changes were often difficult to ascertain in a fragment of a fossil skull, as the brain of any mammal does not make direct contact with the bony case which encloses it.

Teeth are perhaps the most telling of the indicators of subhuman or human status, as they are especially sensitive to evolutionary change. This is fortunate, as a number of early primates left a record of their existence only in the form of three or four molars.

Humanoids chew with a rotating motion, with considerable lateral movement, while apes tend to move their jaws more nearly straight up and down. Primitive forms have larger teeth in an elongated U-shaped palate, in contrast to the developed human with smaller teeth and a parabolic-formed palate.

The relative postures of these early humans are indicated by the curvature and contours of the thigh bones, by the hafting of the skull on the neck, and by details of condyles or joint surfaces which indicate whether the body was carried erect or projected forward. Certain features show a definite relationship, such as the forward thrust of the head and a bent-kneed or simian posture.

There were, of course, a number of other differences between apes and men. The chin and nose are both hallmarks of a modern status. The reduction in the size of the teeth, the recession of the mouth, the lessening of the brow ridges, and the development of a forehead are all criteria recognized by scientists as indicative of the emerging status of a true man from lower and less gifted predecessors.

Geologically, the primates seem to have emerged rapidly after the start of the Cenozoic era. Unimpressive but definite members of this order have been found in the Palaeocene epoch, at the very time when placental mammals were replacing the saurians as the dominant form of life. It would seem from this fact alone that the primates have a family tree going back as far into geological antiquity as many of the other mammalian forms.

In the Eocene epoch, two groups of early primates, the lemuroids and the tarsioids were especially prominent. These two monkey-like groups of animals are regarded by most anthropologists as being the morphological foundations of the primate evolutionary sequence. Although lemurs and tarsiers are now represented in living descendants only in Asia and Africa, fossil remains show that both of these forms were formerly much more widespread. During the Eocene, lemurs and tarsiers migrated to the New World across an isthmus which connected Asia with North America. The earliest history of the rise of the primates is thus seen to be a phenomenon of both the Old and New worlds.

Anthropologists, seeking eagerly for any clues which might clarify the picture of the evolution of man, immediately noted that one group of living primates most closely approximated humans in all salient features. These were the anthropoid apes, constituting four major varieties, all from the Old World—the gorilla and chimpanzee in Africa and the orangutan and gibbon in Asia. If the anthropoid apes were distant cousins of man, the exact point of their divergence from the mainstream of human evolution would be significant.

The first anthropoid apes appear in the Oligocene period. This was the same time when the Alps were uplifted in central Europe by a cataclysmic crumpling of the earth's surface. A sea covered what is now northern Germany. Even though the contours of Europe differed greatly from those today, primate-like beings were ranging Europe, Asia, and Africa, and at the same time developing in a human direction. The Oligocene was also the time of the *Proplio-pithecus,* which was a gibbon-like mammal of the primate order, known from a fossil found in the Fayum district of Egypt.

The Miocene period, in mid-course of the Cenozoic mammalian progression, is the probable keystone of primate development. It was during the Miocene that a genus of great apes, laboring under the scientific name of *Dryopithecus,* made their appearance by evolutionary changes. Dryopithecoids are known from original discoveries in northern India, but also occurred in Europe and Africa. The most significant feature of the Dryopithecine fossils is that their teeth, particularly in the number and pattern of cusps, are remarkably similar to those of modern humans. So significant do anthropologists regard evidence of tooth development that this factor might of itself be sufficient to substantiate the claim that these primates were on the verge of human status.

Many arguments center around the determination of what is usually called the "threshold of human status." When did some primitive ape cease being an ape and become a man?

At this juncture, most fundamentalists boggle at the whole business. Many of the religious arguments which have been leveled at evolution crudely state that "man was not descended from a monkey." Such arguments are technically correct. There is no necessity for a clash between a spiritual point of view and evolutionary facts. The most astounding phenomenon about the creation of man was the pervasiveness of change itself. No form of primate or any other mammalian life remained stable. From geological age through each succeeding time, each form emerged into newer variations. In regard to primate development, an astounding series of changes culminated in man himself. Scientists are still striving to discover the various steps in the story and to determine their sequence and relationships. Certainly the creation of man in this way should be as spiritually gratifying as the more literary accounts of Biblical times which were striving to get across a point to readers unfamiliar with scientific data.

Neanderthal family in front of cave home on Rock of Gibraltar—
Mousterian period.

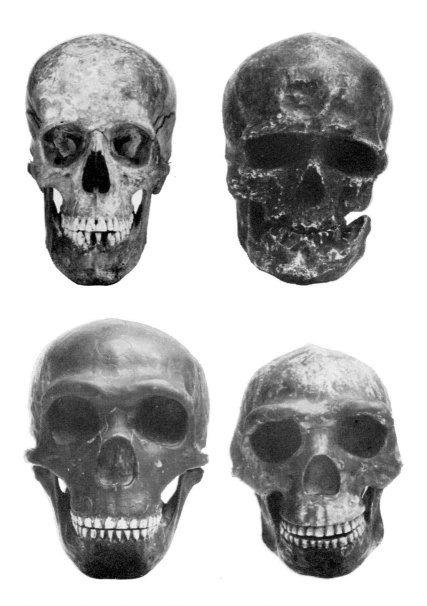

SKULLS OF FOUR TYPES OF MAN *(front view)*

Top, left, modern man, Nordic race, male European (killed by Indians on the Santa Fé Trail); right, old man of Cro-Magnon; below, left, Neanderthal man from La Chapelle aux Saints; right, Pekin man from Choukoutien.

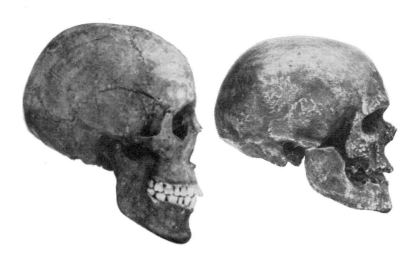

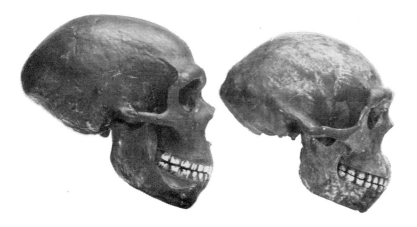

SKULLS OF FOUR TYPES OF MAN *(side view)*

Top, left, modern man, Nordic race, male European (killed by Indians on the Santa Fé Trail); right, old man of Cro-Magnon; below, left, Neanderthal man from La Chapelle aux Saints; right, Pekin man from Choukoutien.

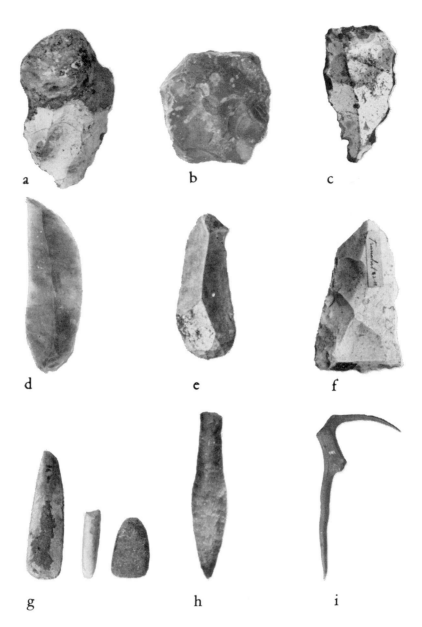

Some Tools of Early Man

(a) Abbeyvillian fist ax; (b) Pre-Crag tool from East Anglia (England); (c) Levallois flake tool (Levallois VI); (d) blade with fine retouch (Magdalenian); (e) end scraper on a blade (Solutrean); (f) tranchet ax (Maglamosean); (g) Danubian "shoe-last" celts; (h) flint dagger (Megalithic), from Dolmen tomb, Denmark; (i) pick made from red stag antler (Swiss Lake dwellings).

Whether spiritually or scientifically considered, however, the Miocene period, some twelve or thirteen million years in the past, is the earliest date considered scientifically possible as the era of human origins. Most anthropologists do not place the origins of man back this far. A few enthusiasts still believe that some orthograde Miocene primate might have been advanced enough in brain, teeth, and body form to be called human. Some supporters of this idea have claimed that Miocene tools made by human hands have been identified. If so, our story begins here.

A significant fossil found by L. S. B. Leakey, a scientist of Nairobi in East Africa, may offer a clue concerning the divergence of true humans from the primate stem. Mr. Leakey discovered a fossil ape in Miocene age deposits on an island in Lake Victoria, also in East Africa. He called this creature *Proconsul*. This ape, although definitely not a human, nonetheless possesses certain human characteristics as well as other features which connect him with the anthropoid apes. Many scientists today place Proconsul at the crossroads where humans on the one hand and such primates as the gorilla and chimpanzee on the other diverged to take their separate paths of evolution.

In spite of the Miocene possibilities, the succeeding period, the Pliocene, appears to be the time when man emerged from primate obscurity. Especially from the late Pliocene or early Pleistocene, a number of fossil possibilities have been discovered which seem to indicate that the trend of primate development had finally crossed the threshold of the human status. It became clear also that most primate forms in North and South America had died out without leaving issue in those continents. Such primates as remained in the New World stewed in their same evolutionary juices for the balance of the Cenozoic period, without indication of any trend toward a human direction. Thus, the culmination of the story occurred only in the land masses of Asia, Africa, and Europe, where certain primates, endowed with some divine spark, evolved into humans.

In attempting to pinpoint the emergence of man, another difficulty arose. Geologists are somewhat vague about the divisions between the various epochs of the Cenozoic period. This is especially true regarding the crucial line between the Pliocene and the succeeding Pleistocene. Many fossil discoveries of significance seemed to be either late Pliocene or early Pleistocene, with no sure decision about which period might claim them. Deposits containing crucial human material were placed by some authors in the Pliocene period, and by others were regarded as Pleistocene. Anthropologists have been distressed at this vagueness, but needlessly so. The difficulty is one of nomenclature alone. It is obvious from all of the evidence that in the late Pliocene or early Pleistocene period, about one million years ago, certain primates, trending in the direction of the ultimate human, diverged from their parent stem to a sufficient degree and assumed the preponderance of characteristics by which we describe man.

The most significant single fact which modern palaeontologists and anthropologists came to realize was that evolution did not move steadfastly in a single line of progression, as had originally been supposed. A few scientists have reverted to a theory of evolution popularized by Jean Lamarck, who preceded Darwin by some decades. Lamarck advocated a simpler principle of evolution without recognizing the factor of natural selection, which was Darwin's main premise. This point of view is related in some of its aspects to the theory of "emergent" evolution, which postulates that innate drive in a species will develop in a discernible direction. Fossil finds from South Africa, Asia, and Europe all demonstrated the asymmetry of evolution. The characteristics by which man is distinguished from the early apes did not evolve simultaneously nor evenly.

Australopithecus africanus, a fossil form of early Pleistocene date recovered from a cave in South Africa, had all of the facial contours of a chimpanzee but a brain and teeth which almost approached those of man. Other African and Asiatic fossils showed features of teeth, jaws, or posture which had outstripped other characteristics. From this evidence it was obvious that evolution had moved by fits and starts rather than by some even combination of changing characteristics which kept in balance.

Especially indicative of the fickle progress of evolution is a series of significant forms brought to light by the late Robert Broom of Pretoria's Transvaal Museum in South Africa and by Raymond Dart of Johannesburg, the scientist who first described *Australopithecus.* Mr. Broom uncovered a cousin of *Australopithecus africanus* which he dubbed *Australopithecus transvaalensis.* This new fossil form seemed to be, in all respects, like an ape, but had a set of very human teeth arranged in an ape jaw. This discovery pointed up the fact that the status of any ape or early man could not be determined by one feature alone.

Not only the morphology of these early forms must be examined with care, but also their time relationships. Throughout the course of evolution, forms representing arrested development have lingered, with relatively little change in some instances for thousands of years, while a parent stalk continued its evolutionary progression toward some predestined end. Thus, evolution has its static as well as dynamic aspects. Two additional fossil forms uncovered by Robert Broom in South Africa are further evidence of the vagaries of evolution. These new specimens their discoverer has called *Plesianthropus* ("Near Man") and *Paranthropus* ("Beside Man"). Although the brain capacities of these fossil primates were small, their teeth were again very human, of a pattern closely related to the *Dryopithecus* form of India, from which, most anthropologists believe, the human stock came. These facts in themselves would not be startling were it not for the fossil limb and pelvic bones of these same South African apes which were in some instances found with the skulls. Evidence from the hip and leg region indicates that these early apes walked erect with the same stance as modern man.

Paranthropus, Plesianthropus, the original *Australopithecus,* and a number of recently discovered South African fossils of the same general sort have now been grouped into a single family of Pleistocene primates called *Australopithecinae.* This important family group is often referred to as the "Man Apes" of Africa, a phrase which describes them rather aptly. Evidence of fire and the discovery of skulls apparently crushed by clubs emphasizes the fact that the Man Apes not only looked but acted in many ways like humans. In spite of the fact that some of the *Australopithecinae* were still living in their South African caves when the Pleistocene period was far advanced, many scientists now believe that the Man Apes resemble very closely the kind of primate from which true humans sprang.

Anthropologists and human palaeontologists have long considered that the human stock evolved from a single center in the Old World. The best choice for the location of this anthropological Garden of

Eden seemed to be in Asia, either north of the Himalayas or in the southeastern reaches of that continent. Choice of the latter locale was pointed up by the discovery in 1891 of a most significant fossil form on the island of Java. Dr. Eugene Dubois, a Dutch surgeon, discovered these remains in the gravel of the Trinil River on that island. He called his find *Pithecanthropus erectus* ("Ape man who walked erect"). The *Pithecanthropus* fossil bones were fragmentary, consisting originally of the better part of a skull, the left femur, three teeth, and a lower jaw. From these bits, however, Dr. Dubois was able to reconstruct a very creditable being with many features of both ape and man. The skull was low and apelike, but with a keel-like ridge along its crest. A heavy yoke of bone lay above the eyes. The skull showed that *Pithecanthropus* had held his head forward, and the thickness of the bone was great. The cubic content of the cranial capsule had originally been about 900 cubic centimeters—approximately midway between that of a gorilla (about 500 cubic centimeters) and of a modern man (about 1,350 cubic centimeters). Even Dr. Dubois changed his mind several times about the human or subhuman status of his fossil find. He finally concluded that *Pithecanthropus* was a remarkable ape. However Sir Arthur Keith, famous British authority on fossil man, deduced from the same evidence that *Pithecanthropus erectus* was the earliest form of man.

Most scientists, following the lead of Sir Arthur Keith, have considered *Pithecanthropus erectus* a point of departure for all studies involving the morphological antiquity of mankind. Recent discoveries, also from the island of Java, made by Dutch palaeontologist R. von Koenigswald, have added considerably to our knowledge of this species. Von Koenigswald found another variety of *Pithecanthropus,* including the skull of a baby Pithecanthropoid about two years old. Other researchers had previously recovered enough fragments of other Pithecanthropoids to piece together two skulls in addition to the original find of Dr. Dubois and the most recent ones of Dr. von Koenigswald.

Dr. Franz Weidenreich of the Union Medical College and the Cenozoic Research Laboratory in Peking, China, drew a number of important conclusions from the extant examples of Pithecanthropoids from Java. It became obvious to him that *Pithecanthropus erectus* and some of his successors in southeastern Asia were gropingly moving in the human direction at the same time that other types were undergoing parallel developments in other parts of the Old World. Thus, modern man did not necessarily stem from any one beginning. *Pithecanthropus erectus* may have been the ancestor of certain of the Asiatic peoples only, or possibly no ancestor at all if his issue died out on the island of Java and left no descendants on the mainland of Asia.

Dr. Weidenreich's conclusions were based, to a considerable extent, upon the remains of another fossil which was discovered near Peking in 1929 by a Chinese anthropologist named W. C. Pei. Chinese and European scientists, under the direction of the late Canadian anatomist Professor Davidson Black, excavating the bone beds of a series of caves at Choukowtien (Chicken Bone Hill) over a number of years, had unearthed a series of human skulls and other skeletal fragments of a different kind of early man. This was called *Sinanthropus pekinensis,* after the place of its discovery.

Sinanthropus had a skull with a low frontal bone and a median ridge in the manner of *Pithecanthropus erectus.* The face, with its large supraorbital ridge and receding apelike jaw, was primitive also. The teeth had an enlarged pulp cavity, but were essentially human nonetheless. Feature for feature, *Sinanthropus pekinensis* closely paralleled *Pithecanthropus erectus,* indicating that the two were undoubtedly related.

Up to the close of the excavations, interrupted by World War II, some thirty specimens of male, female, and adolescent Sinanthropoids had been exhumed from the caves of Choukowtien. These all showed variations on the same pattern. The early Peking people were extremely primitive, but nonetheless human. Certainly, from the abundant evidence of these fossil remains, the human threshold had been crossed with space to spare.

Sinanthropus pekinensis had a cranial capacity of some 1,000 cubic centimeters, as contrasted with that of modern man of around 1,350 cubic centimeters. In spite of this disparity, by more recent comparison *Sinanthropus* seemed more advanced than *Pithecanthropus erectus.* Most anthropologists had considered this fortuitous, and had concluded that Peking man was simply a relative of *Pithecanthropus erectus*. With Von Koenigswald's recent Pithecanthropoid additions, however, it appears that the Java man and Peking cave dwellers were contemporaries, each evolving toward their own anthropological destinies about the same time. Anthropologists now postulate that different human stocks may have been evolving in two, three, four, or even more centers during the latter portion of the Cenozoic period. Because of the obvious relationship between the Java men and the Peking cave dwellers, some scientists have now placed them in the same genus. Thus, the men of Chowkowtien are now called *Pithecanthropus pekinensis* in this system.

Further studies by Dr. Weidenreich of the skulls of the Pithecanthropoids of Java and the Sinanthropoids of northern China show that the ape men of Java were the more primitive of the two. Furthermore, in the caves of Choukowtien were fire hearths and the remains of Pleistocene animals, mostly varieties of deer. There were also crude flakes of quartz which had been made into tools. *Sinanthropus* had obviously been a mighty hunter who had known how to make tools and use them to kill game. This meat he had dragged back to his caves and cooked over a fire. A rather nasty addition to this human picture of the early men of Choukowtien is the evidence that most of the skulls of Sinanthropoids had the base broken out, obviously to scoop out the brains. This was either evidence of cannibalism on the part of the Sinanthropoids or an indication that some other kind of human was systematically killing and eating Sinanthropoids.

When Dr. Dubois first brought his epoch-making fossil, *Pithecanthropus erectus,* to Europe, many Continental scholars began to look for fossil men in their own environs. Distinctive and primitive fragments of mineralized bone had been turned up in Europe even before the discovery of Java man. For the most part, however, the significance of these had not been realized until Asiatic and African discoveries had focused the picture.

Most significant because of its primitive characteristics was the fossil found at Gibraltar in 1848, but not described until a later find of similar nature was made in a cave in the Neanderthal Gorge near Düsseldorf, Germany. Even the scientists of that early day, unenlightened as they were regarding current refinements of evolutionary theory, were able to demonstrate clearly that the human-like bones from Neanderthal and Gibraltar were primitive and unlike those of modern man. Nonetheless, these crude beings had possessed flint tools and knew how to make fire. This type of early human was called *Homo neanderthalensis,* or *Homo primigenus* (primeval man), indicating that he belonged to the genus *Homo* in common with modern man but was a primitive member.

As the picture of an early type of European called "Neanderthal man" began to take shape, several additional fossil finds in Europe amplified the situation. These were the discovery of a human, but primitive, jaw in a gravel pit near the small village of Mauer in the vicinity of Heidelberg, Germany, and a fragmentary skeleton of the same general sort near Steinheim in the same country. Another human skeleton turned up near Ehringsdorf, also in Germany. The Heidelberg jaw, as it came to be called, was classed as *Homo heidelbergensis,* being perhaps a primitive form of Neanderthaloid. The Ehringsdorf and Steinheim skeletons were also similar to Neanderthal but in some respects less bestial and primitive. In this way the European scientists were able to establish a Neanderthaloid family tree, beginning with Heidelberg man and progressing through such intermediate forms as that discovered at Steinheim and the Ehringsdorf fossil. This succession of primitive but human ancestors climaxed in the classic Neanderthaloids.

Examples of the latter did not rest solely on the original find at Gibraltar and that from the gorge of Neanderthal. Neanderthals turned up in such widely separated localities as Spy, in Belgium; Chapelle aux Saints, Le Moustier, La Quina, and La Ferrassie in France; Krapina in northern Yugoslavia; Capo Circeo in southern Italy; caves near the Sea of Galilee in Palestine; and at KüKoba and Podkomuk in the Crimea in Russia. Recently, a young Soviet archaeologist named A. P. Okladnikoff found a fossilized skeleton of a young Neanderthal child in Middle Asia. This find extends the range of the Neanderthals well into the heart of the Asiatic land mass.

Careful studies of all of these Neanderthals showed that considerable variations existed among them. The men and women represented by the Neanderthal skeletons from France, for example, differed in a number of respects from the type of human represented by "Galilee man" from Palestine. In spite of these variations, however, it was obvious that much of the early human story concerned primitive types of humans grouped together under the name of Neanderthaloid. All of these primitive forms were referred to as "Palaeoanthropic man" to indicate that they were an old and outmoded type of human when contrasted with "Neanthropic man," the morphologically modern type.

As Neanderthals universally displayed such characteristics as large supraorbital ridges, low-crested skulls, receding chins, and forward-hafted necks, they could easily be classed as primitive or Palaeoanthropic. In spite of these bestial characteristics, however, it was equally obvious that they were humans. Their cranial capacity, for example, was in some cases even larger than that of modern man, in spite of the thickness of the skull bones and the primitive slant of the forehead.

Neanderthal skeletons were usually accompanied by flint tools, and, at least in one instance, Neanderthals buried their dead as though they believed in a spiritual hereafter, a most human instinct. Thus the Neanderthals seemed to fill in largely the gap between the most primitive types of humans, such as *Pithecanthropus erectus,* and modern man. Human palaeontologists at one time were universally agreed that the beginning of mankind was a unilateral affair. If the evidence could be arranged properly, they believed a succession of fossil types could be demonstrated, one leading into another in gradual progression. Difficulties and gaps were explained by the absence of significant fossils to demonstrate a particular part of this progression. As the asymmetry of evolution became more and more manifest, the universal belief in the single straightforward development of human origins was shaken, but not changed.

Human cultural evidence seemed to bolster such a simple picture of the beginnings of man. The progression had started in a rude and untutored state from some ape such as *Dryopithecus.* First the teeth, then the brain, and perhaps lastly the face of this one strain of pre-destined primates changed under the inexorable force of evolution. In this simple version of human beginnings, anthropologists had only to determine two significant places in the human ascent. The first of these was the threshold of the human status which caused so much difficulty in the case of *Pithecanthropus erectus.* The second hallmark was the point at which Palaeoanthropic man became Neanthropic man. This second point of demarcation promised even greater difficulties, but might be managed if enough fossil specimens could be dragged out of obscure caves and into the scientific laboratories.

There were, however, some grave difficulties in so simple a scheme. For one thing, the Ehringsdorf and Steinheim types of humans, although displaying some Neanderthal connections, nonetheless also had some indubitable Neanthropic characteristics. From this consideration it would seem that the Neanderthaloids became more distinctively Neanderthaloid as they progressed rather than less so. Evidence from several Neanderthal finds, which could be demonstrated as dating from the fourth glacial epoch, seemed to be more primitive looking than the earlier ones. Thus the Neanderthals seemed to have developed into a dead-end line of human evolution with more marked primitive Neanderthaloid characteristics as they went along.

The Heidelberg-Steinheim-Ehringsdorf-Neanderthal progression of events culminated with the last interglacial period of the Pleistocene epoch and with the first part of the fourth or Würmian glacial advance. The Heidelberg jaw was associated with a warm climate fauna of an earlier interglacial. Neanderthals were found associated with both interglacial material and with typical cold-loving mammals of a glacial epoch. For this reason, Neanderthal finds are often divided into "warm Neanderthal" and "cold Neanderthal."

Paralleling these discoveries was a series of finds of non-Neanderthaloid or modern-appearing fossils that were associated with the very last of the Würmian glaciation and thence into modern times. Chief among the latter was a type called *Cro-Magnon* from the French site of that name. It soon developed that Cro-Magnon was not a single form of modern man, but was a mixture of perhaps several strains of human beings, all of whom had essentially modern characteristics.

On the basis of these two series of discoveries, it appeared that Palaeoanthropic mankind, as represented by the Neanderthals, had somehow developed into Neanthropic man, as evidenced by the various varieties of modern-appearing Cro-Magnon finds.

The disturbing difficulty about such an easy succession of human events was that the Neanderthals apparently became extinct sometime near the peak of the Würmian glaciation in late Pleistocene times. Instead of a gradual diminution of Palaeoanthropic or bestial characteristics, merging into an increase of modern details, there was an abrupt break. The Neanderthals had apparently reached an evolutionary end and disappeared. Modern or Neanthropic types of humans appeared to leap into prominence quite as abruptly. Needless to say, any sort of abruptness is not consistent with ordinary ideas of evolution.

To add to the disturbing implications of the demise of the Neanderthals, there were a few signs that these beetle-browed people of the late Pleistocene might have been helped into obscurity by other human contemporaries. At Krapina in Yugoslavia, where Neanderthaloid fragments were found in a cave, pieces of bone showed nicks where flint knives had cut away the flesh, and the bones had been broken for the marrow. Even as far back as the early Pleistocene *Sinanthropus,* there were grisly suggestions of cannibalism and human misunderstandings. A number of the skulls at Choukowtien showed an artificial enlargement of the *foramen magnum* indicating that some human had scooped out the brains, presumably to eat them. Were the Peking people cannibalistic at times? Did the Neanderthals kill and eat each other during periods of stress when game was scarce? Many anthropologists have said that such happenings were entirely likely. After all, many later peoples, with nothing primitive whatsoever about their physical makeup or their culture, practiced the eating of human flesh.

Even those who could stomach cannibalism among the Neanderthals balked at the suggestion that this practice had resulted in the extinction of the race. The disappearance of the Neanderthaloids after they had achieved indisputably human status bothered evolutionists and palaeontologists alike. Assuredly human egotism was at stake, but there seemed no physiological reason why the Neanderthals should have reached a dead-end.

While most scientists were arguing among themselves about whether any Neanderthal blood had somehow bridged the gap to flow in the veins of modern man, a number of other discoveries added novel facets to the argument. A bestial-looking human form was found in 1921 in Rhodesia, Africa, now known as *Homo rhodesiensis,* or Rhodesian man. This individual had enormous brow ridges with orbital cavities quite simian in character. The acromegaly and sagittal crest gave the Rhodesian skull a primitive and apelike appearance. However, in spite of such suggestive characteristics, the Rhodesian find seemed to be a primitive human. Some of the foremost palaeontologists believed that Rhodesian man represented a Palaeoanthropic form very similar to our own ancestral state.

Undoubtedly the most famous fossil and the one which stimulated the most comment was that found in Sussex, England, by Charles Dawson, between 1908 and 1914. Scientifically tagged *Eoanthropus dawsoni* or "Dawn Man [found by] Dr. Dawson," this fragmentary skull and jaw was more familiarly called "Piltdown man" from the name of the gravels which contained the fragments. The discovery was finally adjudged to be a female.

From various restorations of the pieces of bone of the Piltdown find, it seemed that this remarkable skull was primitive, but with a perfectly modern brain case of even larger capacity than many present-day humans. The most fascinating detail of the Piltdown man was the jaw, which was certainly simian and apparently out of character with the skull which accompanied it. Some workers argued that the jaw did not belong with the skull, but simply happened to be deposited with it in the Pleistocene gravel where the fragments were found. Other workers pointed out that the asymmetry of evolution could have produced the modern-looking head and, at the same time, a jaw of retarded and chimpanzee-like development. The Piltdown gravel deposits also aroused a heated controversy. Some authorities identified them as late Pliocene. Others maintained that they were indubitably late Pleistocene.

In spite of conflicting opinions on the contemporaneity of the jaw and the skull or the age of the deposits, practically all experts were unanimous in judging *Eoanthropus dawsoni* what its scientific name implied—a Dawn man. In this way, it was argued, modern humans had diverged from the trend of development before the dead-end of Neanderthal extinction. The Piltdown skull represented a crucial link in the development of modern mankind.

Unfortunately for this explanation of events, *Eoanthropus* has recently received a scientific blow from which it will not recover. Mr. K. P. Oakley of the British Museum has recently disclosed that the famous Piltdown fragments were subjected to a fluorine test.

Further tests involving such advanced techniques as X-ray spectography have conclusively shown that the Piltdown fossil was a cleverly contrived hoax. The simian-like jaw actually is the jaw of a modern ape, probably an orangutan. The fluorine tests showed that the Piltdown skull fragments are possibly those of a prehistoric member of *Homo sapiens,* perhaps 10,000 years old. This is not ancient at all, considering the remote origins of modern mankind. After this setback, it is doubtful that *Eoanthropus* will ever again be seriously considered as a candidate for our most important ancestor.

With the removal of the Piltdown find as a possibility for the origin of modern man it would seem that the picture was more confused than it had been two decades ago. If modern humans had not descended in a direct line from the Neanderthals, and also no near Neanthropic ancestor could be discovered as the progenitor of modern humans, the evolutionary picture was muddled indeed. Certainly Neanthropic man had not suddenly sprung as a phoenix from the ashes of an evolutionary flame.

Actually, the most probable explanation of these disturbing events had lain before scientists for many years. From time to time, fossil finds had been made which did not seem to fit into preconceived theories of the "primitive to modern" evolutionary concept. As early as 1888 a human skeleton was found at Galley Hill on the Thames River in England. The strata in which this human skeleton was embedded seemed to indicate considerable antiquity, possibly early Pleistocene. As the Galley Hill skull showed essentially modern characteristics, most authorities passed it off as too recent to be considered seriously. Some anthropologists timidly suggested that the Galley Hill skeleton might represent an embranchment from the primate stem which ultimately led to modern types of humans. Such taxonomists argued that Galley Hill man may have been a contemporary of the Palaeoanthropic Heidelberg man. However, the morphological concept of antiquity was so deeply embedded in scientific thought that most writers on the subject would not even allow these concessions. All arguments in this direction seemed to end with the irrefutable "if it isn't primitive, it isn't ancient" conclusion. Such a concept blocked studies of the true beginnings of mankind for the last fifty years.

A skull was found in London in 1925 which, although it seemed to be deeply embedded in Pleistocene strata, showed essentially modern contours. More recently an essentially Neanthropic skeleton was uncovered in the French site of Fontéchevade (Charente). The Fontéchevade discovery was made in stratification which placed it in the Riss-Würm interglacial or perhaps even earlier than the Classic Neanderthal.

A convincing argument in this direction was added in 1935 by the London dentist and amateur archaeologist Alvan T. Marston, who dug from the gravels of Swanscombe in Kent, England, not far from Galley Hill, fragments of a skull which appeared essentially modern. The Neanthropic anatomical features of the Swanscombe fragments were again accompanied by seemingly considerable stratigraphic antiquity, as evidenced by the surrounding gravels which dated from an interglacial epoch probably between the Mindel and the Riss. Flint tools found later in these same gravel layers confirmed the date as Mindel-Riss. To cap these arguments, the Swanscombe skull was subjected to the same fluorine test that had toppled the Piltdown man from his pedestal of antiquity. By this chemical means, the Swanscombe fragments indicated that some morphologically modern individual had laid down his life in what is now Kent, England, around the Middle Pleistocene period or possibly as early as 500,000 years ago.

In Africa, also, Neanthropic men made their appearance at a date early in the Pleistocene. L. S. B. Leakey, the same man who had discovered the Miocene ape, Proconsul, also found in East Africa and in the same region near Lake Victoria the remains of two other fossil humans. At Kanam and at near-by Kanjera he found fragments of jaws and skulls. Kanam and Kanjera men both have characteristics which seem to link them with the Neanthropic varieties of humans rather than the Palaeoanthropic-like Rhodesian man.

In contradiction to the evidence of Kanam and Kanjera are three mandibles and some recently found fragments of skull which have been recovered from Pleistocene deposits of large gravel pits near the North African town of Casablanca and another site called Ternefine near Mascara, Algeria. The three mandibles have been assigned the name *Atlanthropus mauritanicus* by their discoverer, C. Arambourg. At the Sidi Abderrahman gravel pit near Casablanca and at Ternefine near Mascara, the stratigraphic evidences place this new type of human in North Africa about the Middle Pleistocene or near the time that the Riss glaciation was forming on continental Europe. That *Atlanthropus* was definitely human seems proved by the finding of a number of stone fist axes in the same strata as the human jaws. The receding chins of these mandibles, as well as primitive features of the teeth and bones, have led Dr. Arambourg to place *Atlanthropus* with the Pithecanthropine group. Thus, these Middle Pleistocene men of North Africa seem to be included in the family tree of the Palaeoanthropic men.

Perhaps Palaeoanthropic strains such as Rhodesian man and Atlanthropus were evolving their destinies in Africa at the same time as Neanthropic forms such as Kanam and Kanjera. In Europe such forms as Neanderthaloids and Swanscombe were contemporaries. Fossil forms as the Ehringsdorf man and the Neanderthaloid people who lived in the Skhūl Cave in Palestine seem to indicate that Palaeoanthropic and Neanthropic humans were occasionally mixed hybrid forms.

From these facts, only one explanation seems possible. Palaeoanthropic man and Neanthropic man were contemporaries. Modern-appearing humans and primitive Neanderthaloids existed side by side in Europe, and undoubtedly in other parts of the Old World as well. It is a tempting possibility that the modern humans, because of some superiority which is difficult to deduce, killed off their Neanderthal contemporaries. This would nicely account for the extinction of Neanderthal man at the end of the Pleistocene.

By these same arguments, we may arrive at not only a double explanation of these events, but possibly a triple or quadruple evolution of humankind. The Neanderthal strain may have developed in Europe or European Asia, since most of the evidences for the rise of the Neanderthals have come from west of the Urals. Neanthropic mankind may have arisen about the same time from some as yet undiscovered center in Asia or in Africa. Certainly, a modern-appearing human had arrived on the European peninsula by the Middle Pleistocene period and probably earlier.

Following the same trends of thought, other sorts of humans may very well have been emerging in India or in various portions of

Africa during the same Pleistocene epoch. It is intriguing to explain the major varieties of present-day man by this means. Thus, a strain of humans may have emerged in eastern Asia ultimately to produce the Mongoloid peoples. Another trend of human development in Africa culminated in the Negroid peoples. And perhaps the Swanscombe skull represents one of the earliest ancestors of Caucasian races.

Such projections of early human beginnings should be exercised with extreme caution, as many crucial links in these chains of events are obviously still missing. However, as far as the European drama is concerned, there were at least two major actors on the stage. Neanthropic man apparently entered the play as early as his distant cousin, Palaeoanthropic man. Indeed, there is some cultural evidence to indicate that morphologically modern humans may have appeared in Europe even before the primitive Neanderthals. However this might be, the European action was played out by both these individuals. Some scenes were dominated by one group. Other portions of the play were carried on by the other.

Some time in the fourth act, the Neanderthals left the stage, never to return. Whether these unfortunates were actually killed by the modern humans in melodramatic style is a matter for future discoveries to determine, but it is certain that the final action was played out by Neanthropic man alone.

CHAPTER 4

Flint and Reason

Many anthropologists, baffled by the difficulties of determining human status on a basis of morphology alone, have turned to another series of evidences in their quest for the earliest beginnings of mankind. Through the processes of evolution, one of the most salient developments in the physical makeup of man was that of the brain. With the increasing size and complexity of this organ, there evolved a peculiarly human characteristic as the working manifestation of the brain, which is normally called *reason*.

Philosophers, more than any other persons, have wrestled with the difficult problem of identifying pure reason. Such philosophers, ancient and modern, vary considerably in their definition of human reason and its manifestations. In spite of these variations, however, anthropologists are satisfied with a major product of reason upon which all authorities agree. Human reasoning power has produced "culture."

Culture, at least in its material aspects, is usually taken as adequate proof that *reasoning* humans existed to produce it. Even though the bony skeleton of some early human might not have been fossilized and thus preserved for scientific inspection, certain products of his reasoning power may have escaped the distintegrating forces of time. Indirectly, such evidences then may constitute adequate proof of the existence of some early human, even though the man himself may have perished and left no trace. Also, cultural remains associated with a morphologically questionable fossil may demonstrate adequately that this form had already evolved into the human status.

The story of early mankind, then, may be reconstructed from two kinds of evidence, physical and cultural. The clues to the latter are varied. Culture, being anything that man makes and does, may be either material or nonmaterial. Non-material culture, such as language, religious beliefs, rituals, and the like, often leaves only indirect traces or no traces at all. Even material culture is not always preserved, although it has a better chance of enduring through time because of its corporeal form. Actually, then, the archaeologist dealing with the earliest phases of prehistory usually utilizes the material side of culture and often only a portion of that.

Most of the products of the first flights of human reasoning power were in the form of "tools." As man's body evolved in various particulars toward the developed human form, it became progressively weaker in contrast to the many powerful mammals of the Pleistocene which were man's early contemporaries. With the rise of reason, however, these early humans utilized the first novel glimmerings of thought to produce tools which might equalize man's puny status in a hostile world. The first tools thus evolved were probably of wood, as this substance would be the most handy in some pointed or splintered form. Even modern anthropoid apes will pick up a stick upon occasion to belabor one of their fellows. As wood is an only passingly durable substance, however, material items of this nature may only be guessed at.

The first concrete evidences of man's material culture are in the form of flint. This one substance became so important during the early phases of man's adjustment to his environment, that most of the initial acts in the human drama may be traced in this one material alone. So crucial was flint in the prehistory of man that, as far as time

INTERRELATION OF CULTURES
Lower and Middle Palaeolithic

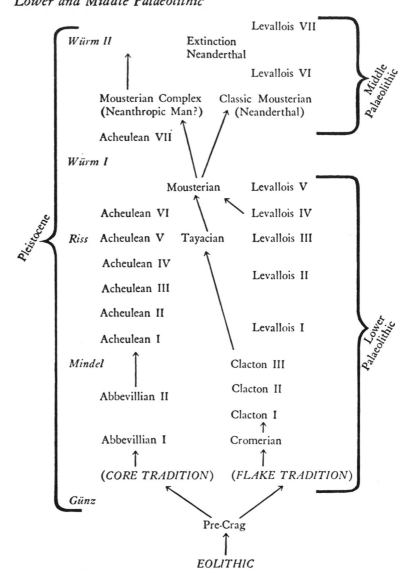

Levallois VII

Würm II　　　　Extinction
　　　　　　　Neanderthal

　　　　　　　　　Levallois VI

Mousterian Complex　Classic Mousterian
(Neanthropic Man?)　(Neanderthal)

Acheulean VII

Würm I

　　　　Mousterian　Levallois V

Acheulean VI　　　Levallois IV

Riss　Acheulean V　Tayacian　Levallois III

Acheulean IV
　　　　　　　　Levallois II
Acheulean III

Acheulean II
　　　　　　　Levallois I
Acheulean I

Mindel　　　　　Clacton III

Abbevillian II　Clacton II

　　　　　　Clacton I

Abbevillian I　Cromerian

(*CORE TRADITION*)　(*FLAKE TRADITION*)

Günz

Pre-Crag

EOLITHIC

Late Pliocene

Pleistocene

Middle Palaeolithic

Lower Palaeolithic

is concerned, we may say truthfully that three-fourths of human experience is recorded only in flint. It is small wonder that archaeologists attach so much importance to this kind of stone.

Flint is an amorphous form of silica with a minute crystalline and fibrous consistency. The homogeneous quality of true flint allows no lines of cleavage. When it breaks, the fracture is conchoidal in form, and extremely sharp on the edges of any fragment. Flint is actually harder than steel, with a designation of seven in Moh's hardness scale.

The origin of flint is still not well understood. Usually it occurs in the form of nodules in Cretaceous chalk beds, apparently by the deposition of silica from the shells of minute animals that lived in ancient seas. Flint also occurs in tabular masses in sedimentary rock. There are many variations of true flint with such names as chalcedony, jasper, or chert. All of these more impure forms possess the same amorphous qualities as true flint, and break with a conchoidal fracture.

Flint may be broken or shaped in a number of ways, the resulting edges and contours of the piece depending upon four major factors. These are the direction of the blow, the force of the blow, the point of impact, and the material or instrument with which the blow is given. As flint is a poor conductor, this stone will not adjust itself to sudden change and readily breaks with a sudden application of heat or cold. These thermal fractures, however, are in the form of concentric rings, leaving a pitted surface which would be of little use in the manufacture of any tool or weapon.

It is obvious from these simple facts that nature can, and demonstrably has, broken flint on many occasions with no human agency involved. The tension of earth movements, solifluction, the action of running streams, and many other natural phenomena have fractured flint, in some instances into very suggestive forms.

Natural flint is usually dark gray to brown in color, although certain variations of amorphous silica run practically the whole gamut of the spectrum. Most flint tools from the very early portions of human history are patinated or discolored on the surface in varying degrees. Patination is a chemical change on the surface of the flint probably produced by substances from the soil or gravel in which the piece of flint is embedded. Patinations vary in color, and may be dark blue, white, brown, or black, irrespective of the color of the original flint. Although thickness of patination is an indication of extreme age, it is no sure criterion of time. Some flint tools of obvious antiquity may be patinated little or not at all, while other specimens of later date display patinations of considerable thickness.

A number of scientists have devoted much time to studies of flint-working techniques. Mr. Leon Coutier, originally a French stone mason, has spent several years in striving to duplicate ancient techniques. Mr. Coutier achieved outstanding success in demonstrating methods by which important varieties of early implements could be reproduced. The lithic laboratory at Columbus, Ohio, has been outstanding in this regard, as have a number of other authorities and institutions that sought by this means to clarify the prehistory that flint had to tell.

From all of these researches, a definite progression of human culture is now well established in flint. This is a series of recognizable types of tools which started with crude and almost undetectable forms in the first beginnings. These evolved to refined and specialized types at the end of the Pleistocene period. From the typology and study of these pieces of flint in relation to stratigraphy, geological evidences, and the infrequent skeletal forms of the humans who made them, the story of the rise of reason has been outlined and the beginnings of mankind established.

This sequence of events, based on the material culture of flint, has been evolved for the most part in France, and the major waymarks of the progression have been named from sites in that country where the different kinds of tools were first found. Originally, anthropologists had arranged these various levels of culture so that one followed the other in an unbroken sequence. Students of prehistory still use this outline of events as a point of departure. However, we now know that the progress of human culture was not so simple as was first supposed. Many of these cultural evidences were first found in France and other parts of the Continent simply because interested scientists looked for them there. Many of the cultural trends which were fitted with some difficulty into the original French sequence, are now known to be foreign not only to France, but even to Europe. Many refinements have been added to the original ideas of European antiquity as first outlined. There have been some changes in nomenclature and many additions in content.

We presume that some early human, with his skull and body already sufficiently evolved to render him capable of human action and thought, hit upon the idea of using flint. We take it for granted that only a human mind could notice the advantages of flint over other substances. Thus, with this single act alone, the human threshold was crossed.

Archaeologists have called the period of the dawn of reason the *Eolithic era*. It is logical to suppose that the first primitive humans who used flint tools did not shape these implements, but picked up natural fragments as need for them arose. Thus, with a jagged or edged piece of flint, such an early fellow was demonstrating clearly his human status. However, as he threw away this flint tool, its usefulness passed, how was some later scientist to identify the piece?

Eoliths are, then, largely a matter of opinion. Various archaeologists in different parts of the Old World have claimed identification of indubitable eoliths. In some instances these "dawn stones" were derived from sources as early as the Miocene period. Mr. Benjamin Harrison, almost a century ago, attempted to demonstrate that certain pieces of flint which he found in Tertiary gravels capping the North Downs of Kent, England, had actually been tools used by the first humans. He based his arguments not only on the position of these tabular pieces of flint, but also on the fact that certain of the fragments were fractured into a nosed form, which would make them handy to use. Opponents of the Harrisonian eoliths argued that the fractures might just as easily have been made in nature, and not by the hand of man.

French scientists also sought to identify eoliths from Miocene, Pliocene, and early Pleistocene levels on the continent. Other eoliths were claimed from Africa, and even from India. There was no sure method, however, by which any of these could be demonstrated incontrovertibly as the first human tools. Undoubtedly some of the eoliths now on museum shelves were actually grasped by an early human hand. Others, possibly, were happenstance fragments broken off by frost action, or chipped into suggestive outlines by waves or currents of some boisterous Pleistocene river.

Promising beginnings of cultural prehistory are provided by a series of discoveries made by Mr. J. Reid Moir along the sea coast of East Anglia in England. Here, a series of deposits of marine origin are known collectively as the "Crag." Many authorities have placed the entire Crag series in the Pliocene epoch. It now appears, however, that at least the upper strata of the Crag are Pleistocene in age as fossil bones of elephant, horse, and ox included within the deposits are referable to Pleistocene fauna. Below abutments of various parts of the Crag, Mr. Moir has recovered an assemblage of flint tools, most of which were apparently shaped by man. Because they are derived from such early levels, these probably constitute the best evidence to date of the possible beginnings of material culture and the initial phase in the period of prehistory known as the *Palaeolithic.*

The flint forms of the pre-Crag of East Anglia have been divided into five groups on a basis of contours, the methods by which the flint was shaped, patination of the pieces, and the evidences of erosive wear which some of the tools display. The earliest implements of the assemblage occur on the littoral of the Crag in the vicinity of Ipswich and Bramford. Typologically, the earliest is a group of eolithic tools from the two localities. These almost shapeless pieces of flint show, nonetheless, evidences of ancient use in the form of small chips along their edges and, in some examples, might actually have been crudely shaped. The eoliths from the pre-Crag may be the only unquestioned eoliths so far demonstrated.

Also occurring, as a distinct group of pre-Crag tools, are some rounded nodules of flint which have been roughly chipped on one end into a snout or point. These pebble picks were first identified at Darmsden in Suffolk, England, and for that reason are often called *Darmsdenian* tools. The Darmsden type of pebble implements were seemingly shaped and may be the foundation of the long series of developments which occurred, in Europe and elsewhere, in the working and shaping of flint.

Also in the pre-Crag assemblage, Mr. Moir found bulky flint implements which he called "rostrocarinates." These derive their name from the fact that the flint has been roughly chipped into a keel-shaped ridge on one side of the tool which ends in a pointed rostum or beak at the end.

Among the assemblage of rough and ready implements from the pre-Crag levels occurs also a number of pieces of flint that had been roughly broken into a pointed beak at one end and a rounded butt on the other. Instruments of a similar shape, on the Continent, had been the first concrete evidences of Palaeolithic man. Here such instruments had been called "fist axes," as they seemed to be designed to be held in the hand without hafting. The fist axes of the pre-Crag levels of East Anglia are rough and crude, in some instances hardly distinguishable from the rostrocarinates. Their presence, however, in this association, is most significant.

Easily set aside from the other implements of this fascinating series are a number of flat slabs, or flakes, of flint which have obviously been struck from a parent core. These demonstrate a totally different technique of manufacture from the hand axes or rostrocarinates. The bulbous flint points, which were roughly chipped to be held in the fist, were shaped by striking off small fragments of flint, leaving a resulting core of the desired shape. On the other hand, the pre-Crag flakes resulted from a contrary process, in which the piece of flint struck from the core was the end product. This difference of point of view will appear of tremendous significance in the later delineation of the Palaeolithic period.

Also included in the Crag discoveries is a group of implements from Foxhall, near Ipswich, in the same region of England. Here a number of significant levels were discovered which terminated in the famous "sixteen-foot" level of Foxhall which seemed to constitute a "floor" stratum upon which early people had lived. The white patinated flints found at a depth of sixteen feet at Foxhall were thick pieces of flint with chipped surfaces, somewhat like the rostrocarinates from the coast. As the Foxhall floor, or floors (since it appears that there may have been two occupied levels), both occur above the Red Crag, the implements from Foxhall usually are regarded as constituting the last in the series of the pre-Crag groups of implements.

If the five groups of implements which Mr. Moir recovered from the pre-Crag levels of East Anglia are actually human tools, they are especially significant from two points of view. The first of these is certainly the time indications, for by any geological calculation,

47

these implements represent the early Pleistocene period prior to the first, or Günz, glacial advance. Some authorities, of course, would reckon the antiquity of the Crag deposits as Pliocene, which would make the implements found beneath them even earlier. Another significant feature of the East Anglian finds is their varied character. In the pre-Crag repertory are not only eolithic forms, but also both core and flake implements. Thus the two great cultural traditions of later times are represented in these groups.

The pre-Crag implements, with their many suggestions of the beginnings of material culture, also furnish another temporal clue to the evolution of the palaeolithic industries of early Europe. Stratigraphically on top of the various levels of the Crag is a group of deposits called the *Cromer Forest* series. In this level have been found large numbers of flakes, seemingly an evolution of the flake tools from the earlier pre-Crag levels. Also in the Cromer Forest bed are included fist axes, roughed out on the core plan.

Obviously, the Cromer levels, as represented in the Forest bed group, are later than those of the Crag. These deposits occurred after the Günz glaciation, and thus are several thousand years more recent than the pre-Crag levels which preceded the Günz. Thus, at least through the first glacial epoch of the Pleistocene period, early humans made both core-tool hand axes and flake-tool cutting implements together.

Unfortunately, the human manufacture of many of these earliest pre-Crag implements is now viewed with suspicion. The arguments of A. S. Barnes, in particular, have tended to prove that these rostrocarinates and the like were produced by frost fractures. Perhaps we will never be absolutely certain of the first tools of man. In this earliest period these crude pieces of flint may well have been naturally occurring eoliths, or may have been roughly-shaped by our earliest human forerunners. Some of the pieces now classified in our collections as fist axes or flakes probably were never made or even used by ancient man.

It will be noticed that no human remains have been specifically associated with these early implements. A human jaw was reported found on the occupation floor in the Foxhall pit, but unfortunately this has been lost. The Heidelberg jaw, which is the only evidence for

Heidelberg man, was associated with the Mauer Sands, which correspond to the same glacial horizon as that of the Cromer Forest bed, although no comparable implements actually accompanied the Heidelberg jaw.

It is logical to suppose that Heidelberg man or his contemporaries probably made implements like the fist axes or flakes found within the Cromer Forest bed. Unfortunately, no human fossil or near-fossil was associated with the pre-Crag implements. The Piltdown type of human was formerly suggested as a candidate for this honor. In view of the spurious nature of the Piltdown skill, some other type of fossil man must be found to fill this vacancy.

On a basis of later evidence, we may make a fair guess at the types of humans responsible for the pre-Crag types of implements. If Heidelberg man, as the precursor of the Neanderthaloids, was the author of some of these shaped pieces of flint, we may conclude that primitive Neanderthaloids were already in existence and making flint tools. The later remains of the Neanderthals are constantly associated with flake implements, suggesting habitual manufacture.

Flaked pieces of quartz, which breaks with a fairly sharp edge, although inferior to flint, were found with the remains of Peking man at Choukowtien in northern China. These flakes of quartz heighten the possibility that Palaeoanthropic man habitually made tools on the general flake pattern.

On the other hand, the core tools such as the fist axes were probably manufactured by a different sort of early human. In later levels, core tools are apparently associated with Neanthropic humans. Such discoveries as that of Swanscombe man in levels which also produced fist axes suggest this connection. As yet, no modern type of fossil man has been suggested for so early a level as the pre-Crag. However, as core tools and Neanthropic man are usually associated in later times, perhaps we may project this connection into the early portion of the Pleistocene. Along this line of reasoning, there existed at the onset of the glacial period, both Palaeoanthropic and Neanthropic humans in western Europe.

With the above arguments, it would be logical to suppose that, as these two disparate human types did not originate in western Europe, probably the flint industries which accompany them did not begin there either. Although the evidences are agonizingly sketchy, the flake tools associated with Neanderthaloids seem to be a product of northern regions, presumably originating in central or northern Asia. Flake industries from northern China may suggest the focal point for such origins, but the proofs are not yet conclusive.

On the other hand, the core tools associated with Neanthropic man are concentrated in western and southern Europe. Recent archaeological finds by a number of authorities, are pointing to Africa as the probable origin of the fist ax and other core-tool implements. Here again the evidence is scanty. Some scientists have suggested that morphologically modern man and his core tools may have evolved in India, and thence moved to North Africa and ultimately to Europe. However, the cradle of Neanthropic man and his coincident typical cores may be closer to Europe in Africa itself.

In Africa, the connections between certain kinds of humans and distinctive tools are mixed. The Kanam jaw from East Africa was found associated with very early Pleistocene fauna and with pebble tools. The Kanam jaw has a well-developed chin prominence which seems to place this early East African with the Neanthropic type of humans. On the other hand, the jaws of *Atlanthropus* from North Africa lack a true chin almost entirely, and for this reason as well as other considerations are placed by Dr. Arambourg with the Pithecanthropines, a Palaeoanthropic variety. However, the tools found with the *Atlanthropus* fossil are fist axes of the core-tool tradition. This seems especially significant as the fist-ax varieties of tools in Europe apparently came from North Africa.

Whatever the exact origin point of the two major tool-making traditions in human prehistory, there seems little doubt that both were foreign to Europe. The European peninsula presented, even at the beginning of the Pleistocene period, a mixed picture. The duality existed not only in the types of humans involved, but in their different ways of working flint as well. The pre-Crag deposits of East Anglia, if we may accept these as man-made tools, already show this mixture.

According to the time-honored nomenclature developed in western Europe, the first significant cultural level was that called the *Chellian*. The name was derived from the type site of Chelles, near

Paris, where the flint tools of this kind were first found. Recently, the French prehistorian, Abbé Breuil, with a number of able assistants, has been reworking the gravel pits in the valleys of the northern French rivers to refine the prehistorical sequence there. The original name, Chellian, has now been changed to *Abbevillian,* from the new site of Abbeville, Champ-de-Mars, on the Somme River, where much larger numbers of Chellian implements were found, in place, in the Somme gravels. However, the original name of Chellian is still used by some antiquarians and the term *pre-Chellian* occasionally designates levels comparable to the pre-Crag.

The typical implement of the Abbevillian was a rough hand ax. The axes are heavy and crudely made, but identifiable as tools. Mr. Leon Coutier has demonstrated that Abbevillian fist axes were probably manufactured by striking a large piece of flint against another stone as an anvil. In this way, thick flakes were detached from a parent core until the latter achieved the desired pointed fist-ax shape. Occasionally Abbevillian tools were dressed with more refined chips produced by a hammerstone. Essentially, however, the Abbevillian technique was one of percussion.

Just as at Cromer and at the village of Mauer, near Heidelberg, the animal bones associated with the Abbevillian hand axes are those of warmth-loving types of elephants, rhinoceroses, and hippopotamuses, indicating an interglacial era with a mild climate. This period is evidentially that between the Günz and Mindel glaciations.

If the core tools such as the Abbevillian hand axes are associated with Neanthropic man, as seems the case, we assume that the Abbevillian people came from the south, from Africa. Apparently at the end of the Günz-Mindel interglacial period, these early fist-ax people retreated southward, withdrawing again into Africa, where warm interglacial conditions persisted. It is in Africa that the continuity of implements from the crudest fist axes to the latest, most developed types is unbroken. Such a complete sequence adds strength to the supposition that the Abbevillian period was but an African interlude in western Europe.

During the development and movements of the fist-ax people, flake-tool men also continued their industries. The next succession of flakes seems to be those called *Clactonian,* after the site of Clacton-on-Sea in Essex, England. Clacton tools are crude flakes which were struck off of a parent core, leaving an obtuse angle at the thick end. The resulting wedge-shaped slab was often dressed with smaller chips to render it a better chopping or cutting instrument. The first Clacton tools were such thickened flakes apparently struck off by a heavy downward blow of a piece of flint on a stone anvil. Later Clacton flakes are much more refined with edges trimmed and thinned with carefully detached chips. Thus, in the Clacton series, there seems to be a progression from early bulbous forms to later refined types. This progression is often formalized as Clacton I and Clacton II.

The earliest Clacton tools are associated with animals of the warm Günz-Mindel interglacial. From this evidence, early Clacton flakes appear to be contemporaries of Abbevillian hand axes. Later Clacton industries persisted, past the time of the Mindel glaciation, into the period between the Mindel and the succeeding Riss. *Atlanthropus* humans at the site of Ternefine in North Africa used large flake tools of the Clacton type.

While the Clacton flake industries were evolving, the core tools of the hand-ax people also progressed. After the Abbevillian, appeared the cultural level known as the *Acheulian,* from the type site of Saint-Acheul, also on the Somme River in northern France. Fist axes recovered from the gravel pits in the vicinity of Saint-Acheul are more almond-shaped than the previous Abbevillian tools. The edges and points are sharper and their cross sections thinner. Although the first Acheulian hand axes were initially roughed out by a percussion technique, the edges were sharpened by a new device.

Mr. Coutier has demonstrated that this refinement was probably accomplished by striking the edges of the flint at a downward angle with a baton of hard wood. Because the vibration of the blow caused by the softer wood is less than that produced by stone, the flint chips thus detached were flatter, with a sharper, straighter cutting edge.

Many French prehistorians now recognize seven stages of Acheulian fist axes. These are essentially chronological, based on stratigraphy. In this sequence, the shape of the fist axes changed from one period to the next. Acheulian I and II featured an ovate fist ax with relatively rough flake scars, retouched only on the edges. Acheulian III and IV fist axes were more pointed than the preceding group. The edges tended to form a sinuous S shape, with better retouching. Acheulian V, VI, and VII axes were progressively more pointed, terminating in a long, slender, pointed form called, from a French site, the *La Micoque* type. The latter development of the Acheulian series featured an over-all dressing with the wood percussion technique which produced a smoothly finished implement with a thin cross section and greater cutting potentiality.

Considering the Abbevillian-Acheulian development on the one hand and the Clacton flake sequence on the other, it would seem that the cultural foundations of prehistoric Europe were distinctly dual, with little connection between the two. As the distances between these various sites are not great, and some sites feature both core and flake implements, it would be strange indeed if the two traditions were unknown to each other. This familiarity is demonstrated by a number of the late Clacton flakes which have been sharpened and trimmed by a technique identical with that of the contemporary Acheulian. In fact many authorities believe that the same ancient people used fist axes and flaked tools together.

The association of some early form of Neanthropic man with Acheulian fist axes now seems a possibility. Recently recovered fossil remains of modern types of humans have occurred with Acheulian material in France and in England. The latter association seems especially irrefutable. At Swanscombe, England, the recently discovered human remains were associated with early-middle Acheulian material. From these suggestive facts, certain enthusiasts again would claim that the core cultures of the Acheulian were an African development which was carried northward into Europe by their makers, an early form of *Homo sapiens*. However, *Atlanthropus,* a Palaeoanthropic type of North Africa is also associated with Acheulian fist axes. Arambourg is convinced that all of the Chellio-Acheulian core tools were made by primitive people such as the Pithecanthropines of the *Atlanthropus* variety.

The study of the place which the Acheulian period occupied in the chronological chart of glacial times is one of particular interest. The French scientists, Commont and the Abbé Breuil, working in the gravel pits of northern France, have found Acheulian material in significant levels of fluvial gravel and layers of solifluction in those areas. Much geological work has also been done in England and in Germany in an attempt to correlate the Acheulian deposits with glacial occurrences. In spite of the disputed status of many of these glacial deposits, it appears quite clear that the early and middle Acheulian are referable to the interglacial period separating the Mindel and Riss maxima. The late Acheulian occurs in the next interglacial period just before the rise of the final, or Würm, glaciation. Thus, again, the fist-ax peoples seem to have invaded Europe especially during the warm interglacial periods.

The late Acheulian implements, in deposits associated with the very beginnings of the Würmian resurgence, are delicately made with the wood-baton technique. This is obviously a significant advancement over the crude beginnings of fist-ax manufacture as represented in the pre-Crag deposits of East Anglia. It must be pointed out at the same time, however, that the development from percussion shaping of flint to wood chipping had occupied almost three quarters of the Pleistocene period. These steps, rudimentary as they might appear, were the major developments of human reason throughout the tens of thousands of years of the first three glacial periods. In the first beginnings, and with inexorable slowness, human intelligence recorded its cultural development in the form of flint.

The flake makers were not idle during this same period. The Clacton industries were carried on, notably in England and northern Europe. A particular development of the thick Clacton flake tools occurred in southern France and is known as the *Tayacian*. The Tayacian flakes show a close association with the Clacton and represent a final development of that technique. Tayacian implements are especially significant since they occurred underneath the French site of La Micoque which featured late Acheulian material. Thus there is stratigraphic evidence for placing the Tayacian earlier than the final stage of the Acheulian.

Perhaps the flake manifestation of the greatest importance was that called the *Levallois* from a site near Paris, France. Levallois flakes differ from Clacton material in that a carefully prepared core of flint was used as a starting point in Levalloisian manufacture. For striking off Levallois flakes, a piece of flint was first hammer-dressed to produce a flat surface on one face and a convex surface on the other. With such a core, the Levallois artisan was able to detach slabs of flint from the edge of the tortoise core by striking the parent flint block on an anvil with abrupt force. The resulting flake-knife tool had a flat striking platform still showing the facets of its original manufacture, rather than the careless obtuse angle of the Clacton flake. In spite of this, however, Levallois flakes were not at first recognized as tools. The first antiquarians eagerly collected the more obvious fist axes from the gravels of northern France and England and ignored the flake tools.

In more recent years, however, the importance of the Levallois industries has been recognized. French archaeologists such as the Abbé Breuil have separated Levallois flakes into seven stages representing a chronological as well as a typological progression.

The first Levallois flakes were heavy, with a prominent percussion bulb. These specimens show an uncertain technique, and the forms of the resulting implements vary considerably. In Levallois II and III, the flakes were struck from better prepared chipping platforms, and the resulting implements are thinner and progressively smaller. Levallois IV features a special type of flake chipped from a more rectangular core, on which a specially prepared chipping platform in the shape of a raised ridge had been previously flaked. The implement, when struck off, still carries on its base end the cross section of the raised chipping platform in what the French call the *chapeau de gendarme* outline. Levallois V features flakes which have been retouched as side scrapers, as well as triangular-shaped slabs of flint which have been retouched with a wood-baton technique. Levallois VI and VII are normally long, narrow flakes struck carefully from more rectangular cores. Some of these approach the form of blades, which is a type of flint working which will appear of great significance in the later levels of the Palaeolithic period. Forerunners of the late Levallois were a few blades retouched along their edges and some angular strips of flint which may have served as gravers.

Unfortunately, the earliest Levallois levels are rarely found in place. Most of the Levallois I and II flakes have been recovered in solifluction levels along the terraces of the Somme River in northern France. As the solifluction is referable to the Riss glaciation, the Levallois series appears to have started before that time. Thus the earliest

Levallois flakes seem contemporaneous with the middle Acheulian. From these beginnings, the various Levallois developments parallel the Acheulian fist axes and outlast considerably the core implement development as such. From various geological evidence in England, Germany, and northern France, it appears that the middle Levallois is associated with the interglacial between the Riss and the Würm. The late Levallois apparently lingered well into the Würmian glacial period.

Even though the fist axes of the Acheulian and the flakes of the Levallois are distinctive in manufacture and in ancestry, the two are often found associated. Late Levallois flakes are often faced with the Acheulian wood-flaking technique. Acheulian sites, with their typical hand axes, often include Levallois flakes also. Conversely, some hand axes appear in places where Levallois flourished. Occasionally, the interchange between Levallois flakes and Acheulian industries produced hybrid tools which are not classifiable in either category.

With such an interchange of material culture, there is the possibility that a mixture also appeared between the peoples who championed these two traditions of flint working. If some form of Palaeoanthropic man made the flake tools while Neanthropic contemporaries and descendants of the Swanscombe individual manufactured fist axes, then who made Levallois flakes? Unfortunately, as yet no human fossil has appeared in conclusive association with Levallois culture. It has even been suggested that the Steinheim type of human, which is usually classed as Neanderthal, might be our closest representative of the kind of man that made Levallois tools. The Steinheim fossil has some modern features which suggest the Neanthropic strain of human development. It may well represent a mixture of the two.

The Lower Palaeolithic period of human cultural development lasted through three-fourths of the prehistory of man. The whole period featured two traditions of flint industry carried on by disparate types of humans apparently originating from two divergent Old World centers. The Lower Palaeolithic in Europe is especially instructive, as the two traditions met in the European peninsula and, in some instances at least, merged there to form new complexes. It was from both of these traditions that the subsequent period of the Palaeolithic evolved.

The old conception of the course of events, which arose from the original work done in France many years ago, was that the Middle Palaeolithic was a simple outgrowth of the Lower Palaeolithic. The name applied to the Middle Palaeolithic period is the *Mousterian,* derived from the cave site of Le Moustier, in Dordogne, in southern France. The Mousterian culture, first delineated at the 1863 excavations of the type site and subsequently elaborated at a number of places throughout Europe, is not a simple one. On a basis of several more recent excavations, the Mousterian now appears to be a series of cultures.

The "pure" Mousterian seems to spring, not from the Levallois, but from the Tayacian of Clacton. This classic type of Mousterian was a flake implement culture, featuring flakes with thick bases struck off from an unprepared core in the Tayacian manner. Usually these thick flakes were dressed along the edge with "resolved" chipping. This was a technique which purposely detached short, thick flakes to produce a scraping rather than a cutting edge. The Mousterian side scrapers produced from this process, are the most typical implements of the period. There were also rough petaloid points, sometimes chipped on one side, and a few nondescript forms manufactured from flint flakes.

Another form of Mousterian from the same period appeared in hand axes of the Acheulian tradition. These are usually small with a triangular shape. In spite of their smaller size, however, they indicate some connection with the old core industries of the Lower Palaeolithic. Mousterian combinations featuring hand axes appear to be lower or early Mousterian.

One other type of Mousterian such as that found at the site of Combe-Capelle in Dordogne, shows a combination with the Levallois. This is not strange, as pure Levallois industries continued into these times.

In addition to the foregoing, there are several other varieties of Mousterian combinations often collectively called the *Mousterian complex.* These associations, which differ widely in various portions of Europe and are even more dissimilar in Asia, show, in some instances, a wide variety of tools. In French North Africa, for example, a most interesting variant of Palaeolithic times is known as the *Aterian*. The Aterian culture, originally thought to be of Mousterian age, now appears much later in time and is actually to be dated at the very end of the Ice Age. The Aterian culture featured tanged points of triangular shape. These points, of fairly creditable manufacture and outline, were apparently hafted, and as such constitute a great development over the cruder hand-held implements of the Lower Palaeolithic period. The Aterian hunters continued to use flint chipping techniques of the Levalloisian variety long after other peoples had progressed to finer and more modern tools. The Aterians may have used their tanged points on bows and arrows which appear only after the Ice Age had come to an end.

Mousterian variations extend throughout European Russia and even across the breadth of upper Asia to north China. Generally, these Mousterian manifestations are characterized by flake industries. There are, in some of these, however, late Mousterian implements which include bone tools, thin flint blades, gravers, and even occasionally stone balls, apparently used as bolas.

From these assemblages, it is quite clear that the Middle Palaeolithic was an extremely complex period, and is not represented by a single classic culture called the Mousterian, as was at first supposed. The Mousterian complex, the loose name applied to the many variations which are not classic Mousterian, seems to be a heterogeneous mixture of all of the many traditions of the Lower Palaeolithic with perhaps the addition of new elements.

All sites of the Middle Palaeolithic that have produced human material have featured Neanderthal-like human forms. The type site of Le Moustier produced a Neanderthal skeleton. The sites of La Chapelle-aux-Saintes and La Ferrasse in south France both produced Mousterian type tools in association with human skeletons of Neanderthal designation. An immature Neanderthal skull from the Devil's Tower at Gibraltar was found with Mousterian tools of Levallois form. The site of La Quina in Charente, France, was associated with Mousterian tools which included hand axes. The Neanderthal remains from Krapina in northern Yugoslavia also accompanied flake implements of Mousterian form embedded in the same magma with the human bones. Indeed, in every instance, Neanderthal or Neanderthaloid human remains are associated with Mousterian cultures wherever those cultures are accompanied by human bones.

Earlier, the evidence seemed suggestive that the flake cultures were carried by Palaeanthropic humans, climaxing in the Neanderthal types. On the other hand, the core-tool cultures were possibly initiated by early variants of *Homo sapiens,* of Neanthropic designation. And yet, in the Middle Palaeolithic period, Neanderthal types apparently dominated the scene as they were associated with classic flake tools as well as some combinations involving core industries.

The obvious fact that the Neanderthal types became extinct at the end of Middle Palaeolithic times and *Homo sapiens* persisted, adds complexity to the picture. This seeming paradox need not be unresolvable.

The answer may lie in Africa, or in outlying portions of southern Europe where Neanthropic man carried on both his blood strains and his flint industries. The very complexity of the Mousterian indicates that more than one tradition was present and presumably, Palaeoanthropic man, with his flake industries, was in contact with and influenced by Neanthropic humans. The site at Ternefine is especially significant. Thus the classic Mousterian was a product of Neanderthaloid humans, and the Mousterian complex, representing peripheral developments, was left behind by Neanthropic or mixed types. This supposition is strengthened by the probable withdrawal of the Acheulian hand-ax makers at the onset of the Würmian glaciation. The major accomplishments of the Neanthropic humans may have occurred in Africa while the Neanderthaloids were dominating the scene in Würmian Europe. The hand-ax makers moved north into Europe during the interglacial periods and retreated into Africa at the onset of the glaciations. Apparently only the hardy Neanderthals doggedly remained during the difficult glacial periods in Europe.

Some enthusiastic prehistorians see a resurgence of *Homo sapiens* as a direct cause of the extinction of the Neanderthaloids. There is some evidence that this resurgence came not out of Africa, but possibly from the Near East. Again the question arises whether any Neanderthaloid blood became mixed in Neanthropic survival. Certainly the

Mousterian complex showed an intermingling of flint techniques and forms. Could not the disparate types of humans who made these cultures have mixed as well? Often the Neanderthaloid skulls from the Skhūl Cave in Palestine are suggested as indications of just such a mixture. These Skhūl skeletons range all the way from classic Neanderthalers to others with distinctly modern characteristics.

The chronological background of Middle Palaeolithic times gives few clues as to the exact succession of events. The Mousterian evolved coincidentally with the rise of the Würmian glaciation. There is Mousterian material associated with the previous, warmer interglacial period which occurred before Würm I. Such early material is typified by the *Weimar* culture, which is the flake industry associated with the Neanderthaloid skeletal remains of near-by Taubach-Ehringsdorf in Germany. This is the Mousterian culture often called the "warm Mousterian," as contrasted with later Middle Palaeolithic manifestations designated as "cold Mousterian" occurring during maxima of the Würm I.

Differentiations between cold and warm Mousterian now seem of small importance, but the fact remains that the Middle Palaeolithic included the first portion of the Würm glaciation, reaching its end within that epoch. In actual years, the Mousterian in all of its variations, occupied a much shorter time than the many millennia of the Lower Palaeolithic. The Mousterian was terminated by the extinction of Neanderthal man around the end of Würm I. The flint industries typical of Mousterian times likewise faded from the scene under the influence of a new technique of tool making which characterized the succeeding periods of the middle and last of the Würmian glaciations.

CHAPTER 5

Refinements in Flint

WITH THE DEMISE of Neanderthal man, and the passing of the period known as Würm I, the Middle Palaeolithic came to an end. This division is marked by more than the extinction of a single human species. There was a definitely notable change in human culture as well. The succeeding periods which occurred during the half-million-year gap between Würm I and Würm II and extending through the remainder of the Würmian glaciation, are called collectively the *Upper Palaeolithic*.

Classic texts on European beginnings have, for many years, pictured the emergence of the Upper Palaeolithic from the preceding Middle Palaeolithic as a simple evolution of time. Based upon French excavations and nomenclature, the Upper Palaeolithic was seen as evolving by easy stages from its predecessor, the Mousterian. Two outstanding difficulties marred such a simple sequence of the events in early Europe. The first of these was, of course, the explanation of *Homo sapiens'* part in these proceedings, as even the most radical

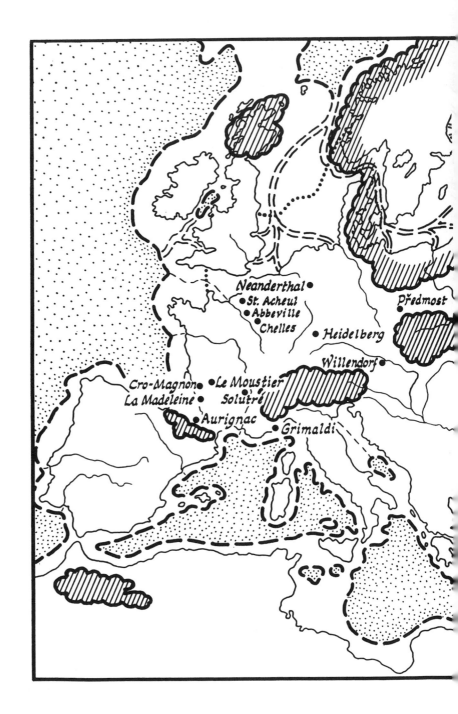

European Coast Line at
Maximum Glaciation

Periglacial Caspian Sea

North River & Tributaries

North European Coast Line
during Interglacial Time

Würmian Ice Masses

• Palaeolithic Sites

PALAEOLITHIC EUROPE
Shows extent of Würmian
Glaciation and locations of
major Palaeolithic sites
0   100   200   300   400   500   miles

physical anthropologist could not derive modern man in a single evolutionary jump from the primitive, lowheaded Neanderthal. The other transitional difficulty was the appearance of a new cultural tool, the flint blade.

The archaeologists of the last of the nineteenth century as well as the modern workers have followed these significant events by changes in flint tools. Most of human history during Upper Palaeolithic times hinges upon refinements and improvements in these implements.

In a French rock shelter site named Abri Audi, archaeologists recovered from an upper level of Mousterian-like mixture a number of long, thin blades of flint. These elongated pieces had been chipped along one edge or backed, so that one cutting edge of the flint knife could be used while the other was purposely blunted to protect the hand of the user. This arrangement was known as the *Abri Audi* knife, after the place where it was found.

At Châtelperron, another French site, similar flint blades occurred as the predominant tool. These *Châtelperron* blades were better made than the Abri Audi, and often dressed along all edges to produce a very creditable knifelike implement.

The introduction of blade-making and the first knife tools made from these blades are typical of a time characterized by some scientists as the *lower Perigordian* period. The name was derived from the region of the Périgord in south central France surrounding the valley of the Vézère River where so many evidences of the first blade-makers have been found.

Two additional cave sites in southern France gave not only the name to the main period of blade-makers and their tools, but seemed to furnish clues to the human makers of these knife-blade, flint tools as well. Buried in a hard-packed cave floor at Aurignac, on the slopes of the Pyrenees, a group of road builders found an abundance of cast-off flint blades of the same general sort, as well as seventeen human skeletons. The blades were well made and had been struck from a parent core with obvious skill. In addition to the long blades of flint was a group of blade scrapers and some chisel-like implements called *burins*. The latter had usually been manufactured on the end of a flint blade by striking off the corners of the flint to produce an angular, but not edged, termination. From these distinctive developments

64

this whole period at the beginning of the Upper Palaeolithic became known as the *Aurignacian*. The name was first given by Gabriel de Martillet when he arranged collections of these tools for the World's Fair held in Paris in 1867.

Not far from Aurignac, in the cave of Cro-Magnon, human remains were recovered from the same strata yielding the knifelike blades of flint and burins. There seemed little doubt that the type of human represented had been the maker of these distinctive tools. Morphologically, however, the Cro-Magnon type of human was not particularly primitive, and displayed little in common with the preceding Neanderthaloids. The Cro-Magnon was quickly judged a type of *Homo sapiens* and regarded as the originator of the Aurignacian culture.

Unfortunately, the road workers who first discovered the cavern of Aurignac thought that the human skeletons represented foul play of more recent times and buried the whole lot in the local churchyard before the bones could be examined by a competent scientist. Later, when the antiquarian Edward Lartet examined the important site, no one had the temerity to dig the seventeen skeletons out of hallowed ground.

Further French studies, especially those by the archaeologist Peyrony, in the region of Périgord, seemed to confirm the local development of the distinctive blade tools of the Aurignacian period. Indeed, M. Peyrony described several versions of Aurignacian blades which became known as *Perigordian*. Until recently, most authorities, following the French opinion, regarded the Aurignacian as a simple outgrowth of the Mousterian by the transitional variations of the Abri Audi and Châtelperronian. The knife blades and burins, typifying the Aurignacian development, were likewise regarded as the products of a type of *Homo sapiens* called *Cro-Magnon*.

Subsequent excavations and studies, not only in Europe but in Africa and Asia as well, have shown that the Aurignacian is far more complex than originally supposed, and is, in fact, indubitably non-European in origin. In addition, Cro-Magnon man is not a type but a combination of several types, some of which had a hand in the development of Upper Palaeolithic events in Europe and elsewhere in the Old World.

Dorothy Garrod, following the lead of Abbé Breuil in the re-examination of many of the long-standing and oversimplified ideas of European origins, found abundant evidence in Palestine that the manufacture of blades had started very early there. Several European workers had discovered evidences in Africa, and in Russia, that blade manufacture, as the definitive criterion, apparently was Eastern in origin. Miss Garrod suggested the Iranian plateau area as the beginning point for this distinctive cultural trait. All evidences seemed to point to the Near East, at least, as the birthplace of blade-making.

Leon Coutier, in concert with several other authorities, has likewise demonstrated that the manufacture of the thin, double-edged pieces known as blades is a complex technique. With the greatest difficulty, M. Coutier, using a bone drift as a tool, has duplicated Aurignacian blades by a method of indirect percussion. Other workers have managed to reproduce Aurignacian pieces with slightly different techniques. All of these have sufficed to demonstrate, however, that the initiation of the Upper Palaeolithic was marked by a new discovery in the refinement of flint tools.

If blade-making was introduced from the Near East, as seems the case, there apparently was an intermingling with techniques already present in Europe. Refinements at the last of the Mousterian, especially in the Mousterian complex, indicate that some of these developments were already present in the European peninsula before the close of the middle Palaeolithic.

As it now appears certain that *Homo sapiens* was present during the middle Palaeolithic, his "sudden" emergence with the lower Perigordian and blade-making does not appear so sudden. Further studies of Cro-Magnon man indicate that he was already a mixture by this time, possibly representing several strains of human development, some of them European carry-overs and others, perhaps, of Near East origin.

Hugo Obermaier suggested some years ago that the Aurignacian may have originated in northwestern Africa. Although this view is now not accepted, it may be partially true in the sense that some of the human elements which compounded into Cro-Magnon mixture may be North African. The usual longheaded skull and short, broad face of Cro-Magnon man indicate clearly a mixing of essential elements. Other features, especially in the later phases of the Aurignacian, indicate even more clearly that Cro-Magnon man was a combination of human strains.

If the humans of the early Upper Palaeolithic were mixed, it is not surprising to find that the resulting cultures also varied. If the name *lower Perigordian* is substituted for early Aurignacian, the original nomenclature may well be retained for the mid-portion of the period. Lower Perigordian featured not only the Châtelperron knife blade, but also simple forms of burins and other tools such as scrapers retouched from various forms of flint blades.

Following the introductory period, there occurs a different repertory of blade tools which are easily distinguished. For these, the name Aurignacian is used, or perhaps better *classic Aurignacian*. The Aurignacian proper featured well-made blades with various refinements. One of these is the strangulated blade which is alternately notched from both sides to produce an elongated capital "S" shape. Presumably, the strangulated blade was used for shaping wooden hafts of other tools. Sometimes the cores from which blades were struck also served as tools. Especially distinctive of the classic Aurignacian are the keeled, nosed, and "busked" scrapers, all of carinated cross section. These were manufactured on purposely thickened blades, which had been stroked at their ends to produce fluted scraping edges for specialized purposes. The *burin busked scraper* is a nosed scraper with a burin stroke added. The presence of these refined tools is the invariable hallmark of the true Aurignacian and their source was apparently to the eastward of Europe.

Also typical of classic Aurignacian are a number of bone forms. The most outstanding of these is the split-based point, obviously a projectile tip with a cleft butt to facilitate hafting. Various other bone tools of the Aurignacian include *batons* occasionally made of antler, which may have been implements or possibly badges of office. Batons reach a climax of development at the last of the Upper Palaeolithic, where they appear ornamented and in a variety of forms.

The classic Aurignacian shows an amazing repertory of burins. French archaeologists, especially, have divided these into a number of named forms, based upon the placement and complexity of the small strokes which faceted the ends of the blades into the typical chisel-like form. Considerable argument has ensued concerning the validity of naming all of the burin types, as many of them seem arbitrary. Much discussion has also resulted from speculations on the use of Aurignacian burins. Explanations vary from tatooing implements for the perforation of the skin to their application as engraving tools for working wood or bone.

Although the Aurignacian receives its name from western Europe, and is best known there, increasingly significant finds of this complex are coming from eastern Europe and the Near East. New Aurignacian material is now known from Rumania, Bulgaria, and Hungary. Recent Russian work in the Crimea and the Ukraine is gradually clarifying the picture of the emergence of the Aurignacian from its Asiatic sources to its ultimate development in western Europe, where it is known so well.

Archaeologists have long recognized that in western Europe a version of Aurignacian culture followed the classic implements of that type. This material, first known simply as *late Aurignacian,* is now designated as *Gravettian* after a site in the Périgord region in southern France. M. Peyrony's "heresy" was to relegate the Gravettian development only to late Aurignacian and only to Périgord and southern France. It became increasingly clear that the Gravettian especially, of all of the early Upper Palaeolithic developments, was not European in origin, but pan-European in its final distribution, and contemporaneous with the classic Aurignacian rather than later, as was first thought. So clear has this become that the Gravettian is now divided into an eastern and western variety.

The *east Gravettian* is known from southern Russia, particularly from the Crimea. This Russian material, such as that found at the sites of Kostienki and Gagarino, appears the earliest of all of the Gravettian manifestations. If the origin of these artifacts is Near Eastern, as seems the case, it would be consistent with logical geographical movements. The site of Mezen in the Ukraine has produced much material of Gravettian nature as well as a series of carvings which are quite unique. The open site of Mezen may have been occupied by hunters for a very long period extending into middle Upper Palaeolithic times.

In southern Russia, as elsewhere, the eastern Gravettian is distinguished by blades with many variations in shape and use. One of the most important of these is a blade which has been chipped at its basal end to produce a shoulder for hafting. These shouldered points are among the most distinctive features of the east Gravettian and appear wherever its influence extended. Although there were some suggestions of the mounting of flint points on wooden shafts as early as the Mousterian, the shouldered points of the east Gravettian are the first sure indication of this refinement. Gravettian points were probably used to tip a javelin or spear with which hunters could kill at a distance. Weapons and warfare developed greatly since the "knee-to-knee" tactics implied by the Lower Palaeolithic fist axes.

In central Europe, especially in the region of Moravia and across the Czechoslovakian boundary in Austria, a large number of open hunting stations have been discovered, which are littered with tools of Gravettian affiliations. C. Absalon, the famous Czech archaeologist, has been active in the excavation of this material. Particularly at the sites of Předmost and Vistonice in Moravia, Professor Absalon has recovered thousands of implements of Gravettian types. Prominent among these is the shouldered point chipped upon a blade of the same sort as the specimens from southern Russia, as well as many other tools made of bone, antler, and mammoth ivory.

Although the early humans of the Lower and Middle Palaeolithic were obviously meat-eaters when occasion offered, the people of the Upper Palaeolithic hunted as a profession. This is markedly true of the Gravettian period, where the evidence shows plainly that the flint tools were used in hunting certain kinds of game. Gravettian hunters favored the horse and the mammoth, which were especially common in the mid-Würmian times. This game was hunted so frequently that many students have called these people the "Mammoth Hunters of Moravia" to distinguish them from other Upper Palaeolithic people. Objects of mammoth ivory and pits lined with mammoth bones indicate that the Gravettian hunters not only successfully killed these pachyderms but used the products of their bodies as well.

The *west Gravettian,* centered in France and extending across the Channel into the British Isles, is chiefly distinguished by the lack of the shouldered point. Also, the west Gravettian tools seem to show some continuity from early Châtelperronian and classic Aurignacian beginnings. The west Gravettian is climaxed by a flint point which had two shoulders. This *Font-Robert* projectile tip is a further refinement made for casting and killing. A well-developed Font-Robert industry has been recovered from Pinhole Cave in Creswell Crags, Derbyshire, England.

The final stage of the Aurignacian, including the Gravettian features of the Font-Robert point, is called by many scholars the *upper Perigordian,* again deriving the name from the region of the Vézère where so much of this evidence occurred. Typical of this late material are pointed blades often called *Gravette points* and a special type of burin called *burin noilles.* Upper Perigordian is then a terminal period for both Aurignacian and Perigordian types of culture. The upper Perigordian occurred during the mid-point of Würmian times and apparently came to an end before Würm II.

A number of excavations in Aurignacian and Gravettian levels have produced skeletal material. These were originally all loosely referred to a Cro-Magnon type. Even a casual examination of this now lengthy series, indicates its heterogeneous nature. At Předmost, in Moravia, and at several other sites in the vicinity of the town of Brünn in the same locality, human remains of the same general type have been recovered. *Brünn man,* as the type is called, shows many differences in stature and in facial features when compared with the original skeletal material from the cave of Cro-Magnon. Indeed, practically all of the human remains occurring with lower Perigordian, Aurignacian, Gravettian, or upper Perigordian levels display many differences and variations. There seems little doubt that *Homo sapiens,* during the earliest periods of the Upper Palaeolithic, was already a mixture, probably containing most of the elements which later produced the typical European races of modern times.

No discussion of the beginnings of Upper Palaeolithic life would be complete without reference to the art forms which distinguished the culture of these early people. Scientists of a few decades ago liked to consider the beginnings of art as a manifestation of the rise of *Homo sapiens.* We now know that this was not the case, as Neanthropic man antedated artistic beginnings as completely as his counterpart, Palaeoanthropic man. There has also been considerable philosophical discussion about the underlying causes of the use of ornamentation and art. No satisfactory conclusion has been reached. We may believe with some that it was the emergence of spiritual beliefs, perhaps in connection with the phenomenon of death, that initiated art. Others see these beginnings as based upon early wonder at the creation of life, and the concept of fertility. Certain matter-of-fact persons hold the opinion that there is, innate in human beings, the desire to decorate.

Whatever the stirrings of reason, there is no doubt that artistic expression began with the Upper Palaeolithic, if not before. Especially famous in this regard is a series of *Venuses*. These repulsive statuettes for the most part Gravettian in age, are the earliest known human attempts to represent, in sculptural form, reproductions of themselves. As the figures are usually female, the name Venus has been whimsically applied to them. Facial features were usually indicated in a rudimentary fashion or not at all. Emphasis was upon large breasts, a pregnant belly, and prominent hips, of a rather florid female type. Of small size and various materials, these figures may represent a female cult, or they may have been only manifestations of Gravettian man's awe at the miracle of birth. Artists see in them, however, much expression of line and contour. Indicative of accomplished creation for artistic pleasure alone, a recently discovered head from the site of Vistonice, apparently carved as a portrait model, would seem to strengthen the concept of an artistic motivation for these statuettes, and negate arguments that they represented a fertility cult.

Gravettian figurines are known from a number of sites of the time, and most of them bear names from the places where they were found. Thus, the famous *Venus of Willendorf* is often cited in this connection. The *Venus of Brassempouy,* from a site in France, is another frequently cited example. Less well-known Gravettian carvings, some of them done in mammoth ivory, occur in profusion in the southern Russian sites. The Ukranian site of Mezen has produced some very interesting figures liberally decorated with incised meanders. A single example of a Venus came from the excavation of Mal'ta on the shores of Lake Baikal in Siberia. The greater frequency of these artistic manifestations to the east again suggests that this trait, as well as blade-making, came into Europe from that direction.

In addition to the Venuses, Gravettian levels have also yielded animal figurines, such as the famous series of Vistonice. It would be strange if these hunters did not reproduce the mammoth, horse, cave bear, bison, and other animals which provided their food, clothes, tools and the like. As early as the lower Perigordian period in western Europe, these early hunters had begun to reproduce on the walls of their caves and occasionally engrave into the surfaces of their weapons reproductions of the beasts they hunted. In a number of caves, such as in the recently discovered cavern of Lascaux, France, floor levels containing distinctive blade tools of Aurignacian types, may be correlated with monochrome paintings of the same age on the rock walls. These are simple, outlined representations of the Pleistocene mammals of that portion of the Würmian period which was familiar to Aurignacian and Gravettian hunters. Many of these early Upper Palaeolithic representations, however, are done with great vigor. A few show not only the outline of an animal figure on a cave wall, but also contour sculpture utilizing projections and irregularities of the natural rock.

It is tempting to derive all of the inspiration for the beginnings of art from some Eastern or Asiatic origin, along with the blade tools which are so distinctive. Most European scientists reject such a premise, and perhaps with good reason. A few compromise with the suggestion that the monochrome paintings on cave walls were European in development, and the plastic art of the Venus figurines was an Eastern derivation. However, if the urge to decorate is innate in modern humans, the beginnings of artistic attainment may well have begun with the development of reason itself.

The Upper Palaeolithic of Europe was not, however, a continuous development of Aurignacian blades and art forms. Coincidental with the second fluctuation of the Würm ice, there occurred a cultural interlude in Europe which sharply punctuated the Aurignacian and served to separate the early Upper Palaeolithic developments from those of later Würmian times. The name of this new period is derived from the village of Solutré, near Mâcon in France. Important excavations at this settlement of Upper Palaeolithic men have been car-

Aurignacian hunter-artist drawing animal figures on the wall of his cave home—Upper Palaeolithic period during Fourth or Würmian Glaciation.

Drawing of bison on a rock, Palaeolithic age.

Painting of a bull from Lascaux Cave, France.

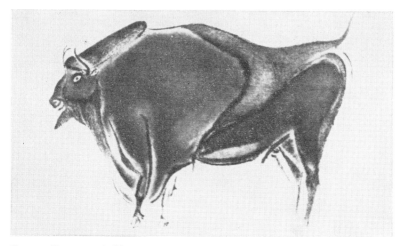

Bison standing, polychrome wall painting from the cave of Altamira in northern Spain.

Modern European bison.

Abbeyvillian man in northern France. One man is making a fist ax by the percussion method. Animals of the Middle Pleistocene in background.

ried on intermittently from 1866 to the present day. From the discoveries at Solutré and other cites where the same type of material has been recovered, it is evident that the *Solutrean* epoch is distinct and different from other Upper Palaeolithic horizons.

The semi-arctic steppe conditions, which prevailed during the second fluctuation of the Würm ice, produced a somewhat different climatic background for the Solutrean Period. The animals hunted by the Aurignacians changed in nature and in number. The mammoth migrated to other parts of Europe. In the open country of Solutrean times, the wild horse flourished, and herds of reindeer found a natural habitat along the peripheries of the ice fields.

It was not, however, the changes in the animal background which differentiated the Solutrean period from the rest of the Upper Palaeolithic. The flint tools of the Solutrean people were manufactured by a new technique. This process was pressure-flaking, by which flakes of flint were forced from the edge of a spall by means of carefully applied pressure with a bone tool. This new idea in the shaping of flint allowed the artisan to exercise more care in forming the implement, to perfect its balance, and to thin its bulk for easy penetration.

Typical Solutrean tools are predominantly projectile points carefully flaked by pressure chipping to form well-balanced, sharp, effective tips for javelins and spears. When the French excavators first uncovered the Solutrean implements from the camp site of Solutré, they heralded these as the finest examples of flint-chipping from the ancient world. This enthusiastic pronouncement may not be entirely true, as other ancient cultures in Egypt, China, and the New World also produced outstanding specimens of the flint workers' art. However, the Solutrean spear points are far more carefully made than any of the stone tools of the preceding European periods.

The full flowering of Solutrean pressure-flaking in western Europe is marked by *laurel-leaf* flint blades. Solutrean men chipped these points on both faces to produce a lanceolate-shaped penetrating point, with the maximum breadth always nearer the less pointed of the two ends. Another distinctive Solutrean form is the *willow leaf,* which is a narrower flint point chipped off sharply at both ends. Willow-leaf Solutrean blades were usually pressure flaked on one face only, leaving the other side flat.

73

In late Solutrean times, the flint craftsmen produced even finer examples of flint penetrating points, embodying the principle of the shouldered tang or haft which was a feature of the east Gravettian of the preceding period. Later Solutrean sites of southwestern France featured these slender, pressure-flaked Solutrean points with graceful tangs. This type of Solutrean blade is usually referred to as a *point-à-cran*.

Still further developments of this remarkable technique are found in northern Spain, where the Solutrean penetrated through passes in the Pyrenees. In Spain, and especially in the province of Catalonia, Solutrean pressure-flaking produced a wide variety of shouldered and tanged points with both symmetrical and asymmetrical outlines. The cave sites of Parpalló in Valencia have revealed a beautiful series of tanged and winged points of careful symmetry and workmanship which represent the Spanish version of the Solutrean.

From a study of the remarkable development of Solutrean pressure-flaking, European prehistorians had no difficulty in evolving a Solutrean sequence of events. The Solutrean period was divided into three sub-periods, lower, middle, and upper Solutrean. Even in the lowermost, however, the pressure-flaking technique was already developing. From this, it was deduced that the Solutrean was introduced into Europe, probably from some unknown Eastern source.

Other clues pertinent to the question of Solutrean origins were found in material recovered from the Szeleta Cave in Hungary. At this site, a number of flint points were recovered from the cave floor; although crude, they showed signs of Solutrean technique. These more roughly formed points have been called *Proto-Solutrean,* indicating their supposed typological position at the beginning of the Solutrian sequence. At the same time, the Szeleta Cave javelin points show a certain relationship to the preceding Acheulian fist axes which lingered on in some parts of Europe to form part of the Mousterian complex. Indeed, a rather small Acheulian hand ax formed with a wood-baton technique is similar to a Proto-Solutrean point roughly shaped with pressure-flaking. From this it would seem that the Solutrean was initiated by hunters living in the mountain caves of what is now northern Hungary. This development then spread westward during Würm II times to culminate in the typical French Solutrean sites such as Laugerie Haute and Badé Goulé with a final flourish in the Spanish Catalonian and Valencian areas.

There are, however, a number of authorities who believe that the true Solutrean was derived from Africa and not from Europe. They base their arguments on a number of African cultures which show laurel-leaf developments. Many of these manifestations in North Africa are difficult to date. The flint points which feature them, however, are quite distinctive, and were formed by a pressure-flaking technique suggestive of the Solutrean. A feature of the Szeleta Cave substantiates the idea of an African origin. At this Hungarian site, the Solutrean-like flints are mixed with split-base bone implements and nosed scrapers which seem to indicate middle Aurignacian connections and suggest that the mountain area had been a backwater of cultural development rather than the place of origin of the distinctive Solutrean. The caves of Parpalló in eastern Spain suggest that an African version of Solutrean may have been transmitted to France from the south.

Whether the Solutrean originated in northern Hungary or North Africa, it formed a distinctive and sharply marked epoch as far as western Europe was concerned. Although the Solutrean peoples lived in these western sites and developed their pressure-flaking technique for less than five thousand years, their presence clearly demarks the middle portion of the Upper Palaeolithic. Solutrean hunters killed the wild horses and reindeer which flourished in the open steppe conditions of Würm II. At some of the Solutrean stations, accumulations of the bones of the animals that they killed show that tens of thousands of carcasses were brought into camp by Solutrean hunters, demonstrating the effectiveness of the penetrating points formed by the superior technique of pressure-flaking.

Skeletons of the hunters have been found among the bones of their kills and associated with the flint points which distinguished them. At the site of Solutré, a number of human remains were recovered. Although some of these skeletons may have been derived from Aurignacian levels which underlie the original Solutrean site, it is quite plain that Solutrean men were modern in most respects. Their closest relationship is with Cro-Magnon types of the preceding Aurignacian times. However, the Solutrean skulls are broader and the indisputably Solutrean remains seem to be a distinctive type in themselves.

A number of physical anthropologists have sought to present Solutreans as the prototype of the later European Alpine race, which also features a broadfaced, broadheaded skull of the same general contours. It seems quite obvious that by the Solutrean epoch several types of modern humans were already present in Europe, Africa, and Asia. These had begun to mix as they moved from place to place with their various flint techniques. In some instances, we may trace these movements and mixtures by the flint tools which defy time so successfully. With other cultures, however, our best evidences may be the human skulls themselves.

The Solutrean epoch was not a lengthy one in Europe, nor was it widespread in its classic form. Solutrean techniques barely extended to England and northwestern Europe. In those places in northern Europe where the Solutrean did not penetrate, the Gravettian continued unbroken, with its blade tradition and shouldered points.

The artistic beginnings which had distinguished the Aurignacian in both the east and the west were not lost entirely by the Solutreans. There is ample evidence that the Solutrean hunters were familiar with their Gravettian neighbors. Solutrean sites feature flint blades, Aurignacian scrapers and gravers, and a continuation of the artistic tradition. As all of these early Europeans were hunters, it is not strange that their artistic depictions were of essentially the same style. Hunting art of this sort was found at Le Fourneau-du-Diable in the Dordogne. One Solutrean site, the cave of Le Roc in the Charente, shows that the Solutrean artisans could depict animals in any medium. Le Roc is especially distinctive since the animals here were formed in a group of relief sculpture. A frieze of horses, ibex, bison, and two human figures was drawn by the Solutrean hunters with as great a skill as any of the preceding Aurignacian depictions. Although Solutrean art is not as common as that which characterizes other periods of the Upper Palaeolithic, the hunters did carry on the tradition.

Though distinctive, Solutrean culture never changed the essential development of European culture. The Aurignacian tradition which lingered on in so many parts of Europe, again asserted itself and gave rise to the next and last period of the Upper Palaeolithic. This period, the climax of the whole Palaeolithic era, was known as the *Mag-*

dalenian, its name being derived from the cave site of La Madeleine in southern France. This new period was first identified from a number of cave sites discovered during the middle and last of the nineteenth century. It was not until the very last of the century, however, that the Magdalenian was identified as a distinctive period following the Solutrean but having little in common with the latter.

Magdalenian times featured not only the climax of the Upper Palaeolithic period but the end of the Würmian ice as well. A glacial climate still continued during the last of the Würmian fluctuations, but the ice-gathering forces had already spent themselves and the fourth or last glaciation was nearing its end.

In northern Europe, the cold tundra conditions prevailed, nurtured by the thawing tongues of ice of the Würmian extrusions. In southern Europe, the climate was already ameliorating. Even the pluvial conditions which moistened the climate on the southern fringes of the continental glaciations became less marked.

Many of the Pleistocene mammals, man's chief source of food through these difficult times, lingered on in Europe. The horse, bison, and mammoth grazed around the peripheries of the retreating glaciers, where they found conditions suitable to their existence. But in northern and northwestern Europe, the severe tundra-like terrain was favorable for the reindeer. Students usually typify the Magdalenian by this one animal, and certainly the reindeer was the most important food source during this period.

At several French sites, the Magdalenian has been found stratified above the Solutrean and below post–Upper Palaeolithic horizons. In spite of this, however, Magdalenian culture derived little from the preceding Solutrean way of life. On the contrary, early Magdalenian flint work and hunting equipment is a continuation of the Aurignacian tradition rather than the Gravettian which had persevered in the northern and northwestern peripheries of Europe while the Solutrean flourished in France. Well before the end of the Würmian period, the Magdalenian had completely obscured the Solutrean, and extended to all parts of western Europe, with the exception of southern Spain. On the basis of Magdalenian tool and weapon development, as well as on the progression of their hunting art, the Magdalenian period has been divided into six epochs.

Most distinctive among Magdalenian tools are the penetrating points with which these hunters killed reindeer and the other animals of late Pleistocene times. The Magdalenian craftsmen, instead of borrowing from the Solutrean's perfected flint-flaking techniques, continued to use bone for their hunting points. The Magdalenian spear points continue in a nearly unbroken series from the Aurignacian forms. These Magdalenian spear tips of bone or antler are usually referred to as *harpoons*. However, as the heads were not detachable, they were not true harpoons, but spears.

The earliest of the Magdalenian bone points was a pointed-base projectile of smooth outline, similar to the Aurignacian javelin heads. In the first and second epochs of the Magdalenian, the base of these points was often beveled for easier attachment to the shaft. Some of the early Magdalenian javelin heads had a groove or depression along one side, apparently to serve as a blood rill. Through Magdalenian III, these javelin points continued to be made with beveled bases and rounded cross sections. In the fourth epoch of the Magdalenian period, the barbed harpoon head appeared. At first the barbs were rudimentary, flat in cross section and cut on only one side of the penetrating point. Later, in Magdalenian V and VI, bone harpoon tips featured barbs with rounded cross sections cut into one or both sides of the elongated, pointed shaft. In these later epochs some of the finest Magdalenian bone work was developed, with saw-toothed javelin points armed with parallel or alternating barbs of hooked outline and fine finish. All Magdalenian weapons are usually stereotyped by the barbed harpoons, but these actually appeared only in late Magdalenian times.

The Magdalenians cast their spears with a spear thrower. This was a contrivance of bone or antler with a hook at one end and a hand grip at the other. The spear thrower greatly increased the leverage of the human arm. The spear was held above the spear thrower with the butt of the spear placed against the hook and propelled with an overarm motion, the hook giving added impetus to the throw. A foreshaft of bone or antler gave weight to the spear so its trajectory would be true.

In addition to bone penetrating points, Magdalenian craftsmen worked bone and horn into awls, needles, and other domestic implements. The fact that some Magdalenian needles are finely made implies the sewing of skins for use as clothing or shelter. *Baguettes,* or wands, of bone manufactured by the Magdalenians seem to indicate some authoritative or magical use. Some *baguettes* served as the foreshafts for spears. Especially interesting among the bone and horn manufactures of Magdalenian craftsmen are the *batons de command- ment.* Some of these problematical implements appear even earlier than Magdalenian times.

Batons usually consist of a section of reindeer antler with an attached tine cut to form a shape like the Greek letter, λ. Where the tine joins the main beam of the horn, a circular hole was cut through the antler. It has been suggested that the hole may have been used to rack or straighten javelin shafts which had become warped. Often these batons were carefully decorated as though for some ceremonial purpose. Both the *baguettes* and the batons, by their manufacture and decoration, follow a progression of development which may be divided into six stages similar to those of the javelin points and harpoons.

In spite of the fact that the Magdalenian hunters, and their women as well, seemed to rely upon bone and antler as working material, they did not abandon earlier flint forms entirely. Indeed, the Magdalenian displays a rich repertory of blades, scrapers, and burins. In general, early Magdalenian flint work was similar to that of the Aurignacian from which it originated. There are backed blades, strangulated blades, and even the shouldered points typical of the Gravettian. Some of the Magdalenian blade work was extremely well done, with the blades struck off to produce slender, razor-sharp slivers of flint. Magdalenian shaping was typically fine, with minute retouching along the edges to produce the desired outline. Especially typical is the parrot-beaked burin, which appeared in Magdalenian VI. This specialized implement, with a snout or beak on one end of the blade, seems to climax the whole Aurignacian-Gravettian-Magdalenian burin development.

Magdalenian hunters did not spend all of their time manufacturing javelin points and flint blades. In many parts of western and southwestern Europe they left abundant evidences of their artistic ability. Magdalenian art is usually divided into two classes—cave art and home art.

79

In southwestern Europe, there are dozens of caves which were occupied by the Magdalenians during late Würmian times. Magdalenian caves, with walls decorated with figures, were among the first discoveries made of Magdalenian remains. Many caves which had been inhabited and decorated by Magdalenians were found in southern France and northern Spain in the last part of the nineteenth century; for example the cave of Massat in southern France, and the incomparable cave of Altamira in northern Spain. Other caves in southern France were the Cap Blanc, Font-de-Gaume, Les Trois Frères, and the more recently discovered caverns of Lascaux. In the Cantabrian region of northern Spain, other Magdalenian cave homes were those of Castillo and Hornos de la Peña, to mention two. On the walls of these caves, Magdalenian artists created a rich assemblage of the mammals of their times. Only occasionally did they depict birds, reptiles, or themselves.

The home art of the Magdalenian craftsmen was carved upon fragments of bone or antler, or, less frequently, on pieces of stone. Such implements as knife handles, baguettes, and batons were engraved with the heads or bodies of the mammals which were the major prey of these hunting people.

The cave art and home art of the Magdalenian period has also been divided into six epochs on a basis of its development and change. In early Magdalenian times, the painting on the cave walls was carried over from the early Aurignacian. Some of these caves, such as that of Pair-non-Pair and Lascaux in southern France, show earlier Aurignacian painting on the same cave walls with later Magdalenian art.

The early Magdalenian mammal pictures were produced by hatching or flat outlines. There is no modeling and the figures are done in monochrome. It was only in the later Magdalenian epochs that two or three colors were used to produce the polychrome masterpieces which are so often associated with Magdalenian times.

As the Magdalenian artists learned to handle color, they also became masters of line and contour. Animals such as horses, bison, wild hogs, mammoth, and rhinoceroses were depicted in death, lying down, running, or charging. Many females are shown, usually pregnant. All of these attitudes and movements were achieved with remarkable skill, even on the unprepared walls of rough caves. Occasionally, Magdalenian artist-hunters showed a weapon piercing the flank of a fleeing beast, or they traced the outline of a trap around the body.

At the last of the Magdalenian art progression appeared a technique called atmospheric perspective. Single animals or groups are shown just as they would appear to the hunter's eye, with many details obscured by distance, dust, or intervening bushes. Thus a herd of reindeer might be pictured with only a suggestion of moving bodies in the general mass and a forest of tossing horns above. Through atmospheric perspective, a mammoth was made extremely realistic by showing only suggestions of the outline of the back and the curve of the tusks.

The purpose of Magdalenian art was probably not pure decoration, although the paintings and drawings served well in this capacity. From the indications of pregnancy as well as the many signs that the artists were interested in their creations from the hunter's point of view, it is evident that this was sympathetic magic of a high order. Animals depicted with fidelity would, by the principle of such magic, be lured before the javelin of the hunter. Females would reproduce large numbers of offspring so that the hunters could take advantage of the easy hunting and be assured of an abundant food supply.

The home art engravings on the handles of tools and fragments of bone were undoubtedly sympathetic magic in their own way and generally follow the same path of development as the cave paintings. In this long progression, it would seem that the Magdalenian craftsmen continually sought to make their carving more realistic, more lifelike, and more typical of the animal portrayed so that the sympathetic magic might be the more potent.

The human figure appeared infrequently in Magdalenian art, and usually as a priest officiating at rites which would facilitate hunting. The masked sorcerer which appears on the walls of the cave of Les Trois Frères in southern France is apparently a priest of this type. Although Magdalenian art was inspired by hunting ceremonialism, it nevertheless achieved a high order of intrinsic merit. In fact, histories of art often start with the Magdalenian period.

Not all Magdalenians lived in caves, nor was the Magdalenian culture known only to southern France and northern Spain. Magdalenian sites occur in Switzerland and in Bavarian Germany. Magdalenian material appears in Belgium and even across the Channel in England. In the northwestern portion of Europe, where the terrain was still tundra-like during the melt-water conditions of Würm III, a Magdalenian type of culture existed, dependent upon the hunting of reindeer. This northern version of the Magdalenian has been called the *Hamburg culture,* because many open campsites of reindeer hunters have been found in the vicinity of Hamburg in northwestern Germany. These less cultured cousins of the Magdalenians followed herds of reindeer as the animals seasonally migrated northward and southward. Such sites as Meiendorf in the Hamburg area show that these hunters had bone harpoons of the general Magdalenian sort. The flint work of the Hamburg culture, however, was a derivative of the tanged-point tradition, apparently a natural outcome of the east Gravettian.

In spite of this peripheral Magdalenian to the north, the Magdalenian was not widespread. Eastward, the Hamburg culture extended perhaps to Moravia. Westward, in the British Isles, the cave deposits of Cresswell Crags show a peripheral version of Magdalenian which is largely Gravettian. Thus the Magdalenian proper seems to have been a development of western and southwestern Europe, where it reached its full flower in the cave areas of Dordogne and Cantabria. True Magdalenian extends no farther south than Valencia in Spain. Elsewhere in the European peninsula, the flint-blade traditions of the Gravettian lingered on.

The human creators of the remarkable Magdalenian developments have been found in a number of instances embedded in cave floors, together with the implements and art which they produced. Magdalenian skeletons are generally classed as Cro-Magnons, although as stated previously, Cro-Magnon humans were a decided mixture. The Magdalenian type of human varies considerably from place to place in Europe, showing quite clearly that a number of human strains were already present in his make-up. All of these characteristics were, of course, Neanthropic, but with enough variation to indicate that most of the elements which were later to make up modern European races were already present by Magdalenian times. A typical Magdalenian type is the *Chancelade man* found at

Chancelade in the Dordogne region of France. The Chancelade skull shows certain Eskimoid characteristics in the keeled shape of the head and in features of the face and jaws. On this evidence as well as the fact that the Magdalenians habitually hunted reindeer under near arctic conditions, these hunters are often referred to as the "Eskimos" of ancient Europe.

The last of the Upper Palaeolithic was marked by continued developments in other parts of Europe. In Italy and along the Riviera, Gravettian-type culture developed into the *Grimaldian*. The Grimaldi Caves at Monaco, from which this culture was named, produced human skeletons as well as flinty material. The Grimaldi humans showed rather distinct differences from other Cro-Magnon variations. Some authorities suggested that the Grimaldi type of human might be the prototype of the Negro. The flint culture of the Italian Grimaldian featured smaller and smaller blades, gravers, and scrapers, worked in the Gravettian manner.

In southern Spain, too, there was an important variant culture at the end of the Upper Palaeolithic. This manifestation, the Spanish *Capsian,* was typical of southeastern Spain in Upper Palaeolithic and later times.

The Capsian culture was, for some years, regarded as a southern version of Aurignacian. This earlier date for the Capsian was based upon the presence of blade and burin tools. However, the Capsian culture also featured diminutive flint-blade forms which foreshadow the post-Upper Palaeolithic period of western Europe. It is now obvious that the Capsian must be placed at the extreme end of the Upper Palaeolithic series, even lasting over into post-Würmian times.

The Capsian was, in line with its supposed Aurignacian date, regarded as African in origin. Such distinguished authorities as Dorothy Garrod suggested that the Capsian was an offshoot of Aurignacian blade industries of Kenya Colony. However, it now seems that the Capsian may not have originated in Africa at all. On the contrary, it appears to be an indigenous, peripheral development of the same blade-making cultures that permeated western Europe.

The Capsian proper, or Spanish Capsian, as it was first called, is divided into two phases. The first of these is Upper Palaeolithic in character. The tools were elongated blades and thick-angled burins.

In the second stage, or late Capsian, the flint work diminished in size to the form of small micro-blades and micro-burins. There appeared also, in the late Capsian, the tiny, angular sections of flint blades called *microliths,* a type of tool which was to become the hallmark of the succeeding period following the Würmian glaciation.

European scholars chiefly remember the Capsian because of its artistic tradition. In spite of the fact that the Magdalenian was contemporary, at least in part, with the Capsian of eastern Spain, the art of the two horizons has little in common. Many of the Capsian sites were located in shallow caves and rock shelters. On the stone walls of these places, the Capsian hunters depicted animals also, but in addition to the animal art, they showed themselves in an equal ratio. Capsian drawings were also linear in style, rather than realistic, although the animation is great and most of the Capsian drawings very successfully show movement and even drama. There is some question about whether the purpose of the Capsian artists was the same as that of the Magdalenians with their sympathetic magic. A large portion of the Capsian pictures are hunting scenes, and Capsian bowmen are shown attacking herds of stags. This is the first clear representation of the bow and arrow in Europe. Since the animals are shown stricken with arrows it would be logical to suppose that this was hunting magic also; however, many of the Capsian pictures also show humans doing menial tasks, such as gathering wood or collecting honey from a bees' nest. The Capsian art, with its abundant use of human figures in all attitudes, differs radically from the Magdalenian.

At a number of sites which extend southward into the western portion of the Sahara Desert, there also occur cave paintings and rock decoration in the Capsian style. These were formerly supposed to be additional evidence of the southern origin of Capsian culture. Some of these picture drawings and rock paintings occur as far south as the southwestern deserts of Africa, in Bushman territory. Most of these African depictions have been assigned a later date than the Spanish Capsian, rather than earlier, as would be the case if the origins of this artistic style lay to the south. As it now stands, Capsian influences may well have retreated in this direction rather than arising from African beginnings, but there may be no connection between Spanish Capsian and its African namesake.

Whatever its origins, the Capsian is obviously not one of the cultural horizons of Europe which shaped the major trend. Rather, eastern Spain, during the period of the waning of the Würmian glaciation, was a backwater of culture where lingering remnants of Upper Palaeolithic ideas of life gradually dwindled and merged with later cultures.

CHAPTER 6

Middle Times

As THE GLACIAL ICE TONGUES of the Würmian melted away to the north, the human drama which was being enacted in these same regions changed also. The last glimmerings of the Magdalenian way of life dwindled with the changing times. Even the peripheral manifestations such as the Hamburg culture in the north and the Grimaldian farther to the east shifted emphasis. The period following the waning of the Würmian ice is called the *Mesolithic* to describe its position following the Upper Palaeolithic and preceding the later peasant cultures of an awakening Europe.

Climatic conditions were not the same throughout western Europe during this post-glacial epoch. In the south, the pluvial climate which had prevailed while the continental ice masses influenced the rainfall had now become progressively drier. The Sahara region of North Africa which had sustained human life during the upper Palaeolithic period because of its pluvial position, was desiccated to something like its present state. Farther north in Europe, the melt-water conditions which had marked the Hamburg culture of the northern Magdalenian still prevailed. The last large ice fields on the continent persisted in Scandinavia. As even these reluctant glacial masses shrank northward, they poured forth melt-water streams and left swamps and glacial lakes in their wake. In northern and northwestern Europe especially, coast lines changed as the earth expanded when the weight of the glacial masses was removed. These, with other complicating glacial factors, produced a succession of water bodies in what is now the Baltic Sea. Human cultures have been blended with this series of late glacial events. It was in northwestern Europe that pollen analysis was first employed to reveal a succession of vegetal changes in the swamps and bogs left behind by the last glacial ice.

The reindeer and other typical mammals of Magdalenian times disappeared to be replaced by the red stag and wild boar, both animals of the forest. Trees followed in the wake of the retreating glaciers to clothe the former open stretches with forest growth. With the changing habitat and mammalian life, human ways of life changed also.

To the pollen-analysis studies and the geological delineation of water bodies, shore lines, river terraces, and the like may be added most recent information derived from analysis of materials from Mesolithic sites dated by the Carbon 14 method. Dates derived from a careful examination of the radioactive carbon content of these specimens agree generally with pollen analysis and glacial studies. The Mesolithic period presumably began about twelve thousand years ago, lasting for perhaps six millenniums.

The Mesolithic way of life generally followed two trends in the traditions of tools. Some Mesolithic people continued to use Upper Palaeolithic implements but reduced their size to microliths, or pygmy flint forms. Other Mesolithic cultures developed wood-cutting tools or axes with which to combat the encroaching forests which covered Europe in the wake of the retreating glaciers. Most of Mesolithic culture was made up of one or both of these traditions.

In southern Europe the Mesolithic is best described by the type of life called *Azilian,* so named from the cave site of Mas d'Azil in the Ariège in southern France. At this place, Edward Piette, the excavator, found stratified above late Magdalenian material a series of fire hearths surrounded by implements distinctly different from the preceding Palaeolithic levels.

Especially outstanding in the Azilian was the use of microliths, small pieces of flint blades purposely chipped into angular shapes. The size of these fragments, however, was small enough to preclude their use by themselves. Apparently these tiny flints were set in slots or notches on bone hafts or wooden armatures to form multiple and tandem barbs, penetrating points, or knife edges. From a few specimens of this kind found at other Mesolithic sites, these small toothlike pieces of flint, when used in series, produced a better penetrating or cutting implement than a single flint tool shaped in the old tradition. Although microliths were found in the deposits of Mas d'Azil, they are not exclusive to that culture, but occur in greater or lesser abundance throughout the Mesolithic, and are, therefore, one of the distinguishing hallmarks of that period.

Microliths did not appear suddenly at Mas d'Azil or any other Mesolithic site, but were presaged by the diminutive flint blades of the late Magdalenian. Likewise, the so-called *micro-burin* technique was a hang-over from earlier times, presumedly an infiltration into southern Europe from Spain. The use of minute flint forms in the Mesolithic period, then, is not a surprise, but a legitimate outcome of tendencies to reduce the size of flint tools which had been in motion during the last centuries of the Upper Palaeolithic.

A most distinctive feature of the Azilian is the presence of small river pebbles which bear upon their smooth surfaces simple geometric designs in dull red paint. Painted pebbles are an invariable occurrence not only at the type site of Mas d'Azil but farther west in Bavaria and in other places where Azilian has been found.

Azilian decorated pebbles are apparently the degenerate art forms stemming from earlier Magdalenian tradition. A possible precursor to these rudimentary, conventionalized designs occurs in the Capsian rock shelters in eastern Spain. The Azilian painted pebbles may then be stagnant symbols of the earlier hunting art in the Spanish area. If this supposition is true, both the micro-burin technique and the painted pebbles are southern innovations in the Azilian.

Another distinctive Azilian weapon was the staghorn harpoon. This type of point, while not a true harpoon, was obviously inspired by Magdalenian prototypes which themselves were nondetachable from their hafts. The Azilian harpoons, however, were heavier, with two or three blunt, wide, barbs as contrasted with the earlier multi-barbed, finely finished Magdalenian examples. Many archaeologists professed to see in the Azilian bone and antler work a decline from the height of the Magdalenian.

The Azilian culture lasted well through the Mesolithic period and extended over much of southern and central Europe. Its center was obviously in southern France, with extensions to the eastward and northeastward in Württemberg and Bavaria. In the latter area, at the cave of Ofnet, a remarkable series of burials have been found which are presumed to be connected with the Azilian. These comprise nests of human skulls, obviously remains of heads hacked from the bodies, which were not interred with them. The skulls were placed in prepared cists lined and covered with red ochre and further embellished with shell and animal-tooth pendants and beads. The peculiar nests of skulls at Ofnet are perhaps examples of a strange Azilian type of burial, or they may have a more grisly significance.

The skulls in the cave of Ofnet, which include those of women and children, show a remarkable range of physical types. Some of the head forms and facial features definitely recall Upper Palaeolithic variations such as those connected with the Gravettian. Both meso-cephalic and brachycephalic types occur among the Ofnet skulls, with indications, also, of longheadedness. The Azilian culture of the Mesolithic was already mixed in population.

The Azilian, representing the continuation of late Magdalenian culture with some Spanish elements, was paralleled in areas of Italy and Great Britain where there was no classic Magdalenian. In these regions, the Gravettian continued practically uninterrupted from Upper Palaeolithic times. The Mesolithic period was marked in these areas by a series of cultures which continued the Gravettian way of life in varying degrees.

A more northerly Mesolithic manifestation which may be distinguished from the Azilian, is called the *Tardenoisian* from the region of Fère-en-Tardenois in northern France where sites of this culture are found. The Tardenoisian is a peripheral Magdalenian offspring which may have originated as far away as North Africa. Typical

89

Tardenoisian featured microliths and related blade implements almost exclusively. Open sites along river terraces in this area show a profusion of the small, geometric pieces of flint which are the hallmark of the culture. A later version of the Tardenoisian type of Mesolithic life extended practically unbroken across Europe, eastward to southern Russia. Tardenoisians also profoundly influenced other Mesolithic groups living in northern and northwestern Europe.

A variation of the Tardenoisian is the *Sauveterrian*. This culture is a more southern version of the middle Tardenoisian named from a site in southern Périgord. The Sauveterrian was also marked by geometric microliths and micro-burins. It differs from the Azilian only in the absence of antler harpoons and painted pebbles. Many French archaeologists now use the term Tardenoisian to designate only the later and fully developed phase of the culture.

As the glaciers waned in the Alpine region and in Scandinavia, several groups of peoples pressing into northern Europe attempted to cling to their former Upper Palaeolithic ways of life in the midst of these changing conditions. The Hamburg culture was one such group which had grown out of the east Gravettian tradition with its typical tanged points of flint. This gave rise to a series of *tanged-point cultures* in early Mesolithic times, which extended from Belgium to the Ukraine.

Perhaps the best known tanged-point manifestation is that called the *Swiderian* from the site of Swidry in Poland. Asymmetrical arrow heads chipped from a blade and the increasing development of microlithic forms are typical of the Swiderian. From this progression an earlier, or late Upper Palaeolithic Swiderian, may be distinguished from a later or Mesolithic Swiderian. The Swiderian is reported as far away as southern Russia and the Ukraine, and may have originated there.

At Ahrensburg-Stellmoor near Hamburg, another tanged-point manifestation has been found together with antler axes of a northern Mesolithic tradition. At Remonchamps Cave in Belgium another version of the tanged-point culture appears. Late and lingering groups of people in Scandinavia continued the tanged-point tradition through the entire Mesolithic period. Such a group was that at Fosna on the west coast of Norway. This remote colony carried on essentially an

Upper Palaeolithic way of life until the end of the Mesolithic and the beginning of the Neolithic period.

As the post-glacial period of the Mesolithic developed, there appeared a whole series of cultures stretched across northern Europe from the British Isles to Finland. Each of these borrowed certain elements from the preceding Upper Palaeolithic and added features of its own. Many of these northern Mesolithic cultures were represented by a single site or by a very small area. Others were more extensive.

Most important of the Mesolithic manifestations of northern Europe was that collectively called the *Maglemosean*, named from the "great bog" area in Zealand. This horizon is in reality a series of cultures concentrated primarily in the region of northern Germany and Denmark with related groups in southern Scandinavia. The Maglemosean was a way of life adapted especially to the post-glacial forest and swamp conditions of this area. Successful existence in this terrain in the post-glacial epoch was made possible by the development of the ax, which was originally found in the Moravian version of the Gravettian at Předmost. Upper Palaeolithic hunters moving northward may have introduced the ax tradition.

The first of these axes was a cutting implement manufactured entirely from antler, usually from the tines of the red stag, a common animal of the period. This antler ax, called the *Lyngby* type from Nørre-Lyngby, was made by cutting the main beam and a single tine of a red stag antler, so that one axis formed the handle of the implement and the other the beveled cutting edge. Some of these may not have been axes at all but clubs or picks. In other Lyngby antler axes, the stub of the tine had been hollowed out to act as a socket for the insertion of the actual ax.

A final Maglemosean innovation was a flint cutting ax called a *tranchet*. This was an obvious improvement over the Lyngby type of implement. The flint tranchet was sharpened at its bit end by a single *tranchet stroke* which was aimed at one side of the ax in such a way as to detach a long flake, leaving a raw beveled cutting edge for the bit of the instrument. The tranchet was mounted in turn in a wooden handle.

Later in the northern Mesolithic, a further improvement was

added to the ax in the form of an antler sleeve, in which the flint ax was mounted. This sleeve of stag antler was in turn fixed to a wooden handle. Thus the development of the wood-cutting ax enabled the people of northern Europe to carve out an existence in the forest-clad terrain. For this reason, many anthropologists refer to these times as the Forest period. The series of cultures which resulted from this development are also often referred to as the *ax cultures*.

The Maglemosean, or *big bog period*, is often characterized as a waterside type of life. In peat bogs, where perishable items might be preserved, portions of dugout canoes, steering paddles, rafts, and piles have been recovered as indications that Maglemosean peoples lived and traveled on water. Sledges and skates were used when the Ancyclus Lake, the main water body of the time, was frozen in winter. But there are inland Maglemosean sites, also, such as that at Gudenaa in central Denmark, where slight evidences of seacoast or waterside life are evident. An early typical site of the standard Maglemosean is Duvensee near Lübeck in northern Germany.

Maglemosean hunters utilized bone and antler in a great variety of forms. Fish-hooks, needles, awls, fish spears, and barbed harpoons were all fashioned of bony materials. Many bone points were slotted on one or both edges for the mounting of microliths in the true Mesolithic tradition. Ax sleeves and adzes of bone and antler were an improvement upon earlier wood-working tools.

On Maglemosean sites on the island of Zealand, the domestic dog appeared in the Mesolithic life as an aid to hunting. This dog was already a developed type, close to the present Norwegian wolfhound, and not merely a wild form kept in captivity.

On the basis of all the implements, as well as on stratigraphic studies, the Maglemosean divides itself into a sequence of Mesolithic people. The Maglemosean culture is divided by many authorities into three stages, of which only the second is Maglemosean proper.

The first of these is called the Lyngby epoch, as the chief feature of this introductory period is the Lyngby ax of antler. The Lyngby period is further distinguished by bone and antler manufacture in the form of adzes, hafts, and crude points of the same material.

The Maglemosean proper follows the Lyngby with a repertory or microlithic and flint forms. The transverse ax or tranchet is typical of this period. Perforated adzes and mace heads also occur. A distinctive Maglemosean implement is the transverse arrowhead. These points were manufactured out of the mid-section of a flint blade, with a cutting edge on the tip of the arrow rather than a penetrating point. The use of the bow and arrow had already been demonstrated earlier by the Aterians of North Africa and by the Capsian paintings of eastern Spain.

In the last period of Maglemosean times, the Mesolithic way of life changed even more radically as the lingering vestiges of the glacial age dried away. This final phase is referred to as the *Kitchen Midden* period and is typified by the site of Ertebølle in Denmark. At this site, as in several others in the area, the inhabitants were forced to subsist on the seacoasts by the ever increasing forest vegetation which thickly covered the land. They ate large quantities of shellfish which lived in the warm Littorina Sea. The large deposits of shell mixed with the bone, stone, charcoal, and other debris of human living accumulated in piles, or middens, which were stratified by the various phases of the human story. In these kitchen middens were found large numbers of flint tools to show that the *Ertebølle* way of life was a legitimate continuation of the Mesolithic. Transverse arrowheads and tranchets also were used. Axes were made by chipping and subsequently grinding the edge to a cutting bit, for example, the *Limhamn ax*. Long picks chipped out of flint show that the Ertebølle peoples varied their tools for different uses. Perhaps the most significant change of stone working was the use of pebble axes. These cutting implements first used in the Maglemosean were pecked and ground on river pebbles rather than chipped from flinty material. The technique of working granitic or nonflint stones was to become common in post-Mesolithic times.

The Mesolithic cultures of the Maglemosean area climax their range of innovations with the appearance of pottery. The Ertebølle or Kitchen Midden phase featured baggy, pointed-bottom clay vessels and oval lamps of pottery. Sherds of Ertebølle pottery at the site of Aamose have been dated from the beginning of the Atlantic phase of climatic history in the Baltic area. No other peoples could have transmitted the idea of pottery to the Kitchen Midden dwellers so eagerly.

There are some as yet uncertain evidences of the manufacture of roughly made clay containers from the upper Magdalenian of Belgium. Indeed, there is a strong suggestion that the peoples of northwestern Europe evolved the making of pottery in its various steps indigenously. In spite of the fact that many Mesolithic groups did not make pottery, the trait was well established in northwestern Europe by Ertebølle times.

It must be emphasized that pottery-making is not simply the heating and hardening of once-plastic clay. The manufacture of true pottery involves a chemical change and a true discovery. When aluminum silicate, which is the principal component of clay, is heated to a high temperature, the water inherent in the mixture is driven out to produce a hard substance with different properties from the original clay. The chemically changed pottery will not remix with water. As such, the vessels so made, or fragments of them, remain in archaeological deposits as valuable criteria for the scientist who seeks to place these cultures in their proper perspective. Archaeologically, the discovery of pottery is most significant. A number of pottery-bearing cultures in northern and northwestern Europe which formerly were regarded as much later, may now be placed in the Mesolithic.

On the shores of the Baltic Sea and in the southern regions of the Scandinavian area were a number of Mesolithic groups chiefly distinguished by various forms of axes, but lacking pottery. These, together with the Maglemosean sequence, are often called the *ax cultures*. Some of the other ax cultures had a less impressive range of tools than the Maglemosean, and retained many Upper Palaeolithic characteristics even into later times.

Such ax cultures were those named after the site of Lihult in Sweden and Nøstvet in Norway. Both of the latter were distinguished by axes made of volcanic stone, shaped by pecking, grinding, and crude flaking. Other types of axes and ax cultures characterized such sites as Limhamn, which featured chipped and ground axes, Aargus, and Svaerdborg. In the northern Mesolithic cultures, such as those in Norway and Sweden which extended to northern Scandinavia, there was a rebirth of art of the sympathetic-hunting-magic variety such as had been used by the Upper Palaeolithic peoples before them.

This style, usually engraved on rocks along ancient shore lines, is often called the *Arctic Stone Age art.* Such subjects as elk, reindeer, bears, and sea mammals were commonly depicted.

Ax-making forest- and shore-dwelling peoples lived also to the eastward during Mesolithic times. Typical of the Mesolithic cultures which inhabited coastal Poland, northern Russia, and the eastern Baltic countries was the *Suomusjarvie* culture in the area of Finland and Estonia. Suomusjarvie tools were chiefly axes, fashioned from basaltic rock. Similar sites in the former countries of Estonia, Latvia, and northern Poland, indicate that ax-using peoples had cleared the forests and killed the animals of Mesolithic times there. A variation of the Maglemosean is exemplified by Pernau in northern Lavonia and Kunda in Estonia, where emphasis was on bone as a universal material. At Pernau and Kunda on the eastern shores of the ancient Ancyclus Lake, bone was used for axes, adzes, and projectile points.

Another variant of Mesolithic life in the north was the *Finnmarkian culture,* named for its location in the Finnmark along the ice-free periphery of the Arctic Ocean. The Finnmarkian apparently originated from Upper Palaeolithic hunters who worked their way northward by way of the Karelian Isthmus from northern Russia bringing with them a tradition of tanged points and blade-making. This Upper Palaeolithic survival in the far north was contemporaneous with the fully developed microlithic and ax-using cultures farther south.

In the region of Belgium, a vague type of Mesolithic has been distinguished under the name of *Campignian.* This culture was supposedly differentiated by the use of a chipped pick called, from the type site at the mouth of the Seine River, a *Campignian pick.* The Campignian peoples also used Tardenoisian-like tools in the form of microliths. Campignian differs from the Ertebølle in the lack of bone, and sites are unmarked by kitchen middens. The Belgian Campignian, however, does feature the tranverse ax and crude pottery similar to the Ertebølle. There seems little doubt that the Campignian version of the Mesolithic was an outgrowth of the Tardenoisian with certain Maglemosean features. In spite of the Mesolithic types of flint tools, some authorities place the Campignian in later times and regard Campignian pottery as a diffusion from early Neolithic rather than an outgrowth of Ertebølle.

95

As the British Isles were still connected with the continent by a tenuous and swampy isthmus in the beginning of Mesolithic times, it is not surprising to find British Mesolithic closely resembling that of the continent. As the separation between Britain and Europe occurred during the *Boreal period,* the variations in the British and Irish Mesolithic are understandable.

In the Mesolithic period the British Isles received three streams of migration and influence representing the three major varieties of Mesolithic life. In the north, the Maglemoseans pressed across the marshy North Sea by boat and landed on the British coasts to occupy the shore line and river valleys suited to their littoral way of life. From the east, the Tardenoisians crossed from northern France, probably on dry land, to bring their typical microliths and the way of life which was adapted to the compound tools which they fashioned from the tiny flints. In the southeast, the Azilians also crossed to British shores from southern France. The Azilians apparently scattered from southwestern England to Scotland. Since the subsidence of the shore lines in late Mesolithic times, most of these coastal regions have been submerged and the remains of many of these Mesolithic peoples lost. At present, the Azilian sites in Britain are preserved for the most part in the higher ground of southwestern Scotland.

As these three continental versions of Mesolithic life became established on British soil, they began to change and to influence one another. Of especial note is the survival of some of the indigenous inhabitants of Gravettian Palaeolithic cultural status from the caves of Creswell Crags in Derbyshire. Some of these Creswellian groups remained in interior Britain and some migrated to Ireland, where the transplanted culture persisted long after the Mesolithic was well established elsewhere.

In Britain proper the Maglemosean immigrants continued their hunting and fishing activities as they had in their forested homeland in northern Europe. Their hunting tools were bone spears, leisters, and fishhooks. To clear the forests around them, they chipped rough core axes of flint and made true tranchets in the Maglemosean tradition. A specialized form of roughed-out ax called the *Thames pick* was developed by Maglemoseans in Britain. Such sites as Broxbourne in Hertfordshire show typical Maglemosean debris. Even off the coast on inundated shorelands, occasional remains are recovered, such as the bone point of typical Maglemosean manufacture which was dredged up by a fisherman from a depth of twenty fathoms off the coast of Norfolk.

Maglemosean immigrants to Britain confined themselves principally to lowland coastal areas or river valleys. Late Maglemosean remains are especially concentrated in the Thames valley. Axes typical of the Forest period have been found as far removed as Pembrokeshire and Cornwall. A few Maglemosean folk crossed over to Ireland and left axes there.

In Britain proper, the Tardenoisians from northern France may have come over to England in two periods or waves. They occupied open country in Britain in areas of sandy soil, where the land was unforested or the trees few. The classic Tardenoisians did not make wood-cutting axes as the forest-dwelling Maglemoseans had learned to do. With microliths they manufactured compound hunting weapons and with these developed a satisfactory existence. The earliest Tardenoisian tools were wide and short. These broad-blade microliths were typical of earlier Tardenoisian on the continent and may represent the first movement of these people to Britain. Another development of the British Tardenoisian was the use of small geometric forms, which may mark the coming of the second Tardenoisian group from the region of Belgium and northern France.

Tardenoisian sites in Britain vary from small, summer hunting camps at comparatively high elevations on the Pennines to lowland winter habitations such as those in the Colne valley in Essex and the pit dwellings near Farnham in Surrey.

In Tardenoisian pit-house sites the microlithic tradition is mixed with the Maglemosean. Classic Tardenoisian hunters lived in open sites in shelters built of brush or ephemeral materials which have left little archaeological trace. The intermingling of Tardenoisian and Maglemosean tradition can be seen in the *Horsham culture* of the greensand area in Essex, Kent, Surrey, and Sussex. The Horsham complex consists of geometric microliths augmented by rough flaked axes of the Maglemosean tradition. Horsham people of mixed backgrounds occupied the pit dwellings near Farnham in Surrey.

The Azilian remains in Britain are now confined only to western

97

Scotland. Flat, poorly barbed harpoons from the rock shelters of Oban in this area resemble the Azilian types from southern France. Azilians along the Scottish shore also used elongated pieces of bone and antler blunted at both ends and long pebbles of the same shape. These may have served as flint chippers. The use of flint did not extend beyond the manufacture of gravers and micro-burins. With this equipment the Azilians of Scotland hunted red and roe deer, boar, and seal. They fished and collected shellfish and nuts.

The Azilian culture was apparently not widespread in Britain, but much of the strand upon which Azilians lived has subsided beneath the sea, submerging possible sites on those shores. However, there is little trace of Azilian life in the area between the Dordogne in southern France and northwestern Britain and Scotland, where they reappear. The now inundated lands of the English Channel may cover such evidences.

In Ireland, the Upper Palaeolithic tradition of Cresswell Crags with its Gravettian background persisted during these times. The implements, associated with a few mammals of post-glacial times, show the survival of the old Palaeolithic stock. In northern Ireland the flint-working techniques showed the carry-over of this old tradition into Mesolithic times. Groups on the Island Magee and Cushendun made broad, thick blades and scrapers of general Upper Palaeolithic varieties, and other local styles developed from this background.

On the beach at Larne, Ireland, axes in the Maglemosean tradition show the intrusion of these people across the Irish Sea. Cresswellian tradition is followed by Maglemosean at Glenarm, Ireland. Here, Movius found core and flake axes associated with the bones of sheep and cows above the remains of an earlier Upper Palaeolithic type of life. Apparently Mesolithic forms arrived late in Ireland from Britain or directly from France, and certain of these Mesolithic types lingered here into the following Neolithic period.

Far to the south, along the coast of the Bay of Biscay and in northern Spain, other Mesolithic people have left abundant traces. There are also some Azilian indications in this area. However, overlaying Azilian sites, in some instances, and extending into areas where the true Azilian did not penetrate are large shell middens formed from the accumulated piles of oyster, limpet, and cockle shells thrown there by an early, shellfish-eating people. This population made rough axes from small cobbles and pointed picks from pebbles. There are scrapers of rough stone and a few bone tools to show that these shore dwellers occasionally hunted land mammals and dressed the skins.

This beachcombing culture, first regarded as Acheulean because of its crudity, has been called the *Asturian,* from the province of Spain where the shell middens are the most numerous, and is found in strata overlaying the Azilian.

A well-known site of the late Mesolithic on the Iberian Peninsula is that of Mugem in the Tagus Valley, with its series of shell mounds or kitchen midden deposits with a large content of shells. A few of the mounds are located some distance from the sea. The shore dwellers at Mugem developed an advanced Tardenoisian-like flint industry of general Mesolithic features. Bones mixed with the shell debris in the Mugem midden are those of present-day fauna, including the sheep, horse, and dog. A large number of human skeletons were also recovered from the Mugem site. These show a wide range of head type and facial contour.

Other Mesolithic discoveries were made in the region of Hungary, Italy, and Sicily. Generally, an earlier Azilian-Magdalenian type of culture was maintained in central Europe. Mesolithic life in the Hungarian Plain was represented by a people who made large axes and heavier implements. This Hungarian Mesolithic has been called the *Avas culture.* Micro-burins were unknown, and there is little evidence of any of the smaller types of weapons and tools that characterize the Tardenoisian. Instead, the Avas culture seems much more closely allied to the Forest or Ax cultures of northern Europe.

The Grimaldian flint tradition persisted in Italy and Sicily. In the south of France and in Spain the late Tardenoisian type of geometric microliths were found stratified over the previous Azilian. In Spain, the micro-burin which originated there remained a dominant form. Southward, nearer the coasts of North Africa, strong evidence suggests that the microlithic technique originated there at the end of the Upper Palaeolithic.

On the coasts of North Africa there were Mesolithic cultures which retained the Upper Palaeolithic traditions. The upper or terminal Capsian was such a culture and lingered in the region of Tunisia. This later Capsian is definitely Mesolithic in date, although its typical tools and techniques are upper Palaeolithic in character. Another blade-making culture, the *Oranian,* in Morocco, perpetuated the Upper Palaeolithic traditions in that part of North Africa.

Formerly the Capsian was thought to have entered through the Iberian Peninsula and evolved into the Capsian culture of eastern Spain. The Oranian also was believed to have arisen in Iberia and as such was called the *Ibero-Maurusian.* Further study has indicated that neither the Capsian nor the Oranian moved across the Gibraltar area to enter Spain. Thus, so-called *Spanish Capsian* was apparently a degenerate version of an essentially indigenous Upper Palaeolithic culture. Consistent with the general character of the Mesolithic, the Spanish Capsian featured knife forms reduced to microlithic size.

In Egypt a Mesolithic culture, the *Sebilian,* proves the extension of microlithic tools to Egypt. Near Jerusalem and Jaffa in Palestine another Mesolithic manifestation, the *Natufian,* excavated by Dorothy Garrod, produced microlithic forms of flint tools in lunate and semi-lunate shapes which were mounted in rib bones to serve as sickles. Many of these were polished with a peculiar gloss which could only result from their use in cutting grasses or straw. It has been suggested that the Natufians may have practiced some primitive agriculture. However, it seems more probable that they simply gathered wild seed-bearing grasses as a supplementary food.

In southeastern Europe, the Mesolithic was separated from the more western Azilian-Tardenoisian tradition. Instead, Rumanian and Bessarabian Mesolithic people used heavy axes, rough flint points, blades, and scrapers that recall the Upper Palaeolithic. The Mesolithic as we know it seems to have originated in western Europe. These origins are significant in a consideration of the appearance of the European Neolithic culture which originated far from western Europe in the Near East.

The latest developments of the Mesolithic appear to have widely influenced the developing Tardenoisian type of culture. The presence of geometric microliths carefully worked in triangles, semicircles, trapezoids, rhomboids, diamonds, and squares suggests this influence. This late Tardenoisian is called *Montbani* from the type site in the

Aisne country of France. Thus, the Tardenoisian sequence from early to late is:

| Azilian | Early Tardenoisian (Tardenois) | Middle Tardenoisian (Sauveterre) |

Late Tardenoisian
(Montbani)

The late Tardenoisian, or Montbani, varieties of geometric microliths are absent in England as Montbani man did not cross the channel that separated the British Isles and France by this time. On the other hand, the late Tardenoisian is found widespread on continental Europe. In the caves of the Crimea, a southern Russian version of Azilian gives way to geometric microliths of the Tardenoisian tradition. Similar microlithic complexes of late Tardenoisian nature were universal from the Ukraine to Silesia and northern Germany. Late Tardenoisian types of tools influenced the Ertebølle tradition of the Maglemosean area.

The middle times of the Mesolithic were, then, both transitional and formational. The roots of the western European Mesolithic were definitely in the Upper Palaeolithic of those same regions. We may legitimately derive all of the major Mesolithic cultures in understandable progression from a preceding way of life. The Magdalenian-Capsian was the forerunner in the south, the Gravettian in northern and northeastern areas.

However, the Mesolithic also contained a number of new elements which were to be the foundation of the new Europe which followed. Among these was the ax, both in its plain antler or sleeved form, and the several stone versions. Several northern Mesolithic cultures had learned to peck and shape basaltic and granitic stones in addition to the old traditions of flint working. Mesolithic peoples of western Europe also utilized the bow and arrow, and manufactured pottery.

The development of housing in this period was significant. Maglemosean hunters, with their new axes, cut logs from the boreal forests to build lean-tos and cabins. Tardenoisian and allied people dug pit houses into the ground and roofed them with poles and skins. These houses were an improvement over the nomadic Palaeolithic man's penchant for natural caves.

There is little doubt that Mesolithic times introduced human society as we know it. People lived and hunted in groups, larger in most instances than those of the earlier Palaeolithic peoples. Their better weapons and tools gave them a greater command over their environment and a greater adaptability to changes in condition.

Although the mixing and movement of peoples had begun in Upper Palaeolithic times, the Mesolithic was an important epoch of great migration. Tardenoisian-type implements influenced a wide area in Europe. Other Mesolithic peoples traveled and shifted their settlements with the changing conditions of the post-glacial period. Methods of water transportation added to the mobility of some Mesolithic peoples. Three waves or more of Mesolithic groups crossed over to the British Isles and Ireland along routes which were to be used by many other migrants of later times. The mixed types of human skeletal remains on almost all Mesolithic sites indicate that the Mesolithic peoples of Europe already displayed most of the physical characteristics of later European races.

Another important contribution of the Mesolithic was the beginning of the domestication of animals. The only indisputable representation of this trend is the dog, noted in the Maglemosean and in Mesolithic remains in Great Britain. Some European authorities, however, pointed to the bones of the European boar as evidence of the domestication of swine and, in other instances, of sheep and even horses. The dog belongs in a special category, however, since it was apparently used as an aid in hunting rather than for food. Nonetheless, the principle of domestication had already appeared. This utilization of animal forms for the use of man was to be one of the major characteristics of the period which followed. Indeed, we may say that the Mesolithic contained all of the elements necessary to form the succeeding foundations of Neolithic Europe with one exception —that of agriculture. When man learned to sow seeds and reap a harvest, he definitely began a new era.

CHAPTER 7

The New Era

FOLLOWING THE TIME of the final waning of the continental glaciers of Europe there were profound changes not only in climate, but in the basic way of life among the humans who depended upon the natural products of this cosmic metamorphosis. During the middle times of the Mesolithic, these differences were already manifest. But even during the Mesolithic, humans still hunted, fished, or gathered the produce of nature. It was only when the changes in human living shifted from a passive dependence upon the foods which a capricious nature offered them to an active production of foodstuffs by man himself that we mark the beginning of a new way of life.

Archaeologists, concerned with the minutiae of these changes, early seized upon changes in the stone tools to designate the new era. The developing period was called the *Neolithic,* which means "new stone age," referring to a new technique for the shaping of stones other than flint or silicious varieties. The previous Palaeolithic, or "old stone age," featured the flaking and chipping of flinty stones,

NEOLITHIC EUROPE

Major Neolithic sites and migratory movements are indicated.

0   100   200   300   400   500 miles

Globe
Amphora

attle-Ax
Zlota

lobe Amphora

Kamkeramic

Warrior
Cultures

Fatyanovo

Tripolye

Warrior Cultures

Painted Pottery

Erösd

ltures

Boian

Gumelnitza

Kuban

Troy

Anatolia

Mesopotamian
Neolithic

elladic

Minöan

eolithic

Merimde

but the archaeologists had noted that the new era was characterized in most places by the use of other kinds of rock, shaped by pecking and grinding. The most typical tool made by this new process was an ax, pecked and rubbed to a cutting bit on one end. This implement is called a *celt* and is found in varied forms in early Europe as well as in other parts of the world.

Actually, the term Neolithic as applied to this new and important period is a misnomer on two counts. Although the celt and certain other pecked and ground forms of stone are indeed typical of the Neolithic period, they are by no means restricted to it. We have already seen that pecked and ground forms of axes were actually developed in the Mesolithic. Also, the method of shaping stone, even had it been confined to this new era, is not the most outstanding of the changes that took place. Celts and their method of manufacture were only incidental to the new life. Although the term Neolithic is now firmly embedded in the literature and used widely by all who refer to these times, it is neither a correct nor a completely descriptive term.

Stone arrow points found at archaeological sites indicate that the bow and arrow were typical of the new era. The previous periods of the Palaeolithic had been typified by the spear and throwing javelin. However, even the bow and arrow were not invented at the onset of the Neolithic. The Capsian rock paintings of Spain show that these people knew and used the bow and arrow prior to the beginnings of the Neolithic. The transverse arrowheads found on the many sites in northern Europe also indicate that the bow and arrow was a familiar weapon there during the Mesolithic. Here, as in the case of the celt, the beginnings of this typical weapon were well within the Mesolithic period.

The use of the loom and the process of weaving are also typical of the new life of the Neolithic. Provident people learned to twist animal or vegetable fibers into threads by a spinning process which actually changed the nature of the material involved. The thread could then be woven into fabrics of various sorts for different purposes. With the loom, the early weaver was again the shaper of nature rather than the passive receiver of natural products, like the hunter who used wild animal skins stripped from the carcasses of his kills.

But even the loom may not be exclusively Neolithic in date. Even before the Neolithic era, baskets and possibly cloth had been woven with natural materials.

Many archaeologists, seeking to find some concrete criteria by which the Neolithic might be differentiated, seized upon pottery as the most distinctive feature. They noticed that archaeological sites which contained potsherds within their strata, were usually Neolithic in date. This is indeed true, for the making of pottery was a typical product of the new era.

But the greatest differences of this new age were not in improvements of shaping stone, in pottery, or even in the greater use of tools and utensils which had been developed in earlier epochs. The two greatest innovations which clearly marked the Neolithic as a new way of life were the development of agriculture and the domestication of animals.

The people who brought forth these revolutionary innovations were not the Mesolithic cultures of western and northwestern Europe, whose progress we have followed through the passing of the Pleistocene period. The humans who first achieved agriculture and animal husbandry were groups peripheral to Europe, perhaps the descendants of those artisans of Hither Asia who first discovered flint blade-making at the initiation of the Upper Palaeolithic period and first spread that trait into Europe.

The changes coincidental with the waning of the glacial age have been cited as the direct cause of these momentous developments. The lush grasslands of North Africa withered as the country became drier with the decline of the glacial influences to the north. Desert and semidesert situations made life impossible over much of this area. Only a few oases punctuated the dry terrain, and human life clustered around these wet spots to survive at all. In late Mesolithic times there was a resurgence of pluvial conditions over much of this area. Around 8000 b.c. the rainfall increased almost to its former status. For this, as well as other reasons, it was not desiccation alone that brought about the new way of life. Indeed, the renewal of the pluvial conditions may have stimulated a process which was already started.

We presume that these early humans, looking for other food in times of scarcity, turned to the cutting of wild seed-bearing grasses to supplement their diet. In the Natufian culture in the Palestinian region, there are evidences of this situation. Wild wheat was native to southwestern Asia. Wild emmer, an important kind of wheat, grew wild in Syria, Palestine, and Iran. Wild barley also was present in this region as well as in North Africa. Several varieties of cattle and sheep were present in Asia.

The first indications of agriculture and stock raising appear already developed in the lowest levels of several sites in Mesopotamia and in the larger area which is often called the *Fertile Crescent,* which extends westward to Palestine and the Mediterranean coast. These places, called *tells,* are actually hills of accumulated debris which comprise records of successive occupations on one spot for great lengths of time. Thus the Tell Al' Ubaid and the Tell of Ur show in their lowermost depths deposits left by settlers who had already developed a well-established Neolithic way of life. There are other sites in northern Syria, such as that of Tell Halaf, which show the same early beginnings of civilization. Recent discoveries in several places in Iraq, Iran, Turkey, and Syria supply other details on this expanding way of life. One of the most important sites is that of Jarmo in eastern Iraq, where Robert Braidwood found evidence of very early farming and stock raising carried on by people who already lived in a village. A date derived from ancient Jarmo determined by the radioactive carbon method was 6,707 years before the present with a possible error of 320 years either way.

Historical and linguistic methods of tracing the origins of agriculture indicate that Hither Asia was the probable center of several species of plants which were the basis of Neolithic living. Actual seeds and husks of early grain products are occasionally found embedded in mortar used in very early buildings or in other sites connected with human civilizations. The search for wild relatives of cultivated plants—if we assume that domestic varieties are simply cultivated plants derived from those regions where the same species grow wild—has been especially informative. Vaviloff and other authorities have sought to discover these beginnings by collecting and plotting the distribution of cultivated plants. In this way the place where the greatest number of relatives and variations of a certain species is found would be the center of origin.

From all of these methods of inquiry into this difficult problem, the main facts are now clear. The first plants were cultivated around the periphery of Mesopotamia. These first cultivated varieties were grains, of which wheat was surely one of the earliest. Wheat has been studied more than any of the others, perhaps for this reason.

Botanists have found, through these studies, that there are three groups of major wheat varieties, each consisting of a number of separate species. There is considerable evidence that each of these three groups may have developed at different times and at different places. As agriculture was developed separately in the New and the Old World, it is possible that the idea may have been developed more than once, even in the Old World centers. For example, there is convincing evidence that one type of wheat was first grown in Abyssinia and another in Mesopotamia. However, it is quite possible that once agriculture had been established, the individual types of plants grown would be a matter of local choice.

Of all of the varieties of wheat, that known as *Triticum dicoccum* or emmer wheat, was the most widely cultivated of the ancient varieties. This is the wheat found in Egyptian tombs, in early Persia, and in Abyssinia. Emmer was the wheat grown in many portions of Europe during earliest times, and even in pre-Roman Britain.

But wheat was not the only grain to mark the beginnings of agriculture. Barley, a wild grain of this same region, was early cultivated.

Although the agricultural idea almost certainly originated in southwestern Asia, it soon spread to other centers. And not only were the original grains domesticated in and around Mesopotamia disseminated with the agricultural idea, but new plants and varieties were initiated in other parts of the Old World. Another center of cultivation sprang up in southeastern Asia. Certainly rice was first cultivated there, as well as millet, soy beans, and varieties of fruit trees. Still another center appeared in the area of modern Afghanistan, and such products as beans, peas, lentils, carrots, and pomegranates were all first utilized by mankind in or near this region of Asia.

The individual species and their exact points of origin are of interest only to specialists. The prehistorian is concerned with the fact that the cultivation of plants produced a revolution in the lives of men. Not only was human food derived from different sources, but the method of procurement necessitated a different kind of human society. Former hunting groups now became agricultural groups bound to the soil.

The domestication of animals was the second great development of the new Neolithic era. If we accept the dog as a true domesticated mammal, the use of animals far preceded agriculture, for dogs of several varieties were already present in the Mesolithic settlements of northwestern Europe. Since dogs were kept as pets or for hunting rather than used for food, most authorities do not accept the premise that the domestication of animals began with the household dog.

Animal husbandry actually began with the herding of sheep, goats, cattle, and swine. All of these animals produced flesh that would supplement a diet of products of the soil. Furthermore, cows, ewes, and goats gave milk which could be manufactured into cheese and other food products, and hides useful for clothing. Thus these domestic animals largely fulfilled all the needs of a simple people.

The progressive desiccation at the end of the glacial era may have brought human groups into more intimate association with animal herds, as both of them were increasingly confined to the narrowing oases and limited spots of moisture. In this way, the transition to the use of animals could be made by close contact. Another school of archaeological thought sees, in the beginnings of agriculture, the ideal situation for the true domestication of animals. The early farmers had fields of stubble and straw and the animals tended to collect and remain near these sources of fodder.

These speculations are interesting but irrelevant. The important fact is that animal husbandry was established coincidentally with the beginnings of agriculture. There were some places in early Mesopotamia where only farming was practiced. In other spots, life was entirely pastoral. The true basis of the Neolithic way of life was a combination of the two.

Studies of the original regions where wild relatives of domestic animals are found have been generally unproductive. For example, there are several species of wild sheep from which domestic sheep may have been derived. Several kinds of wild sheep ranged from Europe throughout Asia before the end of the glacial period. None of them have wool, nor do they show other anatomical features similar to the domestic variety, but almost certainly sheep were domesticated in Asia. The present form of the animal indicates that selective breeding was practiced over a long period. The typical fleece of the present-day sheep was developed from some wild variety by emphasizing the undercoating of woolly hair beneath the stiff outer hairs of wild sheep. In their native state sheep all have short tails. The domestic varieties, of course, have long ones. Perhaps no other domestic animal has exhibited such profound changes under the guiding hand of man.

The goat is less of a problem and, in contrast to the sheep, has changed very little from the wild state. The domestic goat is a descendant of the ibex, a wild form that occurs in several varieties from North Africa to Tibet. Goats were usually herded with sheep in ancient times just as they are today. It is impossible to tell which of the two was the earlier on the domestic scene.

Wild cattle of several varieties ranged over Europe and Asia during the glacial epoch. The domestication of these animals also seems to have taken place in or around southwestern Asia. The development of present-day cattle from wild varieties is not difficult to trace in its major outlines. Large and small varieties of cattle appeared very early in both Hither Asia and north Africa. The earliest form identifiable in Mesopotamia is *Bos nomadicus,* a type of cow which does not differ radically from present-day varieties. A variation, *Bos taurus brachyceros,* had short horns and a small, delicately built body. At the ancient Mesopotamian site of Ur, these early cattle were utilized for their dairy products rather than for their flesh. *Bos brachyceros* appears in Europe, for example, in the Swiss Lake Dwellings as a domesticated form used apparently for dairy products as well as for its flesh.

A quite different kind of cattle, *Bos indicus,* the zebu, was domesticated farther to the east, possibly in India. The zebu or humped cattle became the common variety at such Neolithic sites as Mohenjodaro in the Indus valley. East African humped cattle are probably derived from the zebu form.

The development of swine is no mystery, but the time of first domestication is difficult to ascertain. The pig appeared very early in Europe and was one of the major game animals of the Mesolithic groups that lived around the swamps and seas of northwestern Europe. Probably, however, pigs were not domesticated there, but were simply hunted and killed in the wild state, as was the red stag. Domesticated swine appeared very early in Mesopotamia, and their first place of home use cannot be far from Hither Asia.

The horse and allied forms were not part of early animal husbandry, as were cattle, swine, sheep, and goats. The first horselike animals or donkeys, in reliefs and drawings from early Mesopotamia, are pictured as pulling chariots. Varieties of asses are also shown on slate palettes from predynastic Egypt. There is no doubt that horses were first used as draft animals and were not ridden until much later. The animal first used in Mesopotamia was the onager, a wild variety native to that area whose appearance is between that of a horse and an ass. Onagers were used for drawing chariots and other draft work. The true horse as we know it today was not bred until later in the Neolithic period and was first domesticated in south central Asia. Many variations of horses have appeared in the past several millenniums. Present-day horses are descendants and developments of several varieties of European and Asiatic horse types which probably came from more than one center.

The wild ass was domesticated first in Egypt, where it appears before 3000 B.C. as a burden-bearing animal. The domesticated ass, or burro, later spread to Syria and Mesopotamia. The Moslem invasions of later times took the burro across North Africa to Spain. Spaniards brought the animal to the New World. In the Near East, asses were usually ridden by people of low estate and horses were used by royalty and warriors. Thus Balaam of Biblical times rode an ass.

There are two kinds of camels. The dromedary is single-humped and adapted to desert terrain and sparse vegetation. The Bactrian is a two-humped, shaggy beast of cold, mountainous regions. Both varieties were domesticated late and are Asiatic in origin. The dromedary did not appear in the Near East until perhaps 1000 B.C., although it may have existed earlier in the Indus valley of Pakistan. The Bactrian also appeared late on the Neolithic scene. Neither dromedary nor Bactrian survive in the wild state today.

In southeastern Asia, the water buffalo was tamed from the wild buffalo which still is found in the jungles of India and Siam. It was used for milk, meat, hides, and as a draft animal. It is still used for these purposes in the Orient and the Philippine Islands and is easily the most important domestic animal in those regions.

The Indian or Ceylonese elephant was also domesticated in southern Asia. The elephant was a late addition and did not appear in the early Neolithic. The African elephant has never been successfully domesticated, although one variety originally found in North Africa was successfully trained for warfare by the Carthaginians in later times. It was elephants of this variety that Hannibal employed in his epic march across the Alps against Rome.

In southeastern Asia, also, the wild jungle fowl was adapted to serve mankind as the chicken. Domestic chickens did not reach Mesopotamia until comparatively late; they appear in the New Testament but not in the Old Testament. They reached Greece about 700 B.C. As a matter of rather curious fact, it was sacred or sacrificial purposes rather than eggs or flesh that prompted the spread of this fowl, along with knowledge of breeding them. Early Greeks and Romans used chickens to foretell the future.

The barnyard goose is a tamed version of the wild European graylag. Domesticated ducks are derived, for the most part, from the Asiatic mallard and, in more recent times, from the albino variety of mallard. The various Asiatic and European ducks and geese appeared on the scene relatively late.

The true basis of the new era was, then, the domestication of cattle, sheep, swine, and goats and the cultivation of seed-bearing grains. With these products, humans in the Mesopotamia area began to work out a new way of life. The results of this shift of attitude on the part of human beings to the world around them were far reaching and revolutionary. The subsidiary results are as much a part of the Neolithic as the basic ingredients of agriculture and animal husbandry.

Perhaps the most apparent change in the new era was the fact that human groups became sedentary instead of nomadic, as they had been in a hunting economy. Agricultural people became attached to the soil from which they derived their livelihood. With the development of irrigation systems and better methods of tillage, land became valuable, and a high sense of property developed which had not been present in previous ages.

Especially important with these new and abundant sources of food was the fact that the population increased. Many hazards of human life normally associated with hunting were eliminated. The small farming and pastoral communities of Hither Asia soon became towns and, in some cases, cities. The increase in the number of humans living together produced corollary changes of great significance. All the ramifications of society appeared. Small hunting groups needed no formal government or law. Agricultural communities, with hundreds or thousands of people grouped together, could not exist without recognized codes of behavior and ethics. With the coming of the Neolithic period, civilization as we now know it actually began.

Some of the concomitants of this civilization are strange commentaries on human nature. Warfare became an outstanding characteristic of these times, as differences arose among groups. Stratification of society was another phenomenon of the new development. The first rulers were probably men who claimed to have influence with the mystic forces that produced water for the crops or with the sun which caused them to grow. Priests interposed themselves between these natural powers and the simple beliefs of the early farmers. Later, kingship developed, first in combination with priestly attributes, and then as a natural shift into mundane and secular authority vested in a single person. Certain groups became privileged landowners, whose grounds were tilled by a lower class—of slaves.

Religion as a group activity first manifested itself in the Neolithic period. Earlier hunting peoples had professed belief in spiritual things, and the primitive Neanderthal man occasionally buried his dead in a manner that indicated a belief in a hereafter. But the larger groups of farmers and herders of the Neolithic needed more than simple hunting ritual to influence gods of sky and earth. Ritual became ceremony, and Neolithic groups practiced together to bring about favorable rains and sunshine for the good of all.

Material arts flourished under such an integrated and advanced society as that produced by agriculture and the domestication of animals. Pottery was developed to new heights, with fine firing and rich decoration. Mesopotamia, especially, produced a melange of wares, decorated with all manner of colors and skillful designs.

Weaving, augmented by the wool from domestic sheep, advanced with the development of several varieties of looms. Flax, a product of early Egypt, was used to make fine linen. Woodworking improved, particularly in the building of boats large and durable enough to make coasting voyages along the shore lines.

With a sedentary way of life, architecture became a necessity. Buildings were larger and more permanent, and many of them were erected for communal purposes. Chief among these was the religious structure or temple. Mesopotamia very early made use of wood forms and also sun-dried bricks made from the mud of the valley floor. In early Egypt, where better materials were available, cut stones were employed for building and, of course, had more permanence.

In the new era of the Neolithic, however, not all of the old traditions were completely lost. Knives and arrowheads were still chipped of flint and obsidian. Many of the standard tools of the Neolithic farmer were made in the tradition of his forefathers. There were many peripheral areas also, where the changes from Palaeolithic savagery to Neolithic enlightenment were slight or absent.

The spread of the new way of life from the region of Hither Asia and the valley of the Nile was gradual, extending over several centuries. It is difficult to determine in each case whether the concept of agriculture and animal husbandry spread first, or whether the actual seeds of grain and initial herds of animals were moved over these intervening areas with the expansion of the idea. Most of the movement of the Neolithic took place by expansion from one river valley to another, as more land became necessary. In these river valleys primitive agricultural methods could most easily be utilized. Here were sources of water for irrigation and for domestic herds. But the Neolithic idea also moved over another route—by boat among the eastern Mediterranean islands and along the coasts of other water bodies peripheral to southwestern Asia.

From the regions of the age's first development, Neolithic ideas spread westward into four major areas of Europe and its environs. The first extension was to the islands of the eastern Mediterranean, particularly to Crete. The second area to receive Neolithic culture was the Balkan Peninsula, whence it spread into the middle Danube valley, which proved an ideal place for the growth of the new culture.

The third area was that region north and west of the Black Sea called the Black Earth lands, made up essentially of the broadened valleys and deltas of the large Russian rivers which flow from the north. Western Europe became the fourth area to receive the Neolithic way of life as it moved along the coast of North Africa.

These major regions in which the Neolithic idea flourished were not separated. There were interrelations, especially in the first phases of their development. Early Neolithic settlements in the Aegean area were connected on the mainland with those in Thessaly. Early Danubian beginnings were influenced by Neolithic ideas from Thessaly, the Aegean, and the Black Earth region of the Ukraine. Some of these interrelations are obscure. There were movements from south to north, and countermovements in the other direction. However, the major developments are quite clear.

As the Danube valley was the life line by which the essentials of Neolithic culture reached the heart of Europe, we may consider this development first, although chronologically it may well have been the last. When European archaeologists first began work on the Neolithic sites of the lower Danube, they found evidences of three levels or phases of Neolithic culture. These were distinguished originally on the basis of the differences in the pottery vessels used by these early people, and were called *Danubian I, Danubian II,* and *Danubian III.* Unfortunately, after this original division was established, a level earlier than Danubian I was proved, and it was also found expedient to divide Danubian I into two subdivisions, *a* and *b.* Thus the Danubian sequence is now initiated by a *barbotine* level, followed by Danubian I*a*, I*b*, Danubian II, and Danubian III. Professor V. Gordon Childe has done more than any other single scientist to clarify the Danubian cultural horizons. In spite of the obvious difficulties, the Danubian sequence is still the basis of all discussions of Neolithic culture in Europe.

Archaeologists have long been puzzled by the apparent chronological and temporal lacuna which exists between the Mesolithic of western and northwestern Europe and the Neolithic development as it entered the Danube from its original Mesopotamian beginnings. The Mesolithic of western Europe, rather than the interim that the name implies, was apparently the end result of a long series of cul-

116

tural developments in the European area, which did not themselves lead into the Neolithic. Chronologically, the terminal nature of this European culture seems apparent when we consider that agriculture and animal husbandry were already being developed in Mesopotamia while Mesolithic savagery was prevalent in Europe. Scientists regarded this hiatus as evidence that the entire Neolithic was Mesopotamian in origin.

This concept was not entirely consistent, as most of the material elements of the Neolithic were already present in western Europe in Mesolithic times. The pecking and grinding method of shaping stone, the bow and arrow, and pottery were already in existence. Even the domestic dog was present, and there are some indications that swine may have been kept in captivity in Mesolithic settlements. With these considerations in mind, it is apparent that the only major ingredients of the Neolithic which entered Europe from Mesopotamia were agriculture and the domestication of cattle, sheep, and goats. The new era, as it was lived in Neolithic Europe, was, then, a combination of these native and foreign elements.

The first Neolithic communities on the mainland of Europe probably were the towns established by settlers who came by boat from Anatolia and established themselves on the coasts of Thessaly and Greece. These Neolithic people spread inland along the river valleys and established villages and towns in favorable spots where they could raise grains and keep herds of cattle, sheep, goats, and pigs. The sites of Sesklo, Dimini, and Drakhmani have been excavated by archaeologists and found to contain variations of Neolithic life as the colonists developed differences in various isolated valleys and districts. Sesklo is probably the earliest major settlement of the early Balkan Neolithic. The Sesklo people built houses of timber and brick, made beautiful, intricately patterned, painted pottery, and modeled female figurines. The fortified town of Sesklo, near modern Volos in Greece, is situated on a low headland. The *Sesklo culture,* which extends much farther than the immediate area of the site itself, is quite similar to that of Neolithic towns in northern Syria and the Mesopotamian area. The Sesklo people were probably the first to bring the Neolithic idea to the Balkan mainland, but were forced to protect themselves against either indigenous inhabitants or later arrivals of the same Neolithic background.

117

The Sesklo culture was followed by the *Dimini,* a fortified town, and *Drakhmani* variations. Dimini pottery is typically painted in black or white on a red background, while Drakhmani pottery is characteristically black with mottled orange spots or orange rims. All of these early Balkan Neolithic cultures were, however, much alike and showed obvious similarities to their original homelands in Hither Asia.

From Greece the colonists moved westward and northward through the Vardar valley and across the passes into the Danube basin. Along the Danube itself, archaeologists have identified a number of tells or mounds which are the remains of Neolithic towns built by the settlers pushing up from the south. Undoubtedly also, many indigenous peoples adopted the new way of life once they had learned to cultivate grains and herd animals.

The earliest remains of the Neolithic towns established in the Danube valley are those of a kind of culture called the *Morava* or the *Vardar-Morava.* Evidences of these early farmers and herdsmen are present at the ancient site of Vinča on the Danube near modern Belgrade in Yugoslavia. These Vardar-Morava people were the precursors of several Neolithic groups which followed.

Farther down the Danube, other mounds mark the sites of the *Vadastra culture.* Still farther downriver and east of the Olt River are sites early occupied by Neolithic people of *Boian culture.* North of the Danube the *Körös* culture became established in what is now Hungary.

All of these early colonists are distinguished chiefly by their pottery manufacture and by relatively minor differences in their tools and village life. Basically they are the same. All made houses of mud brick or wattle and daub and grouped their dwellings together into villages. Most houses were rectangular, and some villages were fortified. Typical tools were adzes, bows and arrows, and slings. Knives and scrapers were made of flint or obsidian, and small ornaments of copper also appear. Figurines and other ritualistic objects indicate that religious beliefs were generally similar. All these people raised grains and herded cattle, sheep, goats, and swine.

Once the Neolithic mode of existence had begun in the heartland of Europe, it continued to spread and develop just as it had in the

Near East. The Vadastra culture evolved into the *Salcutsa*. The Boian culture was replaced by one called *Gumelnitza*. The Gumelnitza lasted for several centuries in the Rumanian area and is usually divided into three phases from the stratified evidence at the great site of Vidra near Bucharest. Meanwhile, influences and additional colonists continued to come from Anatolia.

In actual time, the development of the Danubian valley peasant cultures was relatively late. Farming villages were not established on the yellow loess lands in the Danube valley much before 3000 B.C. This was many centuries later than the development of these same ideas among the earliest agricultural villages of Mesopotamia.

Danubian farming hamlets were established in all those places in the valley where primitive agriculture could be easily practiced. As the soil was yellow loess for the most part, it could be cultivated with crude farming implements such as the Danubian peasants possessed. With no knowledge of fertilization or the rotation of crops, the loess soil was exhausted after a century or two of intensive cultivation of grain. The Danubian peasants solved this problem by simply moving up the valley or along the major tributaries. In this way, in addition to the natural spread of the increasing population, the Danubian Neolithic moved upriver into the heart of Europe, mixing with indigenous groups as it moved. When the Danube valley proper had been populated by the spread of these peasant cultures, the Danubian Neolithic moved into other parts of Europe, particularly to the north and west, where there were other river valleys to be farmed. In these more remote regions, there grew up, in Neolithic times, combinations of ideas which produced separate cultures known by separate names. In the Alpine area, and in the valleys of the North German rivers, there evolved distinctive Neolithic variations on the central theme. In western Europe and in the British Isles, another Neolithic tradition was introduced from another direction.

Remains of the Neolithic farming villages of the Danube valley are chiefly marked by the presence of pottery, pits in the loess, and the post holes of house supports. Most of the age differences of the sites can be distinguished through ceramic studies. Dozens of these Danubian villages have been excavated. Perhaps the most famous are those of Vinča, which lies on the Serbian bank of the Danube near the present city of Belgrade, and Starčevo, on the opposite side of the river. A well-known, early Danubian village is that of Köln-Lindenthal near the modern city of Cologne, on the Rhine.

The Neolithic found at Vinča and Starčevo developed differently from that farther downriver, such as the Gumelnitza sequence. Near the present boundary of Yugoslavia and Rumania, a mountainous spur constricts the river in a narrow gorge called the Iron Gates. Below this natural barrier the Neolithic developed a separate tradition, although there was periodic intercourse. After the initial surge of Neolithic influence and people into Europe, the Danube valley, with the upper reaches of the Oder, Elbe, Weser, and Rhine, developed one tradition. The area east of the Carpathians to the Dnieper and the Pontic steppes developed another.

Vinča, as excavated by Professor Vassits, shows a sequence of events which serves as a key for the cultural history of the whole area. There are several occupations and village levels one above the other at the Vinča site, totaling a height of ten meters. At the base of this succession, early Danubian farmers dug rough pits in the loess ridge upon which the village was first located. In the pits are pieces of crude brown pottery decorated on the surface with plastic clay applied in a liquid form. This barbotine pottery decoration gives the name to the earliest levels. Subsequent levels at Vinča as well as Starčevo indicate successive levels of Danubian peasant cultures.

Barbotine pottery, much of it with a crude vegetable temper, appeared early at a number of sites in the lower Danube. This crude ware seems closest to the traditions of central Anatolia. Occasional Danubian Barbotine pottery decorated with fingernail prints is almost identical to Anatolian types.

At Vinča, Starčevo, and along the Körös River, north of the Danube, there were several versions of the basic Danubian Neolithic life. Following the Barbotine period with its typical drip-decorated pottery, there appeared several more sophisticated types of ceramics. There were burnished, ribbed, incised, and red-slipped wares to show that the Danubian potters were capable of a number of variations. Appearing as an intrusive element at Vinča, Starčevo, and especially Tordos were potsherds painted with red designs on a white background. There were also pots decorated with red paint on a buff or brown

Swiss Lake dwellers pulling in their nets. A Lake dwelling appears in
the background with houses perched on piles. Late Neolithic period.

Diorama showing a Neolithic village (Troldebjerg) in Denmark
about 2700 B.C.

Typical Iron Age implements and vessels.

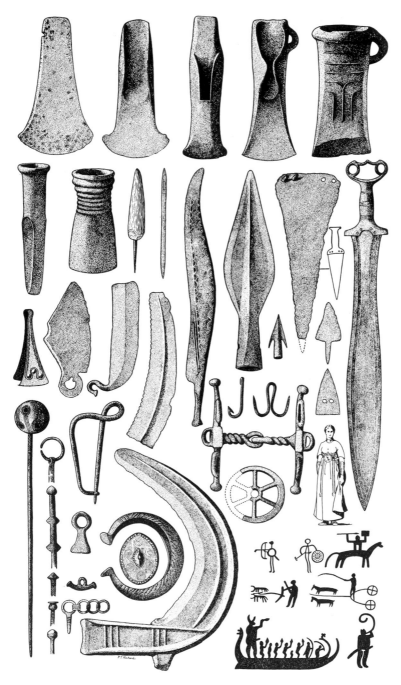

Typical Bronze Age implements and vessels.

TYPES OF POTTERY

Top, left: Danubian bowl of Danubian I*a* type with lugs in the shape
of animal heads. The shape of the bowl is derived from a gourd
(from a site in Moravia, Czechoslovakia). *Right,* Danubian "fruit
stand" dish of Danubian II type (from Jordansmühl).

Below, left: Bronze III or Lausitz pitcher showing circular design in
imitation of human breasts. A cremated human burial was placed
in this vessel (from a grave in Silesia). *Right:* Bell Beaker vessel. This
is the red or eastern type of Bell Beaker. This one was placed in a
grave of a Bell Beaker warrior merchant in Czechoslovakia.

field. This painted-pottery tradition is obviously foreign to the Danubian development and presumably came in from Thessaly. The Danubian family of peasant cultures did not usually paint its pottery. Primarily, the Danubians relied upon incision and burnishing for their ceramic effects. There were, however, other Neolithic peoples to the east of the Carpathians who habitually painted their pottery, who will be described later.

Typical Danubian I*a* settlements were small villages of scattered huts invariably built on the higher elevations of the loess terraces, close to the river. Culture pits, which were apparently storage pits or pig sties, differentiate these villages. Houses were rectangular and of wattle and daub, roofed with thatch, branches, and other perishable materials. In most cases, the culture pits are full of refuse—potsherds, charcoal, broken implements, and fragments of bone. Many of the pits were lined with twigs and then plastered with mud. Excavators have recovered the seeds and chaff of emmer wheat embedded in the wall plaster. Danubian I economy was based on the cultivation of barley, several varieties of wheat, beans, peas, lentils, and flax for weaving. Stock was raised only on a small scale.

A few grave excavations were found in and around the culture pits. A body was usually interred in a contracted position on its side, and was occasionally accompanied by pottery vessels and animal bones. Most graves were those of infants. Evidence of cremations was also present in Danubian I*a*, indicating that even at this time the tradition was mixed. From the physical remains so far recovered from the early Danubian, it is difficult to determine the type of human being represented.

Danubian I*a* pottery differentiates this culture from the later traditions. The vessels are oblated globes, cut off on the top and slightly flattened on the bottom suggestive of a gourd. Later in the Danubian sequence, necks, lugs, and bases were developed.

Almost all of the Danubian pottery was decorated. The earliest motif was an inverted V or the same character with upturned ends to form a simple volute λ. At the height of Danubian I*a*, three essential varieties of incised decoration on this pottery can be distinguished. The first was simple incision; the second was incision with cross-cut designs; and the third was a band arrangement formed by two parallel incisions with the intervening space filled with punctuations. The filled-band variety of decoration is often referred to as *Bandkeramik*, from the German. From this decoration sequence, the Danubian succession is still further refined as Danubian I*a*, I*a*2, I*a*3.

The typical elements of Danubian I*a* incised decoration were used throughout most of the middle and upper Danube valley and in adjoining areas. Design motifs from other regions also show that the Danube was not isolated during these formative times. A double-ax motif on the bottom of a Danubian bowl is reminiscent of a similar design from the island of Crete. Other designs in the Danube valley show influences from the Hungarian Plain and from the Black Earth region of the Ukraine.

In addition to the typical Danubian pottery vessels, the Danubian I*a* peasants also made crude clay models of the human figure. These figurines presumably served some magical or religious purpose in connection with agriculture, perhaps to augment fertility. As the Danubian culture progressed, the making of figurines became a common practice.

Scattered about the Danubian I*a* villages are abundant reminders that the stone-working traditions of earlier Europeans had not been abandoned. Flint was flaked into knife blades and scrapers. Obviously, from these tools, the Danubian peasants still hunted game to supplement their agricultural foods. Most of the fine-grained stones which the earlier Danubians used were hard limestones, shales, and igneous rocks which they worked by pecking and grinding. The Danubian celt, however, was distinctively asymmetrical, with one face of the implement flat and the other highly rounded. From this peculiar outline, these tools have received the name *shoe-last celts,* because of similarity to an old fashioned shoe last. This type of celt is one of the commonest implements of early Danubian times.

In addition to celts, the Danubian I*a* farmers made mace heads of the same materials, and rough oval slabs which probably served as hoes and mattocks for their fields. Later versions of the shoe-last celt are also perforated with a tubular instrument, probably a section of bone, which, with sand as an abrasive, would gradually wear through the hardest stone. It has been suggested that the shoe-last celt itself was utilized as a grubbing implement in connection with the farming activities of the Danubian peasants. However, these celts do not show the type of wear which would occur with this use. It has even been suggested that the shoe-last celt served as a plowshare on some crude wooden contrivance which was dragged through the ground to cultivate the soil. Perhaps the best explanation is that the shoe-last celt was used as an adze for the clearing of woodland areas in the Danube valley necessary for the expansion of the fields.

The Danubian I*a* people also used bone materials from their hunts in the surrounding hills along the valley. Bone awls, needles, and perforating points were commonly found mixed with the other debris of the culture pits of the Danubian villages. The bone spatulae which these people carefully fashioned from larger fragments of bone are particularly notable. These usually have an expanded shovel-like blade and a long tapered handle. They may have served as polishers or as means of smoothing pottery.

Shell was also utilized, primarily of the variety *Spondylus,* which looked something like an oyster. These shells came from the Mediterranean, an additional indication that the Danubians had trade connections outside their valley. *Spondylus* shells were usually drilled and used as pendants.

In addition to the wild game which the Danubian farmers hunted on occasion, there are also the remains of domesticated animals. Short-horned cattle, swine, goats, and sheep supplemented the barley and wheat of the Danubian peasants and provided a firm basis for their economy. Apparently some of the villages had only sheep or only goats, but both animals were known to them. The bones and teeth of horses from Danubian culture pits are apparently those of wild European horses which the Danubians killed and ate when they had the opportunity. Dog remains of several varieties are present, especially a lanky canine of the hound category.

The Danubian complex known as I*a*, with its distinctive pottery types and other tools and weapons, was closely paralleled by that type of ancient farming life known as Danubian I*b*. Danubian I*b* is delineated almost entirely on the basis of pottery differences, and there may be no time differential at all, for I*a* and I*b* materials are often found in the same settlement. Danubian I*b* may have arisen in the region of the Sudeten lands of Czechoslovakia, and would thus be a middle Danubian innovation, inspired entirely from the peasant beginnings of the Danube valley within Europe. In general, Danubian I*b* settlements occur in the same localities as the I*a* peasant villages. The I*b* type of life in Saxony, in Germany, is known by the local name of *Rössen*. Late Danubian I and Rössen settlements were typically fortified. In the Köln district, still farther to the northwest, I*b* material appears under the provincial name of *Hinkelstein*. In other parts of Europe, also, this variation on the Danubian theme appeared with individual characteristics that were different from those of the Danube valley. Again, here, most of these distinctions are made on the basis of pottery.

Danubian I*b* pottery is usually described as *punctuate ware* or *pointillé*. It is typically decorated with long, fine furrows or strokes made on the surface of the clay. Rows of punctuate indentations were usually made in the form of garlands or zigzags and covered the whole area of the vessel. There are a few rare instances in which Danubian I*b* decoration followed a checkered pattern.

The forms of the vessels also were different in Danubian I*b*. The globular shapes of previous pottery variations became more pear shaped in the I*b*, with the greater diameter toward the bottom of the vessel. A widemouthed cauldron of clay called the *puten* also became popular, as did the storage jar, a large cylindrical vessel used for storing seeds or for purposes other than cooking. Bowls were also manufactured, as well as angular vessels which seemed to be clay imitations of earlier leather forms, with squarish corners where the leather had been gathered together with stitching. I*b* vessels were often fitted with pointed or hooked lug handles. In many instances, wartlike lugs were scattered around the bases of the vessels as a decorative addition. Ladles began to appear, as well as short pedestals or ring feet.

Later Danubian I*b* variations on the pottery theme accentuated these same tendencies. Late I*b* vessels were noticeably elongated or carinated. The new Danubian II from surrounding areas also influenced pottery styles. The noticeable tendency to elevate vessels on hollow bases or pedestals was a Danubian II innovation. Lobate rims and the further use of lugs as ornamentation were typical of late I*b* pottery wares.

Zoomorphic and anthropomorphic clay figurines were common in Danubian I*b*. Some of the figurines are obviously cattle, while others are nondescript and might be any animal. Humans were modeled both standing and seated. The sexual features of the female figures were strongly emphasized. Little attention was given to faces or realistic detail. The same *pointillé* indentations that characterized the pottery vessels appear on the figures. In addition to the figurines, there were some spindle whorls made of potsherds.

Other than the pottery, there were few real differences betwen Danubian I*a* and I*b*. Settlements maintained similar economies with the same repertory of domesticated animals and the dog. The burials of I*b* settlements contained more cremations. In fact, so few skeletons remain from this punctuate period that the physical type of these early peasants is uncertain.

The tools of the I*b* complex were generally better made. Even flint-working had a brief revival in the workshops of the I*b* artisans. The first arrow straighteners appear, for the straightening and abrading of arrow shafts. Danubian I*b* artisans were especially skilled in making ornaments of limestone and marble. At Rössen in Saxony, a series of skillfully made bracelets of these same materials has been recovered. The use of the *Spondylus* shell again indicates a wide trade area.

In both the Danubian I*a* and I*b* there is ample evidence that the potter-peasant cultures of the Danubian valley were becoming firmly established and developing a sound economic basis. These Neolithic communities were complex and, although this was a new era, were apparently functioning smoothly. The Danubian peasant villages were the foundation of much that was to come in later Europe.

The pottery, as well as the other material culture of the Danubian peasants, was largely indigenous to the Danube valley. It was only the basic expedients of agriculture and animal husbandry which motivated the Danubian expansion, which continued up the Danube valley and spilled over into other European river valleys, especially to the north. With this spread, many European Neolithic cultures developed. Some of the differences were formed by various mixtures of the old Mesolithic peoples and their culture, overawed by the Danubian expansion. Generally, the previous Mesolithic was absent from the loess lands which were the domain of the Danubian peasants. In certain other instances, Mesolithic developments seem to have prevailed, little affected by the new ideas. Local minor discoveries and different ways of making pottery produced distinguishable regional variations which archaeologists consider significant. In spite of this heterogeneity, however, it is relatively easy to detect the Danubian variety of Neolithic as it spread up through central Europe. The Danubian brand of Neolithic culture spread over the loess lands of the Elbe River valley, the Saale, and the upper and middle Weser. Danubian peasant farmers settled the upper Danube valley to its headwaters, and established settlements in the valleys of the Main, the Neckar, and the Rhine, particularly in the vicinity of Cologne. From this distribution, which had been traced for the most part on the basis of the typical incised Danubian pottery decoration, it may be seen that the Danubian expansion was a central European development. On the peripheral areas of Europe, there were other types of Neolithic cultures which will be described subsequently.

The site which illustrates best the Danubian peasant life in its expanded form is the great settlement of Lindenthal near Cologne. This site has been skillfully excavated and has revealed a Danubian town consisting of four periods of occupation. The inhabitants of Köln-Lindenthal, as the place is usually called, raised wheat and barley on the surrounding loess lands. They stored their grains in sheds and oblong barns which they placed in orderly rows. The post molds of the excavations at Köln-Lindenthal show that most of the buildings were elevated on stilts to keep the grain dry. In the second village built at this site, two contiguous circular ditches were added to enclose a protected space for herds of domestic animals. The town of Köln-Lindenthal also shows clearly that it was once abandoned completely and then reoccupied by new settlers who also carried the Danubian culture. The fourth and last occupation of Köln-Lindenthal was the most populous and distinctive of all of the periods of the village. Dwelling huts, granaries, and oblong barns were built not only within the enclosing ditches of the original site, but also in an outlying addition to the town. Köln-Lindenthal gives a very clear picture of the importance of the Danubian expansion into the northwest. Its fortification presupposes warfare in Danubian life.

Perhaps the Köln-Lindenthal farmers were afraid of the Rössen people to the east or of other contemporary groups covetous of their agricultural lands.

The pottery of the Lindenthal Danubians was typically I*a* and I*b* in type. By the time the Danubian culture had spread to northwestern Europe, however, Danubian II developments were already under way elsewhere. In relative chronology, Köln-Lindenthal was a lingering version of earlier Danubian culture.

Danubian II is best characterized by that type of culture often called by the hybrid name *Lengyel-Jordansmühl.* Lengyel was a settlement and cemetery site west of the Danube. Jordansmühl was a large village and cemetery located in Silesia to the east. Material from both of these sites is later than Danubian I*a* and I*b* and was for the most part a development from these earlier beginnings.

The Jordansmühl culture, typifying Danubian II, featured a number of new pottery forms in addition to the globular and pyriform vessels of previous cultures. Jordansmühl potters evolved a pitcher with a rounded or angular shoulder and a band handle. A variation appeared in the Jordansmühl amphora, a pitcher with double handles. Also at Jordansmühl, a fruit stand or shallow dish mounted on a hollow pedestal was recovered. An oval tublike bowl was also typical. These new forms of Jordansmühl pottery, as well as old Danubian types such as the puten storage jar, cauldrons, and ladles, were decorated with incised designs. The decoration, however, was usually done in chevrons or crosshatched triangles. Dimpling and furrowing with a blunt tool was also practiced. Occasionally, the Jordansmühl potters reverted to punctuate ornamentation, reminiscent of earlier Danubian traditions.

A peculiar type of pottery, obviously intrusive, also appears in the Jordansmühl repertory. This is called *South Moravian Crusted,* from the place of its occurrence and the practice of placing the painted decoration on the surface of the pot after firing. The paint flakes off easily and is fugitive in all instances. Painted pottery seems incongruous among Danubian ceramics. Most authorities believe that the South Moravian Crusted ware, which appears sporadically at several points in central Danubian territory, is evidence of slight influences from areas to the southeast and in the Black Earth region where painted pottery was common. Of these *Painted Pottery* people, we shall have more to say later.

In spite of pottery differences, ethnically the Lengyel-Jordansmühl development was obviously the same as Danubian I. Settlements were in the loess area. The villages of these Danubian II farmers are marked by single storage pits or complex pits dug into the loess. Wall plaster and post impressions suggest rectangular houses and granaries of woodwork and wattling. Graves of the Jordansmühl people are usually plain pits. At the Jordansmühl cemetery site, the graves are lined with stone and the skeletons are contracted. It is noteworthy that many of the graves at Jordansmühl contain copper trinkets.

Of the weapons and tools of the Danubian II people of Jordansmühl, there was little change over preceding forms. The shoe-last celt was still typical, both in compressed and cylindrical type. Axes and perforated hammer-axes appeared, and blades, scrapers, and arrowheads were still manufactured from flint. Mace heads also occur, as well as forms of mattocks and other implements of hard stone. The same bone implements as those used in Danubian I were carried on by the Jordansmühl people. Disk beads were special favorites, and were probably sewed on clothing for decoration.

The Lengyel-Jordansmühl culture was, then, little different from the preceding farming cultures of the Danubian I peasants. Even the religion seems much the same. The famous rain figurine from Jordansmühl exemplifies the way that the Jordansmühl and Danubian peasants sought to influence those forces which could bring moisture from the sky.

In distribution, the Lengyel-Jordansmühl version of Danubian II actually covered a smaller area than that of Danubian I. In many places on the peripheral areas, classic Danubian I*a* and I*b* was contemporaneous with Jordansmühl. The Lengyel-Jordansmühl type of culture influenced the Bavarian sector of southern Germany, where it is known regionally as the *Münchshöfen* culture. The Lengyel type of Danubian II extended to southern Moravia, where it developed into the *Wolfsbach culture*. On the middle Danube, Jordansmühl is apparently contemporaneous with the second level of the site of Vinča, or Vinča II. Thus the Danubian II development was a logical and chronological development of those peasant cultures which had been established in the central Danube valley. However, as indicated by the Moravian crusted pottery, the copper trinkets of Jordansmühl, and the *Spondylus* shell ornaments prevalent at a number of Danubian sites, these people were not entirely isolated. They obviously had trade connections, in some instances to considerable distances. The Danubian life of central Europe was not entirely self-contained. The story is not complete without some record of the developments in surrounding regions.

A notable deviation from the central Danubian theme occurred in the region of northern Hungary, east of the Danube. Here, in the vicinity of the Bükk Mountains, a specialized version of Neolithic life developed. This was the same area where, previously, upper Palaeolithic hunters and later Mesolithic groups had evolved their distinctive cultures. Curiously, many of the Neolithic peoples of the Bükk Mountains area continued to dwell in caves. There is, however, in the *Bükk culture* which resulted, an obvious admixture of Mesolithic elements.

As is usual with Neolithic variations, the divergence of the *Bükk* was chiefly manifested by differences in pottery. The Bükk potters manufactured well-constructed vessels of globular form. They made one type of thin-walled pottery which is especially distinctive. The latter was decorated with parallel bands of finely-incised lines, usually in volute or Gothic arch motifs. A regular progression of Bükk ornament was distinguished by Ferenc Tompa, who has elucidated the progression of events in the Bükk Mountain area. The first decorative motifs of Bükk pottery featured meanders of fine, parallel lines. The second stage was characterized by the dominance of volutes and angular designs. In the third and last period of development, the designs became extremely complex, with a great multiplicity of incised lines, skillfully cut. The chief distinction of Bükk ware is the novel appearance of red or white painting which was used in connection with the linear work. In many Bükk vessels, the white paint was rubbed into the incisions to accent their effect. In all examples, the paint supplements the fine incised work. Bükk pottery is definitely not a painted ware as such.

The importance of the painting tradition of the Bükk people has been greatly stressed. Presumably this was a far extension of the

Painted Pottery traditions to the south in Thessaly, and still farther beyond in the Aegean area. Presumably it was the painting of the Bükk potters that inspired the peculiar crusted ware which occurred in Moravia, to the west. There are even those who see in the Bükk painted pottery the inspiration for the multicolored styles of decoration which were popular far to the east in Moldavia and Transylvania. Certainly the Bükk area, isolated as it was, was influenced by other, distant Neolithic centers.

Aside from pottery differences, the Bükk culture paralleled almost exactly the Danubian, with which it was contemporaneous. Bükk farmers grew the same grains and herded the same animals as the Danubians. Tools and weapons were similar, and the shoe-last celt was the typical ax form. Obsidian occurs locally in the Bükk area and was a favorite chipping medium.

From studies of trade pottery and correlations of a few sites which contain both typical Danubian material and distinctive Bükk elements, it seems clear that the Bükk people correspond to Danubian I*b* in the main valley. Late Bükk actually extends into the Danubian II period. About this same time, when Danubian I*b* was merging into Danubian II, the Bükk tradition, combining with some of the original Danubian elements, gave rise to a new culture which also centered in the Hungarian area. This new development is called *Tisza,* after the Hungarian river valley where it principally developed. The culture of the important Neolithic center of Polgar, in the Tisza valley, has been designated the *Tisza-Polgar.*

From the site of Polgar itself, and also Kenezlö, another Neolithic town of the Tisza culture, an abundance of pottery which accentuates these differences has been recovered. On the basis of ceramics, the Tisza culture has been divided into two distinct periods—Tisza I and Tisza II.

Tisza I was a transition from the Bükk tradition. The pottery forms follow the globular Bükk types of the later versions. Early Tisza also featured such forms as the cruce, pedestal stands, and small amphoras, forms derived from the lower Danube. Some of the early Tisza decoration is likewise Danubian. Crusted or post-fired pottery continues the Bükk tradition. Much of the early Tisza work is a poor imitation of the Moravian crusted ware.

Plastic art, in the early Tisza culture, included zoomorphic vessels, clay figurines, and modeled rim figures decorating the edges of the pots. Pedestal tables, spindle whorls, and loom weights were also made of pottery materials. The presence of *pintaderas*, which are pottery stamps for the imprinting of a design on some flat surface, is interesting. The inspiration for the pintaderas was almost certainly the cylinder seals of the Near East. Here again is a telling proof of the direction from which these Neolithic inspirations were derived.

Early Tisza material was, in other respects, quite Danubian. Local Hungarian obsidian was used for most chipped work. The shoe-last celt was still the prominent tool of that type. Early Tisza hunters and fishermen used harpoons of horn, many of them barbed like Magdalenian forms, and antler axes reminiscent of earlier Mesolithic types. However, except for the distinctive pottery, the Tisza was, as these other variations were, simply another adaptation of the Neolithic way of life.

Tisza II corresponds to late Danubian II. In this late Tisza version of the Neolithic, the Bükk pottery traditions had essentially faded. Tisza-Polgar material features fruit stands, chalices, and pots with elaborate bases. Dimples and rivet-like knobs became the typical decoration, many of them seemingly an imitation of metal work. The fruit stands were often elaborated with cut-out bases to produce an intricate fretwork of clay. Perforated bases of this sort continued until, in the succeeding period of the *Bodrogkeresztur* culture, they reached a climax of development. The Bodrogkeresztur will be discussed subsequently, as this is the period of Danubian III in Hungary and also the Copper Age. Even in Tisza II, however, there were copper ornaments. Bits of the metal were used as decoration, as they were at Jordansmühl. These trinkets constitute the first beginnings of the knowledge of this metal among the Neolithic people of the Danube.

A notable variation of the Tisza culture occurs at Butmir to the southwest in Bosnia. Butmir, the central site of this development, indicates that here in Yugoslavia, also, local Mesolithic traditions combined with the central Neolithic theme to produce a distinctive variation. The pottery of Butmir is different and easily recognized. The decoration features running spirals as a main motif, with hatchwork, checkers, and tatoo-like forms also prominent. Although the Butmir pottery shows a great similarity to the Tisza tradition and some connections with the central Danubian, it is nonetheless a distinctive style in its own right.

European archaeologists stress the significance of the various pottery shapes and the traditions of their decorations. These may be traced in currents and crosscurrents among all of these Neolithic centers as they borrowed or were influenced one by the other. In this way, the movements of small groups of farmers and herdsmen from place to place may be traced, who otherwise would leave no record of the exchange. Trade contacts from one village to another are reflected in pottery styles. It is not the pottery itself which is important, but it is through this means that the intricate web of European Neolithic beginnings may be traced. By these studies, it is evident that Butmir was not properly Danubian at all, but was a distinctive Neolithic mixture. Butmir farmers grew *Triticum vulgare* or bread wheat and barley; they kept herds and lived in rectangular houses. The shoe-last celt was their typical stone implement.

When the first European archaeologists began to outline the beginnings of the Neolithic period as it had evolved in central and southern Europe, it became increasingly apparent that there was a distinct Neolithic development in southeastern Europe and the Black Earth region of the Ukraine. With continuing excavations, it became clear that there were several groups of agriculturists and stock breeders in southeastern Europe who were chiefly distinguished by their painted pottery. For this reason, these Neolithic peoples have long been designated as the *Painted Pottery* people.

The excavation of the first site of the Painted Pottery people was at Tripolye in the Ukraine, and later discoveries were made at a number of sites in the Tripolye area near Kiev in the middle Dnieper region. Russian diggers also excavated the Painted Pottery village of Bilče in Galicia and the important settlement of Košilovci. The most significant sites of Cucuteni and Izvoare were discovered in Moldavia. Transylvania was found to contain abundant material, especially in the valley of the Alt to the east, where the type site of Erösd yielded Neolithic remains obviously connected with the Painted Pottery problem. Professor Szombathy from Vienna excavated the site of

Schipenitz in the Bukovina area, where again the typical polychrome pottery showed a totally different tradition from that of the Danubian peoples. From all of these evidences, it is clear that a number of allied Neolithic peoples, whose distinguishing characteristic was their painted pottery, had occupied these regions. From the intrusive painted wares and painting techniques which appeared in such Danubian centers as Starčevo, Lengyel, and Bükk, it is also clear that the Painted Pottery people had generally developed during the same centuries as the Danubian peasant cultures. On a basis of all of this information, the Painted Pottery problem has been separated geographically into a number of groups or allied sites with their relative chronology as follows:

	UKRAINE	MOLDAVIA	TRAN-SYLVANIA	MIDDLE EUROPE
3000*	Neolithic beginnings	Neolithic beginnings	Neolithic beginnings	Neolithic beginnings
2700*	Volute	Izvoare	Boian A	Volute Danubian I*a*
2500*	Tripolye A–1	Cucuteni A	Erösd	Punctuate Danubian I*b*
2300*	Tripolye A–2	Cucuteni A–B	Erösd	Jordansmühl Danubian II
	Transition		Coţofeni	Danordic Danubian III
2100*	Tripolye B–1	Cucuteni B	Coţofeni	Danordic Danubian III
2000*	Tripolye B–2	Cucuteni B		Corded Danubian III
1900*	Costes, Corded		Schneckenberg	

* Approximate date B. C.

Early Painted Pottery seems most closely connected with Danubian II. These Danubian influences were augmented by continued influences from the eastern Mediterranean. The Tripolye culture is divided into four phases which show increasingly less Danubian influence as they progress. During late Tripolye times this culture of the Painted Pottery group expanded eastward across the Dnieper. Late Tripolye corresponds with Danubian III in central Europe.

In the Ukraine, Professor Kandyba has worked out a sequence of four phases with a transitional period between the first two and last two groups.

> A-1—Nezvyska (Niezwiska)
> A-2—Zališčyky
> Transition—Horoduycja
> B-1—Bilče
> B-2—Košilovci

Similar time designations from other parts of the Painted Pottery area indicated that these Neolithic people passed through a number of distinct periods which paralleled the Danubian. By means of pottery interrelations, it is possible to make a rather exact parallel between their developments.

The origins of the Painted Pottery people are patently the same as those of the Danubian peasants in that the inspiration for their agriculture and animal husbandry was derived from Hither Asia. The routes over which these influences moved, however, were probably different, although there is some evidence that Painted Pottery inspiration may first have traveled over the Vardar-Morava route from Thessaly into the middle Danube area. Indeed, the Painted Pottery people were obviously intimately connected with Aegean Neolithic beginnings. During later periods of their history, there were even Painted Pottery influences in the opposite direction, that is, from north to south. Undoubtedly, also, there were Neolithic infiltrations of ideas and peoples around the Black Sea directly from Anatolia. However, no Painted Pottery materials occur much farther east than the left bank of the Dnieper River near Kiev.

In its greatest extent, the Painted Pottery area included the lower Danube below the Iron Gates in the Wallachian Plain of Rumania, Moldavia, Transylvania, and the Ukraine, to southeast Poland. There were also decided southward extensions of the Painted Pottery area in Thrace and Macedonia.

The basis of Painted Pottery life was the raising of the grains, wheat and barley, as well as millet and rye. The herding of cattle, sheep, and goats was also important. Probably horses were used, as the bones of these animals are found in some Painted Pottery sites and seem to indicate their domestication. Apparently the climate in most Painted Pottery regions was wetter than at present and ideally suited for the Neolithic culture. These people also hunted chamois, elk, and bear and fished for sturgeon to supplement their economy.

Their tools were similar to those of the Danubians. Shoe-last celts and chipped stone celts are typical. They also used flint for blades, scrapers, and arrowheads. Awls, daggers, and spatulae were fashioned from bone, and wool was probably woven. There also occurs, in the Painted Pottery repertory, a considerable number of copper objects, such as beads, awls, and an occasional dagger. In addition to ordinary implements, the Painted Pottery peasants left behind them abundant evidence of their spiritual beliefs in the form of figurines. These include humans, both male and female, and animals in the form of bulls, sheep, pigs, horses, dogs, and bears. These plastics are for the most part schematic and nonrealistic. Details were put on with punctuation or, in some cases, incision or paint. Even the animals are rudimentary, and many of them cannot be identified by species.

The villages of the Painted Pottery people show a number of differences when compared with Danubian sites. Painted Pottery towns in Moldavia and Transylvania were fortified. These military works included fortified hills, ditches and, in some settlements, wooden palisades. At the Painted Pottery site of Erösd in eastern Transylvania, a very large area was surrounded by earthworks and a moat. Within these works, the Painted Pottery people lived in several kinds of dwellings. The earliest houses at Erösd were pit dwellings excavated into the loess. In later phases, rectangular houses appeared at Erösd with wickerwork walls built above ground. These rectangular dwellings had gabled roofs, a vestibule or porch at one end, and were equipped with hearths of clay and stone. The houses were placed in regular rows in a formal arrangement. This type of house is called the *megaron,* from the Greek term for the rectangular and formal type of dwelling. In Ukranian centers, however, the sites are marked by *zemljanki* or house pits. These are subterranean dwellings one or two meters in depth, with steps or a ramp leading down into them. At the rear was a stove arrangement with a chimney or, in some instances, a raised hearth. Other Painted Pottery centers show variations of pit dwellings and megaron types. The Painted Pottery houses are consistently more architecturally progressive than the Danubian. Occasional clay models of houses, such as those from the sites of Popudna and Suskivka, indicate that superstructural details were even more elaborate.

Most of the Painted Pottery material from eastern sites has been recovered from Točki. These houses had been destroyed, perhaps intentionally. Occasionally, cremated human bones occur in the Točki, and complete skeletons are also found in the zemljanki or dwelling pits. These demonstrate that the skeletal type of the Painted Pottery people was already mixed. Some of the dolichocephalic remains appear close to the racial type called *Mediterranean*. Others are sub-brachycephalic in form, showing a mixed tradition.

The pottery of the Painted Pottery people is obviously, then, their most distinguishing feature. The sequence of decorations and the forms of vessels have perhaps best been worked out in the Ukranian area. There are some differences when compared with Painted Pottery progressions in Moldavia, Transylvania, and peripheral areas.

Even in the early phases of Painted Pottery development, the forms of the vessels were sophisticated. In the Nezvyska stage, a few crude pots with *Unio*-shell temper appear, but these are intrusive wares of hunter-nomads of surrounding areas and not Painted Pottery proper. Very early in the Painted Pottery sequence, these people developed a number of typical vessel forms which may be followed in their evolution. Perhaps the commonest shape was the amphora, with a conical neck and two horizontal handles. Another usual type was an amphora with an outflared neck and two vertical handles. A plain openmouthed pot with a round belly was also popular. A beaker form with incurved edges appeared consistently, and covers for the amphora forms and beakers were used. These covers were vessels in themselves, often having horizontal handles. Bowls, in a number of variations, were present, and were usually a narrow-based dish with steeply flaring shallow sides.

Perhaps the most inexplicable and distinctive of the Ukranian Painted Pottery types were the binocular vases. These were dual vessels joined by small bridges of clay. The two vessels attached in this way had no bottoms, which increased the illusion of binoculars. Several authorities have suggested that the binocular vases were used as incense burners; however, their surfaces are not burned except where they were recovered from Točki or burned houses. Cossina thought that they were pottery drums with skin heads stretched over their tops. This theory, however, is implausible because the painted decoration is carried over the lip of the vase to the inside of the top opening, which would scarcely be the case if a skin drumhead were stretched over this portion.

The decoration on these various forms of vessels evolved in a recognizable sequence of types. In the Nezvyska stage, decoration was sometimes incised and occasionally encrusted, but usually painted. The painted form was on a red ground with white motifs outlined in black. Predominant among the forms of this polychrome arrangement were spirals done in a broad belt around the vessel. Indeed, this running spiral, in many variations, is by far the most typical design.

In the Zališčyky phase, red or black designs were placed on a white surface. White on red, outlined with black, was also used. Many thin white lines replaced the broad-belt arrangement of the previous Nezvyska treatment.

In the transitional or Horoduycja phase, only bichrome designs were featured. Most of the vessels were highly polished and thin-walled. In this intermediate period, the running spirals of previous decoration had degenerated into elliptical figures with pendants. In some cases, "S"-like forms with intermediate slanting lines, were all that remained of the former advancing spirals.

In the Bilče phase, sophisticated vessels with accentuated profiles were elaborately decorated with black and red on a polished red surface. Hooked spiral decorations are typical of the Bilče period. Much of the finest Painted Pottery material is of this sort.

In the final Košilovci phase, white and black designs were placed on a red background, or red and black motifs on a white background. In this final phase of Ukranian Painted Pottery decoration, the advancing spiral had disappeared almost completely. There was much geometrication and a tendency to cut the design into panels. Sworls were the common motif used on bowls and open vessels. However, in many instances in the Košilovci phase, there was no decoration at all.

It must be emphasized that, paralleling the distinctive and highly ornamented Painted Pottery vessels, crude domestic pottery appears in all phases. Some of this was made in the tradition of the *Kamker-amik,* or comb-ornamented pottery, which was a persistent tradition in European Russia at this time.

Moldavian Painted Pottery, as evidenced by the most important Moldavian site of Cucuteni, is only slightly different from the Ukranian. Cucuteni itself, as excavated by Hubert Schmidt, showed only two levels. These, with their transitions, correspond well with the Ukranian phases. Considerable Moldavian pottery is done with a negative technique, featuring "S"-shapes, spirals, and degenerated spiral forms.

In early Moldavian, or Moldavian A, the decoration was somber, in brown and black on a white background. In the transition between Moldavian A and B, designs were executed in black and white on brown, or red and black on a white background. In the final Moldavian phase, or Moldavian B, the decoration was for the most part black on white, or simply black designs on a natural background. Some variations occurred at the Moldavian sites of Fedeleşeni, where a black-and-white-on-red type of decoration occurs which closely parallels that of the Ukraine.

In Transylvania, as evidenced at the sites of Oltsein, Priesterhügel, and Erösd, the clay was for the most part dark, and white decorations were popular. Transylvanian vessel forms and general decoration motifs were, however, very similar to those of the Ukraine and Moldavia. The stratigraphy in most of the Transylvanian sites is obscure. At Erösd, the excavator distinguished three strata. Two periods, or phases, occur at other Transylvanian sites, however, which correspond to the general situation at Cucuteni. Transylvanian decoration featured many combinations of white on red, or white on black. Red outlined with buff was used, and spirals and meanders were the favorite decorations. Paralleling the Ukrainian, much of the late Transylvanian material shows disconnected spirals and degenerate forms. Several types of painting on the pottery from Erösd show interesting connections with Thessalian material. From its geopraphical position and the nature of its cultural elements, Erösd may be regarded as an intermediate site with connections in all other Painted Pottery areas.

Also present in the repertory of pottery products from Erösd are a number of pintaderas or pottery stamps, similar to those at Butmir. Other tools and implements show little variation between Ukranian, Moldavian, or Transylvanian sites. Plastic clay figurines were manufactured by all three Painted Pottery groups. Stonework was of Danubian types, and the general economy and products were similar.

The Painted Pottery peoples of southeastern Europe were not isolated from the other Neolithic groups in the Danube valley or in the Aegean area. Crusted pottery and various painted types extended into southeastern Poland and well over into the middle Danube area above the Iron Gates. Such Danubian settlements as Lengyel, Starčevo, and the Bükk group show Painted Pottery influences. Perhaps most significant were those connections which lay to the south, in Macedonia and Thessaly. Many archaeologists see, in the similarity of the Painted Pottery motifs and the Thessalian wares, a movement or resurgence from north to south.

Neolithic life, as at Sesklo and Dimini, was quite unlike that of the island of Crete and appears to be more closely connected with Painted Pottery cultures to the north. The ancient farmers of Sesklo farmed and herded much like the Danubians and the Painted Pottery people. Connections with the Painted Pottery area are especially evident at the last site of Dimini. Dimini was a fortified town protected by enclosing walls very much like the military protections at Erösd and Cucuteni in the Painted Pottery area. It is significant, also, that at Erösd in Transylvania the rectangular or megaron type of house appeared. Because of these similarities, some authorities would classify the Thessalian Neolithic as a derivation of the north rather than as the parent Neolithic stock from which the Danubian and northern cultures were derived. Sesklo and Dimini appear to be the older; therefore, the original movement was northward, although later influences may well have moved in the opposite direction.

In western Europe, a type of Neolithic tradition appeared which was distinct from the Danubian in both content and source. Neolithic peoples had early spread from the Nile valley along the northern oases of the African coast to the region of Tunisia. Probably this type of Neolithic life stemmed originally from Merimde on the western periphery of the Nile Delta. These colonists pushed steadily westward and ultimately moved across Gibraltar into Spain. In the Spanish area the African strain of Neolithic gave rise to the *Almeria culture*. The Almerian sites of El Garcel and Tres Cabezos were the first settlements of the western Neolithic on European soil.

The colonists of El Garcel brought with them a type of dark pottery with a shape which was probably derived from leather forms. They also knew the use of copper. The working of metal from the rich mineral deposits of the Iberian Peninsula became an outstanding feature of later phases of Almeria developments.

The western colonists did not all stop in Spain, however. Many continued into southern France and thence north by way of the Rhone valley to northern France and Switzerland. Other western colonists, or their descendants, formed the earliest farming communities of Brittany, Britain, and the western coasts of Europe, in places favorable to their new culture. Consolidating these holdings in the west, they soon pushed eastward into areas already held by peasants of the Danubian expansion. The westerners crossed the Rhine and moved into the Elbe valley, into eastern Switzerland, and into northern Italy. The fortified settlements suggest clashes between the western Neolithic settlers, and the Danubians. In fact, most of the western settlements were fortified.

A major part of the western Neolithic economy was based on stock raising and trade. Many of the western Neolithic settlements depended almost entirely upon their herds. Others raised cereal grains—wheat, barley, and millet—as well as beans, peas, lentils, and apples. Flax was grown for weaving. Many of the western towns in Switzerland were built on the Alpine lakes for defense, with the rectangular, gabled houses supported on piles driven into the mud of the lake floor. Of these pile dwellings, we will hear much in the late Neolithic. In the mountainous regions such as Switzerland, the new Neolithic colonists relied mostly on cattle and pigs, with farming on a minor scale. In other regions such as the British Isles and especially Scotland, sheepherding was a major activity.

In spite of many regional differences, the western Neolithic tradition is much the same from southern France to Scotland and from the Atlantic coast to the Alps. The pottery is universally the baggy, leathern forms reminiscent of their origins in distant Egypt. In northern Europe and Switzerland, the presence of tranchets, transverse arrowheads, and barbed bone harpoons indicates that the Mesolithic societies such as the Maglemosean contributed to the western Neolithic. Undoubtedly some of these groups were Mesolithic peoples who adopted the new way of life. However, a dolichocephalic type of people, whose burials are widely associated with the western Neolithic, are close to the Mediterranean race which undoubtedly represents actual immigrants from north Africa.

Thus the Neolithic way of life became a part of European prehistory in two major traditions and a number of minor ones. These variants, each with its pottery styles, house types, and individual tools, though different in particulars, were all part of a fundamental Neolithic pattern. As this pattern developed, divergences became more marked, but the underlying structure remained the same. The growing of grains and the herding of domestic animals remained the economic basis of European existence to historic times. Each European group borrowed in varying degrees from the preceding local Mesolithic or was influenced by individual strains of tradition. As each developed new pottery types, methods of burial, or other differences, prehistorians have named these plateaus of development and sought to trace their growth and movements. Following the Danubian II and the developed western Neolithic in central Europe, there were a number of cultures in different parts of the continent. These late Neolithic variations arose not only from the Danubian, western Neolithic, and Painted Pottery beginnings, but also from patterns which were continually brought to the coasts of Europe by sea routes from the Mediterranean.

CHAPTER 8

Farms and Ships

As THE ARCHAEOLOGISTS began to identify the ramifications of the Neolithic way of life in Europe, they noticed a number of variations which were obviously not simple outgrowths of the Danubian or of the Western Neolithic. As was usual, most of these differences were distinguishable in pottery, but there were other criteria as well. The form of life represented by these variations was obviously much the same as the preceding, and yet these differing cultures were distinct versions of Neolithic life recognizable in different parts of Europe. Curiously this later period displays pottery differences as did the preceding times, but in the late Neolithic the ceramic lines of demarcation are more difficult to distinguish. Several ceramic forms or styles are widespread but show local variations. Many hybrid forms were present which are difficult to divide into distinct cultures.

In other respects also, the late Neolithic in Europe had characteristics which were almost universal. Perhaps because of slash-and-burn agricultural practices which exhausted the soil rapidly, the late Neolithic peoples turned to stock raising on a larger scale, particularly sheepherding. Figurines of rams and bulls show that religious thought, too, had turned in this direction, whereas previous Danubian peasants had worshiped a Mother Earth Goddess in the form of a female. Villages were universally fortified, but the houses were smaller. Some cultures of the late Neolithic were entirely nomadic. Most worked in metal or had begun to copy metal forms in stone. Battle-axes of stone or copper are characteristic of the late Neolithic. Warfare was prevalent because no new land was available for excess population and expansion was possible only through force.

Especially distinctive of this late period were several groups found in North Central Europe, which were demonstrably different from the earlier Danubian II. This type of Neolithic was at first called *northern Neolithic,* or *First Northern culture,* or sometimes *Nordic* because of its supposed connection with the origin of the Nordic people.

This combination of Neolithic materials was soon found to be a complex rather than a single culture. It apparently originally centered in Denmark and Schleswig-Holstein and was based upon the Ertebølle Mesolithic tradition in that region. The original Mesolithic inhabitants there had absorbed the Neolithic idea with its grazing and farming practices. However, they were not bound to the loess soil regions as were the Danubians. By 2500 B.C. these Nordic Neolithic people were expanding, with their increased populations, eastward along the coast and southward, absorbing other Mesolithic groups in their path. Variations of this northern Mesolithic spread southeastward to the headwaters of the Vistula River and the Bug in Galicia. Southwestward, the northern Neolithic reached Moravia and Bohemia, where the Danubians were already firmly entrenched. The northerners generally occupied the rougher country back from the rivers, whereas the Danubians lived on the loess in the valleys.

The northern Neolithic is usually distinguished by three readily recognizable pottery forms. These are a beaker with a flaring or funnel rim, a round-bodied jar with two small loop handles which vaguely recalls the amphora form, and a small flask with a ridge or collar around its constricted neck. These three, the funnel-neck beaker, the amphora, and the collared flask, all with incised designs on their surfaces, are everywhere indicative of the spread of the northern Neolithic. Even in local variation these three pottery forms are outstanding.

To the south, the northern Neolithic came in contact with the Jordansmühl variety of Danubian. Inevitable fusion occurred. The resulting mixtures sometimes have been termed the *Danordic* as a combination of Danubian and Nordic. The Danordic peoples represented several versions of late Neolithic life and undoubtedly several tribes. The Danordic includes such cultures as the *Altheim* and *Baden* which are often regarded as distinct and separate.

In the Danordic, Danubian I*a* and I*b* elements were absorbed. Obviously the ethnic element of the Danordic was much the same as the preceding Danubian. The farming type of life continued with its basis in the growing of grain and the herding of domestic animals. Settlements of the Danordic are of two types—open valley sites and hilltop forts. At both of these types, excavators have encountered pits and rectangular huts. Post molds and wall plaster show the Danordic dwellings to be less sophisticated than those of the Painted Pottery people. There is evidence, however, of specialization of labor among the Danordic peasants with the greater emphasis on stock raising.

As an indication of the widespread trade connections of the Danordic and the Danubians there were distinctive pottery forms and bits of copper from the far south. Outstanding among the pottery forms were small pedestal bowls with scalloped bases and lobate-bottomed pots. These specialized forms are similar to those from the site of Laibach Moor, in the old Austro-Hungarian crownland of Carniola. A Danordic cup with a high, arching loop handle is similar to pottery from the site of Drevenik in Slovakia and suggests a southern influence.

The Danordic pottery traditions also seemed to have been influenced by many other types of Neolithic known in central Europe. The Neolithic culture called *Baalberg* is represented by typical narrow-necked jars with pierced lug handles. Baalberg Neolithic was a distinct culture located between the Elbe and the Harz Mountains. The widespread Neolithic tradition known as the *Corded* exerted a considerable influence over the Danordic, especially in the matter of impressed, twisted, cordlike decorations on the surface of vessels. Corded ornament from the late Corded tradition is common in the

Danordic. Indeed, there are few types of ceramic ware prevalent among late central European Neolithic developments that did not appear occasionally in the Danordic area.

In addition to ordinary pottery forms, the Danordic people also modeled a few figurines in clay, although this tradition seemed to be dying out. A scattering of human forms and occasional animals were present. Generally, these figurines were poorly formed, with the usual lack of detail. Clay spools and loom-weights were found. Spindle whorls in conical and discoidal forms are typical of the Danordic, suggesting an extensive use of wool for weaving.

Shoe-last celts were still a common tool of the late Neolithic. A specialized small type of the shoe-last celt in the Danordic is called the *Slanska Hora* type. Axes also appear in Danordic combinations, particularly a round-butted type with a drilled perforation for a handle. Stone disks and mace heads were recovered. Arrowheads appeared in Danordic settlements for the first time in large numbers. Most of these were bone points; the others were fashioned of flinty materials and obsidian where it was available. Bone was still utilized by the Danordics for a variety of purposes, such as chisels, spatulae, bodkins, and needles. Phalanges of animals were perforated for use as necklaces and charms. Antler was also formed into pick and ax heads, some of them indistinguishable from Mesolithic types. Shells, especially of the *Glycimeris* variety, were used for ornaments and bracelets.

From these tools and ornaments it is evident that the Danordic groups were typically Neolithic in their economic background. There had been few changes in pattern since the earliest advent of the Thessalian peasant cultures. It is true that the Danordic pottery shows a much wider field of trade and travel than that of the preceding cultures, but this would be a natural development, as most of the terrain and the river valleys were utilized. There are evidences of warfare in the fortified Danordic sites, but as military installations were already present in the Painted Pottery traditions, this feature is not entirely new. The Danordic is, then, simply a combination of elements which were already present, but in a new and interesting grouping.

Perhaps the best-known site in the Danordic groups is the settlement of Homolka in Bohemia. This was a fortified village associated with the Baden culture. Another well-known Danordic settlement is the hilltop site of Altheim in Bavaria, again a fortified village. Altheim is often regarded as a separate culture, as it obviously was formed of a combination of Danordic and western elements. In Austria, the Danordic culture is called Baden. The Baden culture introduces the Copper Age in those regions, and is often used as the name for a group of cultures centered in the Carpathian area and extending as far as the Elbe in one direction and the Drave in the other.

Even before the development of the Danordic, another variation had already appeared in Europe. This was the so-called *Corded culture,* named for its distinctive pottery decoration. The Corded is a series of cultures identified almost entirely by pottery and graves. These are also known as the *Battle-ax* cultures.

Many investigators had noticed that a peculiar pottery decoration occurred in several variations from the Ukranian area of south Russia, northwestward to the old Ertebølle region of the Mesolithic, and to Holland. This decoration involved the use of cord imprints pressed upon the surface of pottery vessels while the clay was still plastic. In some instances, a twisted piece of cordage was wrapped around the thumb of the potter, who, by this means, made distinctive imprints in the soft clay. Other vessels were decorated by linear cord imprints in which twisted cordage was used as a stamp to mark the pot surfaces, usually in vertical series. In the easternmost section of this interesting development, cord types of pottery decoration blended with the *Kamkeramic* or comb-ornamented pottery of the Russian forest lands. Much of this peripheral corded and comb pottery was unaccompanied by other Neolithic elements. Many of the groups in extreme northern Europe, while adopting pottery traditions and other material culture items from Neolithic neighbors, had not as yet adopted the growing of grains. Most of the Corded Ware people herded animals and were at least seminomadic.

While it is impossible to determine precisely the origin of the Corded Ware type of decoration, it was most strongly developed in central and north central Europe. In Silesia, Bavaria, north Slovakia, Poland, and northwestward to the mouth of the Rhine a number of graves were found which were the focus of the Corded Ware development. An especial concentration of graves occurs in Saxo-Thuringia. These were usually single interments with the body contracted and lying on its side. In the Saale valley, Corded graves were stone cists covered by a tumulus or mound. Most of the Corded Ware graves were those of male skeletons. Accompanying the body on the right hand was usually a battle-ax of stone. These axes were finely made with a drilled perforation for the insertion of a haft. In addition, the battle-axes of Saxo-Thuringia were faceted and fashioned with a flaring bit. Occasional celts or hammer-axes accompanied the skeletons in lieu of a faceted battle-ax. Because of this association, many archaeologists have called the Corded people the *Battle-ax cultures,* or *Warrior cultures,* and these have been much discussed in connection with the origin of the Nordic race and the Indo-European linguistic complex. These Warrior cultures have a broader scope than the Corded Ware Neolithic itself. Emanating originally from the steppe lands of eastern Europe, they became identified with cord-impressed pottery, the battle-ax in various forms, and individual burial.

Corded graves in central Europe contained, in addition to the martial equipment, one or more pottery vessels with typical cord-impression decoration. It is for this reason that the term Corded culture has been used. Actually, a wide spread of Neolithic peoples had developed cord-impressed pottery before the coming of the Warrior cultures. The Corded Ware area of Saxo-Thuringia was a center of this development; the warrior element was foreign to central Europe.

The Corded beaker, a tall pot form with the neck constituting about two-thirds of the entire height of the vessel, occurred frequently. Rarely, the beaker form had a band handle. Cord impressions usually occupied the entire neck of the beaker and a considerable portion of the body. Sometimes incised decoration simulated cord impressions. The myrtle twig pattern was common and was made with incision or cord impression. These beakers, which occurred with all varieties of Corded cultures, although not always with corded or myrtle twig decoration, were associated with other beakers from western Europe. The beakers were drinking vessels, presumably for some kind of mead or fermented brew.

Another Corded Ware form was a pitcher with an outline suggesting derivation from the Jordansmühl tradition. The body of the pitcher was usually embellished with the cord impressions or incisions done in triangles after the Jordansmühl manner.

The amphora was also recovered from Corded graves. This two-handled vessel may be a deviation of the amphora form of the Painted Pottery people, and is certainly from the southeastern regions of Europe. In early amphora forms, two handles were provided. In later variations, four handles were added high on the neck in addition to the original two on the belly of the vessel. Amphora were usually ornamented with the myrtle twig design, herringbone patterns, or, in some cases, appliqué. Certain forms of the amphora of the Corded Ware graves were connected with the Danordic.

Bowl forms also occurred in the Corded culture graves. The bowls were, for the most part, plain, and innocent of cord impressions, although they were found with typical Corded vessels of other forms.

Amber and copper ornaments were present in the occasional female interments of Corded affiliation. Copper was fashioned in the form of small rings, thin bracelets, and bangles. It is, however, significant that the Corded people were familiar with this new material. Many stone battle-axes in Corded graves simulate metal forms, even to the casting ridge on top and bottom, which is often faithfully reproduced in the stone.

Triangular arrowheads of flinty materials, flaked knives, and occasional scrapers were also found in Corded graves. Disk beads of bone or shell, perforated animal teeth, and decorated shell pendants were likewise typical.

With the exception of the settlements of Grosslehus and Stössen in the Saale valley which do not give a satisfactory picture of Corded backgrounds, few towns of these people are known. The usual adjuncts of the Neolithic way of life, such as permanent habitations with evidences of animal husbandry and agriculture, are absent. Because these elements were missing, it has been suggested that the Corded Ware people were traders and warriors, and some have considered them dealers in salt who moved through the Neolithic communities of their time peddling their wares.

Professor Childe prefers to group all of these Corded or Battle-ax cultures into eight groups, including peoples from the North Sea to the Pontic steppes of Russia. These groups are: (1) Beaker culture

of southern Holland and northwestern Germany; (2) the later Jutland Single-grave culture; (3) the Boat-ax culture of Sweden and
southern Norway; (4) Saxo-Thuringian culture; (5) the Oder culture; (6) Drevohostice culture of eastern Moravia; (7) Fatyanovo
culture of the upper Volga; (8) Yamno culture of the Pontic steppes.
Because most of these people (except the Boat-ax culture and the
Fatyanovo culture) buried their dead in graves surmounted by barrows, this whole group has been termed the *Barrow cultures*. In spite
of the names Corded cultures or Battle-ax cultures or Barrow cultures there were obviously many differences among the various components of this loosely associated group. Perhaps the greatest differences were the warrior elements in the easternmost groups as contrasted with less nomadic and more peaceful aspects of the Saxo-Thuringian and northwestern German components.

The battle-axes occurring in the graves suggest that these warrior
elements intruded from the east of Europe. Warrior peoples brought
the Painted Pottery cultures of the Ukraine to an end. About the
turn of the second millennium before Christ, these Warrior cultures
were dominant throughout the steppe region and its environs. Penetrating into southeastern Europe, they dominated the Schneckenberg
and Coțofeni versions of the Painted Pottery life of Transylvania.
Warrior peoples penetrated to the Hungarian Plain and to the Baden
culture area of Austria. They apparently introduced horse-breeding
and the use of horses as draft animals. Horse bones occur in Holland
Corded graves and in graves of the Yamno culture. The use of horses
accentuated nomadic tendencies.

The warriors brought copper hammer-axes from their eastern
homeland where copper was plentiful. As they pushed into Europe
and could no longer obtain copper, they made stone copies of their
original metal weapons. Across central Europe the warrior invasion
is marked by a whole series of battle-axes in stone. The Corded Ware
people of Saxo-Thuringia made a specialized version of this stone
battle-ax with facets. Other Neolithic people to the north, in Denmark,
adopted a type of battle-ax called the boat-ax, which gives its name
to the Boat-ax culture of south Sweden.

In addition to the First Northern, Baden, Altheim, Danordic, and
Corded manifestations of the late Neolithic, there were several other

149

cultures in the European area which are distinctive enough to be separately named. Among these are the *Mondsee, Slavonian, Horgen, Cortaillod, Michelsberg, Rinaldone, Glina, Baalberg, Nosswitz, Walternienburg, Bernburg,* and the so-called *Globe-flask culture.*

The Mondsee culture, named from the famous pile-dwelling site on the eastern slope of the Alps in Austria, was a culture covering a considerable area of Alpine terrain. Sites of this variety, all in the eastern Alpine region, developed late and extended into a Chalcolithic period when the Mondsee Lake Dwellers were dealers in copper derived from local mines. Mondsee pottery is typically incised, but Corded Ware also appears. The pile-dwelling type of fortified village was adapted by several varieties of late Neolithic peoples.

The Slavonian culture is named from sites in Slavonia in Yugoslavia, with typical sites at Sarvaš and Vričedol on the Drave River. Slavonian pottery was very distinctive and typically ornamented with carved-out designs filled with white paint. The Slavonian culture was also late in its development and showed evidence of Corded influences as well as connections with the Balkans and the Aegean. The Slavonian continued into later metal periods and contributed pottery techniques which became typical of later Bronze periods both in Slavonia and in contemporary Italy.

The Horgen culture is a term used for a late Neolithic grouping of cultures in Switzerland. Horgen follows both the Cortaillod and Michelsberg cultures in Switzerland. In the Alpine area, a number of Neolithic peoples had protected their villages by placing them on pilings driven into the mud of the lake bottom, by crib work placed in the water of rivers, or by wooden platforms in peat bogs. One of these groups was derived from the western Neolithic.

In the various areas of France, just as in other parts of Europe, the incoming Neolithic fused with the Mesolithic cultures which were already present. This was especially true in the old Azilian area. A mixture of the Azilian-like culture with the incoming Neolithic from the south produced a most distinctive variation in the western Alpine area. This, from one of the sites on the shores of Lake Neuchâtel, has been called the Cortaillod culture. Various sites in the Lake Neuchâtel area indicate clearly that the basis of the Cortaillod development was a combination of the western Neolithic with its round-bottomed pottery of the same sort as that at Camp de Chassey, and the indigenous, lingering, Azilian Mesolithic with its antler work. The Cortaillod type of Neolithic extended east to Zürich and northward into the Black Forest region. It was a part of a larger development which is usually referred to as the Swiss Lake Dwellings.

When the lake dwellings were first discovered at Meilen in 1855, the initial find stimulated a whole series of explorations in the Alpine area. These curious settlements were designated as Swiss because most of the sites lay within the boundaries of Switzerland. However, the type of life represented by the Neolithic people who built their villages on pilings around the shores of lakes, extended well into the Italian Alps and into Austria, Bavaria, and eastern France around the periphery of the Alpine region.

Early investigators, because of the distinctiveness of the type of architecture involved, were inclined to group all of these remains together under the heading of a single *Lake-dwelling culture*. Subsequent excavations at a number of sites and more careful analysis of the early material has shown conclusively that the Alpine Neolithic was in reality three major developments with a number of minor variations. Chiefly because of the nature of the terrain, the Neolithic cultures in the Alps had much in common. They were, however, of diverse origins.

Possibly the first of these developments was that which intruded into the Alpine region from the west. This Neolithic strain has already been referred to as the Cortaillod culture, and was a combination of Neolithic influence which entered Europe by way of southern France and an indigenous Mesolithic background of Azilian affiliation. The Cortaillod sites, such as those on Lake Neuchâtel, excavated by P. Vouga, showed these Neolithic people built habitations of logs supported on piles, placed in the shallow water around the margins of the lake. Abundant cultural evidence has been recovered by the excavators from the mud and sand around the stumps of the piles which once supported these villages. Generally, the axes, antler sleeves, picks, arrowheads, blades, and microliths show the tools and weapons of the Cortaillod people to be a combination of new Neolithic ideas with older Mesolithic traditions. The Cortaillod residents of the pile dwellings around Lake Neuchâtel ornamented themselves with bone pendants and stone beads. They made fishing nets and baskets. Clay loom-weights indicate that they wove clothes of various fibers, probably vegetable as well as animal.

Stone and antler hoes, querns or grinding stones, and flints which served as the teeth for sickle blades indicate that the Lake-dwelling people were agricultural in spite of the fact that the terrain is ill suited for cultivation by primitive methods. Charred wheat grains are additional evidence that the Neolithic economy was firmly implanted. Also, the bones of cattle, goats, sheep, pigs, and dogs round out the picture of a full Neolithic economy. However, there are ample indications that the Lake Dwellers hunted extensively also, notably for the deer which abounded in the mountains.

Apparently at the same time that the western Neolithic influences were finding a foothold around Lake Neuchâtel and developing the distinctive pile-dwelling villages there, a similar intrusion was occurring in the eastern Alps. Danubian peasants, perhaps driven by necessity or warfare, entered the Alpine region from the other direction and established pile dwellings of a similar sort around a number of lakes to the east of the Cortaillod people. Typical eastern lake dwellings were those at Aichbühl and Mondsee. At Aichbühl on the Federsee, for example, Neolithic people influenced by Danubian backgrounds built a village on the shore of the lake. They constructed long platforms of logs and rectangular megaron-like houses, faintly reminiscent of the architecture of Erösd and Dimini. At other eastern Alpine settlements, the houses were built on piles erected in the shallows of the lakes.

The pottery of Aichbühl was of the Danubian tradition. Cups, pedestaled bowls, and large, rough, storage vessels recall Jordansmühl material. Actual Danubian imports of pottery were present at Aichbühl, from trade or intermarriage with Danubian villages farther east.

The Mondsee culture is a later version of the eastern tradition and shows, by its connections with the Corded and its use of copper, wider trade connections than other eastern Alpine towns. Because of these differences as well as many variations in pottery, tools, and other items of culture, the Mondsee is usually regarded as a separate culture.

Danubian shoe-last celts and hammer-axes of Danubian design

emphasize the connections of the eastern lake dwellings with the Danube valley. Agricultural products include wheat, oats, millet, lentils, and beans. Domestic animals were most commonly sheep, pigs, and several varieties of dogs. The eastern Lake-dwelling economy, however, was not comparable to the farm-herd development in the Danube valley. The Lake-dwelling people had at their disposal only small tracts of level ground around the littoral of the mountain lakes. They supplemented their agriculture and stock raising with hunting just as their contemporaries of the western lake dwellings did.

The Lake-dwelling cultures, then, were divided into an eastern group and a western group, each of separate derivation and influence. Both of these developments apparently took place during the period of Danubian II. Aichbühl pottery is normally ornamented with a type of stroke technique similar to Danubian I*b*. Late Aichbühl materials were closely analogous with Jordansmühl of the Danubian II period. Allowing for cultural lag, it would seem, therefore, that the bulk of the pile-dwelling period paralleled Danubian II and Danubian III. The Cortaillod culture to the westward has been correlated by lake, flood deposits with the eastern material. These deposits indicate that the Cortaillod peoples were building their pile dwellings around the shallows of Lake Neuchâtel at about the same time that the Aichbühl residents were establishing themselves in the east.

Not only is the Lake-dwelling development divided into an eastern and western grouping, but also there is considerable evidence for a succession of events based upon the evolution of certain tool forms which they used. Usually, Lake-dwelling material is divided into three periods, designated as lower, middle, and upper Neolithic. However, it has already been pointed out that even the first of these developments did not begin until roughly Danubian II times or around 2400–2300 B.C. Mondsee and Horgen developments succeeded the Cortaillod and Aichbühl in western and eastern Alpine regions.

A typological sequence of Lake-dwelling material is based upon changes in the form of the antler sleeves which they manufactured as sockets for their celt axes. The custom of fitting celts into antler holders or sleeves is a probable carry-over from the Mesolithic. In the early part of the Lake-dwelling development the antler sleeves were simple, with tapering outlines. Usually the base of the beam of a stag horn was utilized, with a small stone celt set into a prepared socket. Then the antler sleeve was mounted on a wooden handle.

In the mid-course of Lake-dwelling developments, the antler sleeves acquired a sharp shoulder. The bases for insertion into the wooden haft were squared and angular. This change in outline of the antler sleeve was presumably to secure better attachment to the wooden handle. In late Neolithic times the antler sleeve was even more highly evolved and became a more elongated form with a bifurcation at its base. Apparently the Lake-dwelling toolmakers felt that this was an improvement in hafting.

Other tools and flint work generally follow a sequence of improvement and change in form from early to late Neolithic times in the Alpine area. Pottery also indicates change and foreign influence. From occasional imports and adaptations from surrounding regions the time correlation may be rather exactly made.

A third and later development peripheral to Lake-dwelling life was to the north and west. This northern area included not only lake dwellings such as that on Lake Constance but also some sites which were not lake dwellings at all. A number of villages on dry land, some of them fortified, are typical of this culture on the northern edge of the Alpine area. Perhaps the most famous of these is that of Michelsberg in Baden which has given the name to this culture.

The Michelsberg version of the Alpine Lake-dwelling material was essentially an outgrowth of the western Neolithic. Michelsbergers pushed down the Rhine and overawed the Danubian peasant cultures there. The Michelsberg Neolithic people also invaded northeastward through the Rössen Danubians and finally reached Bohemia, which had long been a Danubian stronghold. The Michelsberg, a derivation of the western Neolithic, was responsible for the final blend of the Danubian and the western Neolithic. The Michelsberg also moved into the Belgian region, establishing such fortified sites as Boitsfort in Brabant.

Michelsberg pottery is essentially western, with some forms still reminiscent of the original Egyptian prototypes. The typical tulip beaker was another intrusive element in the Danordic combination. The Michelsberg type of antler ax sleeve had a sharp shoulder or tang. The settlements featured rectangular log houses. The walls of some of these consisted of small poles and wattle and daub bent inward to form a curved dwelling. This peculiar type of structure was also found in a number of the other settlements allied with the Michelsberg, such as various pile-dwelling sites in the northern Alpine area.

Altheim, which gives its name to the Altheim culture and was built on top of a hill for defense, was closely allied with Michelsberg and apparently was a later version of the same trend of Neolithic events. Much of the Altheim material was similar to that called Danordic. Among the pottery, for example, storage jars and open bowls closely parallel Danordic forms. Typical of the many crosscurrents found at Altheim are the pouched jugs similar to western forms of round bottom and "baggy" pottery. Pointed-butted celts of pile-dwelling type occurred also at Altheim as well as faceted hammer-axes from the northern Neolithic. Even the copper celt appears here to indicate that the Neolithic people that fortified themselves on the Altheim hilltop were familiar with at least one metal.

The Cortaillod culture was brought to an end by floods which raised the lake levels and destroyed the villages. There are indications that eastern pile dwellings were affected by the same catastrophe. The Cortaillod people never re-established themselves on Lake Neuchâtel after this inundation. Some of them retreated southward into the Italian Alps and rebuilt other lake dwellings of the same sort. Others of the Cortaillods moved northward mingling there with Danordic elements and groups of eastern derivation.

In the original western Alpine area the Cortaillod people were supplanted by new invaders from northern France, represented at the site of Horgen on the lake of Zürich. These were the people of the Horgen culture, and their variation on the Lake-dwelling theme adopted many features of the preceding Cortaillod and Michelsberg. Most of the late, western Lake-dwelling material is of the Horgen variety.

While the important Lake-dwelling cultures of central Europe were developing in the Alps, other Neolithic people in far corners of Europe were establishing other cultures. The Rinaldone culture, from the site of Rinaldone in central Italy near Viterbo, evolved a distinctive culture with unique architecture, pottery, and tools. The

Rinaldone people were not completely isolated, however, for battle-axes of the type used by the Corded Ware warriors of central Europe have been found at their Italian centers.

The Glina culture of Transylvania also shows the influence of the warrior cultures in the symmetrical battle-axes which occurred as far south as the site of Glina in the Wallachian Plain. The Glina culture had its roots in the same early beginnings as the Danubian at Vinča and the original settlers who began the Painted Pottery traditions in this same area. Trade items of Danubian III suggest that the Glina persisted until the late Neolithic. Glina, as well as Rinaldone and other southern towns of the late Neolithic, seems to have been overwhelmed by an invasion of peoples from the north. Perhaps these were groups of the Battle-ax people expanding southward.

Other kinds of late Neolithic people are distinguished almost entirely by their pottery. The Baalberg group of northern Europe is known from a peculiar kind of pottery usually found in large cist graves. The Baalberg area is centered between the Elbe River and the Harz Mountains. Accompanying the contracted skeletal burials in these cists were distinctive, usually undecorated pottery jars and flasks. Baalberg pottery shapes are easily recognized as different from northern Neolithic Danordic or Corded. The Baalberg people did much to pass the Neolithic traditions on to retarded Neolithic groups beyond them. The influence of the Baalberg people was marked in many surrounding areas. For example, a number of Corded Ware pottery variations are obviously Baalberg shapes adopted by the Corded peoples.

The Nosswitz culture, named from the type site in Silesia, was a variant of the First Northern Neolithic, but again with distinctive pottery variations. Baalberg and Nosswitz are often combined in a Baalberg-Nosswitz axis of Neolithic influence.

The Walternienburg also was a variation of the northern Neolithic theme. Late Walternienburg material is often separately designated under the name of *Bernburg,* from the site of Bernburg. East of the Walternienburg-Bernburg sequence, another culture, the *Havel,* developed in Brandenburg. These three are distinguished by their pottery, but had much in common. They are often grouped together as Walternienburg-Bernburg-Havel. Here in the Elbe and Saale basins, these northern Neolithic people developed pottery types in the form of low, open cups with sharply angular shoulders and band handles, tall jars with accentuated profile, and cylindrical beakers. The decoration was incised, usually as parallel lines or groups of zigzags. Apparently the Walternienburg-Bernburg-Havel development of the northern Neolithic evolved from the Rössen culture during middle Danubian times. The Bernburg material seems later than the classic Walternienburg. Of special interest is the Bernburg drum, which is a pottery drum with lugs for the stretching of a skin head.

It is interesting to speculate about the reasons for these variant pottery forms and culture in a comparatively small area.

The Globe-flask, or Globe-amphora culture is the result of a movement of herding and hunting people from the east mixing with the Danubian and First Northern Neolithic. These easterners made typical round-bodied pottery vessels which are often described as globe-amphora in shape. The Globe-amphora tradition was an apparent outgrowth of fresh Neolithic influences entering southeastern Europe directly across the highlands of the Caucasus to the east of the Painted Pottery region. Globular pottery, together with stone battle-axes, was common in southern Russia early in the Neolithic progression. The same typical globe-shaped pottery moved northwestward, perhaps with an invasion of steppe people, into the region of Poland and ultimately to north central Europe. The Globe-amphora people penetrated into central Germany, where the tradition mixed with the Nosswitz and the Corded styles in those areas.

An additional item carried by the Globe-amphora people was a flat-stone-cist type of burial. Flat-stone-cist graves were a persistent tradition in the Russian area, which at its greatest extent was carried to northern Germany and to Denmark during later Neolithic times. Here the Globe-amphora vessels, the battle-ax, and the flat-stone-cist graves mixed with local elements to produce some interesting variants.

While the Danubian Neolithic tradition was permeating Europe through its heartland and the more easterly strains of the Neolithic were influencing northern Europe through the steppe lands, western Neolithic influences were moving into Europe by southern and western routes. The western Neolithic moved not only along the shores of north Africa where there is sporadic evidence of its passing, but

157

also by sea. Much of the Neolithic life of western Europe was brought by sea trade and travel.

There is ample evidence that several of the more advanced Neolithic peoples of the eastern Mediterranean had already begun to build ocean-going boats by the beginning of the third millennium. By 2500 B.C. various strains of Neolithic culture were already beginning to appear on such distant shores as Sardinia, Sicily, and the Balearic Islands. It must not be supposed that the Neolithic people that carried these influences sailed boldly up the middle of the Mediterranean Sea. On the contrary, they moved hesitantly from place to place along the coasts, establishing themselves in favorable littoral spots when they could.

The first of this sea-borne Neolithic culture was, of course, that which established itself early on the island of Crete and ultimately on the adjacent Balkan mainland. The Cretan Neolithic tradition was intimately connected with the Mediterranean coasts to the eastward and greatly influenced by Egypt. As the Cretan was ultimately climaxed by the Minoan civilization, which was, in turn, the foundation of Classic culture, the Cretan and Minoan together will be discussed separately in a subsequent section.

Neolithic life typical of the eastern Mediterranean and Egypt began to work its way westward throughout the Mediterranean world. In Italy, the Painted Pottery tradition of the Dimini variety of Thessaly appeared, apparently carried in by sea. In Sicily, African versions of the Neolithic established themselves by the beginning of the third millennium. Both open sites and cave settlements in Sicily indicate African affiliations of a people who came there by boat. The pottery which they made was decorated by incision in the form of crosshatching or box design. Some of the Neolithic people in these coastal areas practiced agriculture or animal husbandry on a limited scale. Others adopted only herding or incipient farming. Seldom were their settlements marked by large-scale agriculture or areas of intensive cultivation such as occurred in the Danube valley. It was, however, the Neolithic economic basis, nonetheless. Because so many of these sites are in caves, this peripheral Mediterranean Neolithic is often referred to as the *Cave Culture*.

Still farther to the west in the region of the Strait of Gibraltar, other cave sites indicate the arrival of the Neolithic idea from African origins. Some of the movement to the Gibraltar area may well have been overland by way of various oases and ultimately across the strait into peninsular Spain. Pottery forms occurring in cave sites on both sides of Gibraltar Strait indicate a close connection. The pottery, as usual, was the most sensitive criterion of influence and interrelations. Certainly ideas of Neolithic pottery and tools had moved overland across the north African coastal areas by the middle of the third millennium. Professor Bosch Gimpera, who is concerned with Spanish origins, sees both an inland African influence on the first arrival of the Neolithic in Spain as well as a coastal movement of the same ideas.

While the western and eastern Neolithic traditions were merging to bring about the distinctive cultures of the Alpine regions, Neolithic mariners were pushing farther along the European coasts and into the British Isles. Several groups of western Neolithic people had established themselves in northern France and later moved across the channel to southern Britain.

On the continent, strong strains of the Mesolithic cultures still persisted well into the late third millennium before Christ. The situation was both conservative and provincial. Many sites in northern France and Belgium, for example, show a mixture of pygmy flints and Mesolithic bone work, mixed with round-bodied celts of Neolithic affiliation. Pottery of the most rudimentary western form with baggy, round-bottom bowls was used by these various people with little change. There is some evidence of the western pottery tradition mixing with the old Ertebølle style of pottery-making farther to the north. Generally, however, the Neolithic, of northern France was a very simple form of stock raising, and rudimentary agriculture of the sort which had entered southern France from the Mediterranean and spread northward.

Early in the process of the northern spread of the western Neolithic, the culture passed over into southern Britain. There is little evidence that the Neolithic was first carried by a sea route along western Europe. Rather, it crossed over from the chalk lands of northern France to the similar chalk areas of Sussex and Wessex. As there has been no appearance of the later Michelsberg type of development, the first transition apparently occurred before that time. The Neolithic colonizers quickly spread over southern Britain, reaching Lincolnshire, Yorkshire, southern Scotland, and northeastern Ireland.

The early Neolithic in southern Britain is known from a number of entrenched towns but best from the famous site of Windmill Hill in Wiltshire. The earliest levels of Windmill Hill feature that type of British Neolithic called *Neolithic A*. In form, the great site of Windmill Hill is a causewayed camp. Three concentric ditches enclose a total of twenty-three acres. The ditches are interrupted by frequent gates or causeways, possibly for the convenience of herdsmen who wished to drive cattle into the enclosure for safety. Material from the ditches was piled on the inner side and surmounted by a stockade. This form of fortified village was typical of the culture, and a number of other causewayed camps are known such as White-hawk on the race course above Brighton.

The early inhabitants of Windmill Hill kept cattle, sheep, goats, pigs, and dogs. The emphasis seems to have been on the raising of a long-horned breed of fairly large cattle. They also grew barley and wheat in small plots near by. The grains were ground on stone grinders or saucer querns.

Perhaps the outstanding characteristic of the implement repertory of the early British Neolithic as evidenced at Windmill Hill was its conservatism. Mesolithic forms were preserved, and the initial tradition of early Mediterranean stone implements was continued. Even bone and antler implements of general Mesolithic style were common.

Grain was reaped with flint-toothed sickles. Serrated saw blades, lanceolate arrowheads, and occasional transverse arrowheads of Mesolithic form, flint knives, and scrapers were utilized with little change from preceding forms. The celts were often of chipped and polished flint of the western form, in contrast to the Danubian shoe-last. Manufactures of fine-grained stones have been found at Graig Lywd in Wales, and flint axes of the period were mined and chipped by specialists at the famous flint quarry of Grimes Graves in Norfolk. Flint mining was a specialization of the Neolithic which extended into the later periods.

Neolithic A pottery was typically in the form of plain round-bottom bowls, inspired from leather prototypes and similar to those of the earliest continental types in Neolithic France. The rims of the vessels were simple flaring forms and lug handles were common. Decoration was usually entirely absent.

Later in the development of the causewayed camp at Windmill Hill, as well as in other British Neolithic settlements, the pottery changed. Pot shapes became more complicated, with sharp shoulders and angular bowl forms indicating increased skill in pottery-making. Ornament was provided by incised and comb-stamped, simple, linear designs on the shoulders of the vessels. Occasionally the rims were ticked. These forms may have been the result of later Michelsberg influences crossing the Channel to Britain, and are called A–2. Variations of the Windmill Hill type of Neolithic were affected by the incoming Megalithic peoples and other foreign elements. Such variations are found in Scotland in the *Beacharra culture* and in the north of Scotland in the *Pentland culture.*

The type of British Neolithic life termed *Neolithic B,* or *Peterborough,* is typified by more complicated pottery with comb and tooled decoration. The forms of the vessels suggest that fresh waves of Neolithic influence were constantly coming across from the continent with new ideas in pottery-making and other items. This suggestion is augmented by the fact that Neolithic B pottery ornament became most firmly entrenched in the east.

The influences which brought in Neolithic B were demonstrably more northern than the French impetus of Neolithic A. Pottery decorated in the Neolithic B style occurs in the Baltic area, especially in the Ertebølle region. Routes across the North Sea were undoubtedly shorter and easier than those of today. Submerged sites of Neolithic and even later times show that the subsidence of shore lines in this region has continued into comparatively recent millenniums. These peoples who came to British shores from the Baltic settled and traded along the waterways accessible from the North Sea. Because the site of Peterborough characterizes this type of Baltic-derived Neolithic, this name is often used instead of Neolithic B. British scientists frequently speak of Peterborough pottery.

Peterborough settlements were characteristically in lowland areas,

161

whereas the Windmill Hill peoples had settled the uplands. Peterborough colonists occupied valleys and marshy coastal areas similar to those regions of the northern European Forest cultures of the Mesolithic. Although the Peterborough newcomers presumably practiced agriculture and possessed oxen, pigs, and sheep, they were still largely hunters and fishers of the Mesolithic tradition. They were also traders and middlemen, as evidenced by their import and trade of foreign rocks and raw materials to other Neolithic people.

British Neolithic colonists of both A and B varieties were roughly contemporaneous. Neolithic A herders and farmers knew and traded with the lowland Peterborough people. Both A and B Neolithic cultures were present at Grimes Graves and profited from the mining of flint there.

Neolithic B pottery, or Peterborough ware, shows no Megalithic affiliations. The movements of early peoples from the Baltic area to the shores of Britain occurred before the sea-borne Megalithic influenced the Baltic area. Therefore, Neolithic B and Neolithic A were entering Britain at roughly the same time but from different directions.

An interesting variant of Neolithic life was that found at Skara Brae on the Bay of Skail, Orkney. These people bred sheep and cattle but did not raise crops. They gathered great quantities of limpets to supplement their diet. Since in the treeless islands there was no timber to build shelter, they constructed houses of local flat stones; these are remarkably preserved and still contain many interior fittings made of the same flags of stone. The *Skara Brae culture* may well have lasted late into Bronze Age times in the Orkneys.

In Ireland several variants of the Neolithic culture appeared as the result of Neolithic immigrants crossing to Irish shores and mixing with Mesolithic hunters and fishers. Such a combination brought forth the *Bann culture,* so named from the River Bann. These people chipped flint in the Mesolithic tradition and were familiar with pottery of Windmill Hill type.

British Neolithic colonists disposed of their lower-class dead in casual burials. Their important members, however, were usually buried under long barrows, or elongated mounds of earth. The burials were usually multiple. This type of interment was apparently introduced into Britain by sea, although the origin is uncertain. The fact that most of the long barrows of Neolithic Britain are located along the mid-channel coasts strengthens the theory of sea-borne entry.

Neolithic colonists in Britain also had other forms of burial, indicative of mixed influences and origins. Mound cremation, perhaps, was an importation from the Belgian area, as well as the rite of destroying the deceased's hut to serve as his tomb. Even round barrows were used in Neolithic times.

Scattered along the coasts of the British Isles, Ireland, and continental Europe are a number of Neolithic tombs, many of which are constructed of large rough stones. These monuments have long been known as the *Megalithic,* which was a religious movement which greatly affected many Neolithic peoples of the Mediterranean, the Atlantic, and the Baltic coasts of Europe. The term Megalithic is not always applicable, for many of the tombs were built with small stones, rubble, or, in a few cases, no stones at all. However, in form, the Megalithic graves are patently part of a central religious idea to which the name Megalithic has been generally applied.

Megalithic tombs were at first regarded as belonging exclusively to one culture. Comparisons in various parts of northwestern Europe, Scandinavia, and the British Isles, however, as well as excavations in those Megalithic monuments which had not been looted by later cultures, indicated that no one people, in terms of tools and pottery, was associated with the Megalithic burials. Rather, the grave goods were of local varieties, indicating that many groups of Neolithic peoples, each with its own culture, had adopted a foreign mortuary religion as their own.

A possible clue to the origin of the Megalithic religion may lie in some interesting monuments on the island of Malta in the central Mediterranean. Here are temples built of carefully cut stones laid in regular ashlars to enclose buildings. These buildings consist of series of rectangular rooms with rounded or apsidal ends. Such temples as Hagiar Kim and Hal Tarxien on Malta are typical examples. Some of the stones of these apsidal temples were carved with the motif of the advancing spiral. Also on the island of Malta and in connection with the curious temples are underground buildings which reproduce the same features as those above the ground. The subterranean form is known as a hypogeum, one example of which is the famous Hal Saflieni.

The island of Malta, with its apsidal temples and hypogea, seems a logical origin point for the sea-borne diffusion of the Megalithic cult. However, Malta gives every indication of being only the purveyor of these ideas rather than their originator. The stimulus of the Megalithic idea may well be from the island of Crete or even Cyprus, possibly carried there from the coasts of Syria.

If the inception of the Megalithic cult may be traced to Crete and Syria, it was centered around a complicated building of the tholos type. In Crete and the Aegean, this form was known as the beehive tomb because of its domed shape. The sides of the building were built up of cut masonry, so that each layer extended farther inward than the one below to produce a cross section which tapered to a rounded point at the apex in the manner of a beehive. An open oculus, at the very center of the apex, was closed by a single stone. The chamber was entered by a slanting runway or dromos, also lined with cut stone. A doorway outlined in stone separated the dromos from the tomb chamber.

In Syria, a tholos type of building apparently served as a temple; but on the island of Crete and elsewhere in the Aegean area, this distinctive building was used as a tomb, usually for multiple burial. On Malta, the apsidal structures were temples. The hypogea such as those at Hal Saflieni were also temples used later for the burial of large numbers of human bodies. Thus the temple and the tomb were closely connected.

There is no doubt that the tholos tomb and the multiple-burial rituals which accompanied it extended to the western Mediterranean. At the great site of Los Millares, on the Andarax River in Spain, was a large settlement established by traders who had come there by sea. Los Millares and the neighboring site of Almizaraque were trading towns with a number of stone buildings. At Los Millares, these seafarers erected a great cemetery of tombs with many of the features of the Cretan tholos.

The islands of Sicily and Sardinia were also affected by the Megalithic cult and its mortuary ideas. In Sardinia, so-called "Giants' Tombs" were constructed with a burial chamber, portal, and forecourt. The Los Millares tombs combine many Aegean tholos features and peculiarities of plan from Sardinia and elsewhere in the Mediterranean islands.

It was in the western Mediterranean that the idea of building tombs with rough stone slabs evolved, apparently from these imported Aegean ideas. By 2500 b.c. the Megalithic cult was established in Sicily, Sardinia, Spain, Portugal, and southern France. By sea, these religious ideas were carried to Brittany, the British Isles, Ireland, and ultimately to the Baltic. Overland also, certain Megalithic ideas moved from southern France northward and westward. By 2000 b.c. the Megalithic cult was well established from southern Spain to southern Scandinavia.

However, as these ideas spread along the coasts of the Iberian peninsula and western Europe, mixing with the indigenous Neolithic inhabitants and their religious conceptions, it was inevitable that the cult should change and the distinctive stone architecture should vary in technique.

At the famous cemetery of Alcalá in southern Portugal, for example, the corbel-arch tomb chamber was entered by a long passage. At other contemporary sites in Portugal and Spain, circular burial chambers and long entrance passages were also built, but in a number of variations.

In southern France, rough slab sepulchres were built. In the Languedoc area, for example, there is abundant evidence from these rough stone monuments that the Megalithic ritual idea spread northward from this center. All manner of slab-made tombs may be traced from Languedoc northward to the Atlantic coast of France and westward to the peninsula of Brittany. As the cult of the Megalithic progressed northward and was adopted by one Neolithic group after another, the form of the tombs changed with local ideas or materials. In a few places where no stone was available, turf or timber was substituted. However, the mortuary practices of the cult which were the hallmark of the Megalithic idea influenced all this area.

In the final form of the Megalithic sepulchre two typical plans were followed in western and northern Europe. The *passage grave* was one in which a rectangular or circular tomb chamber was covered over with large slabs of stone to form a corbelled roof. The chamber was approached by an entrance passage, often long and narrow.

The second major variety of Megalithic tomb was the *long-cist* type. This was an elongated burial chamber roofed over with stone slabs. The long-cist type had no entrance way or separate burial chamber. This type is often called a *covered gallery grave,* or in its shorter form, a *dolmenic cist.*

Entrances to passage graves in southern Spain or long-cist tombs in the north were often closed by slabs of stone with a circular or near-circular hole in them. These are called *port hole stones.* Occasionally the port hole is achieved by notches in the edges of two adjoining slabs of rock.

Megalithic tombs in Sicily and Sardinia were usually entered through a forecourt cut into the rock. Such a forecourt flanked by upright slabs appears in the Giants' Tombs of Sardinia. The forecourt plan was adopted in some Megalithic tombs of southeastern Spain and Portugal and is an integral part of the plan of the *horned cairns* of Scotland and north Ireland.

In Britain, these various Megalithic tombs are divided into several groups—long cists or gallery graves, unchambered long barrows and collective tombs, and passage graves. No British tombs were dug into the ground, and only a few were excavated in rock as in the Mediterranean area. However, in spite of these differences, the ritual of the Megalithic burials in Britain was remarkably similar to that on the coasts of Europe and in the Mediterranean area. The differences that did occur over these great distances undoubtedly may be explained as the work of several sects of the central religious idea.

When the Megalithic cult reached the British Isles, the Neolithic A or Windmill Hill people were already established. Perhaps the new mortuary ideas of the Megalithic priests with their collective burial rites gave rise to the long-barrow form of burial, which became typical of the British Neolithic. The Peterborough type of Neolithic was little influenced by Megalithic ideas. It is certain that we must presuppose several waves of influence and many voyages to account for the variations of the Megalithic architecture along the Atlantic and North Sea coasts. However, from the eastern Mediterranean to Denmark, the burial customs of the Megalithic cult were quite uniform. The tombs were used for long periods for successive interments probably by one family or group. Offerings of pottery, food, tools, and jewelry were placed with the dead. Often, previous interments and offerings were set aside or disturbed by later burials as the tomb was used by successive generations. Fires were a part of the funerary ritual in the tomb, and in some cases cremation was practiced.

Some of the most notable Megalithic monuments of this tradition have been found in Ireland. Megalithic builders left passage-grave tombs across central Ireland northwestward. Such a monument is the famous one of New Grange in County Meath. Here a beautifully built grave of stone 80 feet long was covered with a cairn 280 feet in diameter. The cairn was ringed by a circle of standing stones and the grave itself was embellished with a number of abstract magical carvings on its walls and entrance.

Megalithic seafarers of the passage-grave variation of the cult brought with them a type of architecture which had its closest parallels in graves of Portugal and southwestern Spain. They left a marked route through Ireland, Scotland, the Western Isles, the Orkneys, and thence to Jutland and Scandinavia. In Denmark and southern Sweden the passage-grave version of the Megalithic cult was later than the dolmen, or cist, form which had come by a shorter route from the Pyrenean area.

The Megalithic sect of the covered gallery tomb, originating perhaps from the Giants' Tombs of Sardinia, became established around the Gulf of Lion and Catalonia in Spain. From here this cist form of the Megalithic was adopted in southern France and the Pyrenean region. The Megalithic version of the cult on the Atlantic coast of south France was then the cist type of tomb. From these regions the long-cist sect moved to influence certain areas of Britain and the Baltic.

The long-cist tombs were less spectacular than the passage graves. The long cists were low roofed and not really buildings in the sense that some of the passage graves were. One form of the long cist was divided into several compartments by transverse slabs which did not reach quite to the low roof. These segmented cists were covered with a ritually constructed cairn or mound. The northern Megalithic builders always covered their tombs in this way; it was only in the Mediterranean area that tombs usually were dug into rock or buried below ground.

167

Another variety of the Megalithic cist tomb was the dolmen. This was a tomb made of upright slabs to form a crude chamber, with a single large horizontal stone for a roof or table stone. The dolmen might be covered with a mound or left open. It was the dolmen form of Megalithic grave from its origin in the Pyrenean region that first reached the coasts of northwestern Europe. Segmented cists such as that at Maranzais, Haut-Poitou in France, and dolmen forms such as those of France or Valdygaard on the island of Zealand in the Baltic show the spread of this form of the Megalithic idea. The Beacharra culture of the coasts of the North Channel including northern Ireland, southwestern Scotland, and the Isle of Man was a Megalithic cult brought to those shores by people building the cist type of tomb. Variations of the long-cist sect built tombs in the form of the wedge-shaped cairns or *Paris cists*. These are specialized gallery graves usually divided into a short antechamber and long burial chamber. Paris cists are found in Brittany, the island of Jersey, and at a few points in the British Isles and Ireland. The horned cairns of the British Isles are cist-type graves with the forecourt feature of the original Sardinian prototypes maintained.

As the Megalithic sects of both the passage-grave and long-cist versions moved northward and established themselves at various places in northwestern Europe and the British Isles, the local Neolithic inhabitants were the groups who accepted the new cult practices. There may have been a few priests or families who actually traveled to bring the new religion to the local inhabitants. It has been suggested that these priests enlisted the labor of the local Neolithic people to build the tombs for themselves and their families. However, there is no Megalithic culture apart from the burial practices. Rather, the western Neolithic people were those who adopted the idea of cist and dolmen tombs and their ritual in France. Local Neolithic groups in Spain and Portugal carried on the idea in those places. In most of Britain the Windmill Hill type of pottery occurs in association with Megalithic structures, indicating that it was these people who adopted the religion of Megalithic burial.

Especially distinctive are a number of abstract designs which are often carved on the Megalithic grave stones. Originally these signs were apparently representational, but in their finished form they were

Cow with her young—Cretan faïence, Middle Minoan II (1800–1600 B.C.), relief.

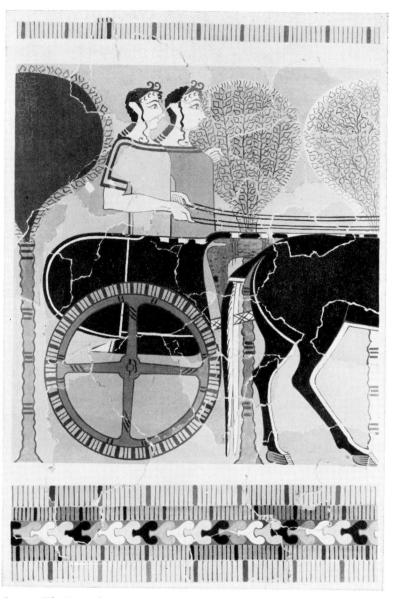

Water color of fresco, detail from a boar hunt. The women in a chariot watching the hunt, Late Minoan (1350–1100 B.C.). Found at Tiryns, Greece.

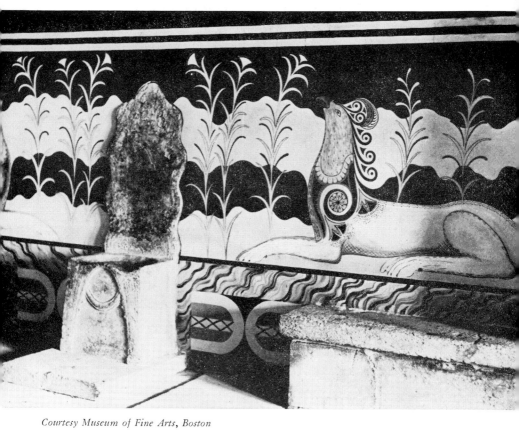

Throne room, Palace of Knossos, 14th century, B.C.

Palace of Knossos, court and stairway (restored).

Grave circle, Mycenae, from the 16th century, B.C.

purely abstract and presumably magical. Such signs were distinctive of the passage-grave type of monument but sometimes occurred on the pottery of the builders of the long-cist burials.

When the Megalithic was studied in the Baltic area, monuments and their contents were arranged into a sequence. As the Megalithic blended well with the preceding Mesolithic in the Baltic area, the transition seemed almost unbroken in some sites. For these reasons, many of the archaeologists working in the Baltic believed that the Megalithic, as well as its distinctive stone monuments, evolved there with little foreign influence. In light of the demonstrable Megalithic beginnings in the Mediterranean, however, the possibility of a Baltic origin for this complex now seems impossible. Indeed, the Megalithic is extremely late in the Baltic region and only reached that area around 2300 B.C.

When the Megalithic cult, carried by sea traders, reached the Baltic coast, the First Northern Neolithic was already well established there. The typical pottery was the triad of the funnel-necked beaker, the collared flask, and the ball amphora. Weapons were chipped and polished flint axes and other chipped implements of previous tradition. Farther north in Scandinavia, a Mesolithic type of life still lingered. Many of the groups in this area were arctic hunters, whose weapons and living patterns differed little from the preceding Forest cultures of the Mesolithic.

Into this Baltic situation, the Megalithic funerary ritual intruded. Apparently the idea took hold quickly in southern Scandinavia, Jutland, and along the Baltic coast of Europe. Generally, dolmen graves and variations of the dolmen were the first form of the Megalithic to be adopted. Megalithic ritual was accepted along the coast as far eastward as the eastern Baltic area. In the region of Poland were the *Kujavian graves*. These were elongated triangular barrows with two or three burials under the broad end. No dolmen was utilized in the Kujavian grave.

Many regional variations were developed by the Baltic groups. Differences in pottery and other grave goods in the Megalithic tombs reflect the influences of trade routes. These routes ran north and south through the body of continental Europe over paths which had already been established by Danubian peoples as they traded for shells and copper to the south. Other routes had been used for transporting salt overland. A movement of people from interior Germany northward to the coast brought Danubian elements to the Baltic Megalithic and a distinctive pottery form of decoration reminiscent of Danubian I*b*.

The incoming Megalithic in Baltic Europe was taken over by the several Neolithic cultures already there. No new western ethnic elements appeared. Pottery forms of the northern Neolithic, the Danordic combination, and other related cultures were those associated with the Megalithic tombs. In the Baltic area, throughout the development of the Megalithic, there was a strong undercurrent of the Mesolithic prevailing, especially the Ertebølle type. The pottery of the early dolmen, Megalithic tombs was a derivative of Ertebølle forms. It was this influence which produced the funnel beaker pot which appeared so often in the Neolithic of northern Europe.

Several periods of Megalithic development in the Baltic area have been recognized following the work of Montelius. Some Scandinavian scientists added a preliminary period representing a transition from the Kitchen Midden to the Megalithic. It now appears that the Megalithic sequence in the Baltic is not due to the localized growth of these ideas, but to a succession of introductions from the direction of the British Isles.

The first form of the Megalithic cult to reach the Baltic was the dolmenic cist type of the religion. This form of grave was a variety of the cist type of burial which early was derived from the Pyrenean area and became implanted on both sides of the North Channel of the British Isles and Scotland. This type of Megalithic is called Beacharra culture from the Megalithic cist tomb of Beacharra in Kintyre. The incoming Megalithic voyagers brought to the North Channel country a cist form of ritual, probably in a segmented cist variation, and also a different kind of Neolithic pottery, similar to pottery from southern France and Brittany, termed Beacharra ware. Beacharra pottery occurred in some Megalithic tombs with Windmill Hill ware, indicating contemporaneity.

It was the Beacharra type of Megalithic which first reached the Baltic as the Beacharra people sought wider trading territory in more remote regions. Perhaps their greed was motivated by the desire to find new sources of metals or to trade in these new materials.

Later, from Portugal, other Megalithic voyagers brought the passage-grave type of ritual which became firmly established in the North Channel country. These passage-grave Megalithic adherents followed the same route to the Baltic and later brought that type of tomb to west Baltic regions. The Beacharra cist Megalithic probably reached Denmark around 2300 B.C. The passage-grave Megalithic appeared there two centuries later, or about 2100 B.C.

Megalithic I in the Baltic area features the single dolmen, Megalithic type of structure. Within this dolmen, collective burials were found with abundant grave goods. Often subsequent burials disturbed previous ones. The grave goods included pottery, flint tools, and occasionally amber, jet, and callais.

The pottery forms of the early Megalithic are usually classed as the *Early style*. The Urbecker or simple pointed-bottom vessel of the old Ertebølle tradition developed in the early Megalithic into the flaring-mouthed, funnel-necked beaker. In addition to the funnel-necked beaker, the collared flask appeared. Designs in the Early style of the Megalithic sequence were occasional whipped cord impressions, or simple vertical incisions. Many of the vessels were undecorated.

In the early Megalithic period the typical flint weapon was the thin-butted ax, skillfully chipped from flint. In form, the body of the ax head was chipped to a thin, rectangular cross section. The tradition of flint-working seems to be that of the old Mesolithic tranchet ax done with a refined technique. The thin-butted ax also suggests that it may have copied a flat copper celt such as those already in use in many parts of southern Europe. As metals were not yet available to these northerners, they may have simply copied the form.

In addition to thin-butted axes, Megalithic dolmen-builders also manufactured thin-butted chisels and thin-butted gouges. The gouges were celts with a curved cutting edge for hollowing out dugout canoes and other similar work. These people also chipped with great skill spear points and dagger blades as well as arrowheads of flint. The early spear and dagger outlines were long and narrow with little differentiation between blade and hafting.

In Megalithic II, the dolmen was augmented by a stone passage made of larger slabs of rock lending the appearance of the passage grave. Burials were made in the passage as well as in the dolmen itself. In the final development of the passage grave, the passage became longer and more elaborate and the dolmen disappeared entirely.

In Megalithic II, the funnel-necked beaker and the collared flask were joined by another typical pottery form, the Kügel or ball amphora. Four small handles were usually present on the decorated vertical neck. A large-mouthed cup with a sharp shoulder and a band handle also appeared. Funnel-necked beakers, cups, and collared flasks were more elaborately decorated with incising, grooving, and stamping. This style of decoration is usually referred to as the Megalithic *Grand style*.

Megalithic II dolmen passage graves usually contained a flint weapon called the thick-butted ax. These, like their thin-butted predecessors, were bulkier versions of the earlier Megalithic axes. Thick-butted chisels and thick-butted gouges were also typical of Megalithic II. Spears and daggers of this period showed increasing skill in chipping technique, particularly in hafting. Dagger handles were differentiated from the blade. Spearheads show a rudimentary tang.

In some parts of the western Baltic, especially in the Danish islands, a third period may be recognized. The form of burial was a long-cist type. Rough slabs were still used to outline the burial area, but the dolmen disappeared entirely.

Pottery of Megalithic III was a seeming degeneration of earlier Megalithic forms. The Kügel amphora became more open-mouthed. The funnel-necked beaker evolved to a flowerpot form. The collared flask was more elongated and onion-shaped. Megalithic III decoration was a more refined version of earlier work, and the best of this is called the *Refined style*. At the end of the period, the style begins to break and disintegrate. This degeneration is manifest in the lack of care and precision of the ornament.

In the Megalithic III period, flint forms of tools still persisted and probably reached their most finished form of chipping and polishing. Gouges and chisels were splayed at their cutting end. All of these tools were chipped with great precision and were undoubtedly as effective as any implements of stone could be.

The daggers of Megalithic III represent some of the finest flint work of prehistoric Europe, surpassing the best chipping of the Solutrean of the Palaeolithic. Megalithic III daggers have well-differentiated handles with lozenge-shaped cross sections and flaring hilts. The flat blades of these daggers were chipped with such skill that they blended into the more thickened handle section exactly like a metal dagger of the same outline. Spears of the Megalithic III matched the daggers in their precise workmanship. The spearheads were provided with good tangs for secure hafting.

Semilunar and triangular knives of flint were also common in this period. Flint sickles, chipped from a single piece of flint, as well as saws with serrated teeth, were made with the same skill as daggers and spearheads. Flint arrowheads with deeply concave bases, were also perfected. There is no doubt that Megalithic III saw the peak of the flint-working technique of ancient Europe. As the period of Megalithic III already overlaps the beginnings of metal-working in more southerly regions, there seems little doubt that the Megalithic flint workers knew of this material and tried to copy it in their flint forms.

The Megalithic sequence in Jutland and northern Germany was abruptly ended by the invasion of a new people who moved down the Elbe. These warlike newcomers cut off the Megalithic development in Schleswig-Holstein first and then moved farther north to occupy the inland portions of Jutland, pushing the Megalithic out to the islands and the remote northern tip of Jutland. This movement forced some Megalithic peoples into the Drenthe region of Holland, where they continued to build tombs. As the passage-grave tradition was strong there, these *Huns'-bed tombs* were long mounds which covered stone-made passage graves or passage dolmens beneath. Pottery associated with the Huns'-bed Megalithic consists of late forms of funnel beakers and collared flasks. The northward push of the invader people also disrupted other groups of the northern Neolithic or pushed them aside. Because these warlike intruders buried their dead in distinctive graves dug into the earth and covered by a round mound, they are called the *Single-grave* people. The Single-grave invasion produced a sharp break in the continuity of the northern Neolithic peoples and the Megalithic religion.

As the single graves, which are the major manifestation of this culture, are remarkably like the burial practices of the Walternienberg and Bernburg types of Neolithic peoples, there seems little doubt that the inspiration for the Single-grave culture came from the upper Elbe and Saale region in Saxo-Thuringia. Pottery of the Single-grave culture is similar to the Baalberg Neolithic and was affected also by the cord-impression decoration which was distinctive of the Corded Ware Neolithic development.

As the Single-grave people used their own barrows for successive interments, often opening a hole in the top of the barrow to make a later burial, three phases of development may be distinguished.

In Phase I the original burial was placed in an earth-dug grave below ground, and a mound or barrow erected above the spot. Typical grave goods in Phase I were pottery vessels such as a beaker pot with an ovoid body, the neck ornamented with cord impressions. A thick-butted flint ax was often present. A type of battle-ax with a bit of wide, flaring design and a drooping butt was often found in Phase I. This type of ax may be a stone copy of copper or bronze implements of the same shape in more southerly regions.

In Phase II of the Single-grave culture, the grave was dug into the barrow and the body placed at ground level. The typical battle-ax of Phase II was an implement of the same general sort as the first phase, but without the decided flaring of the ax bit.

In Phase III, the separate graves were dug into the tops of previous barrows and constitute the top graves or the last burials made there. The implement appearing in Phase III was the hammer-ax, or shaft-hole battle-ax. One end of this implement was a stump. The bit had little flare, and is in decided contrast to the preceding wide-bitted types.

Often accompanying separate graves were stone maces, amber buttons, and amber rings. Occasionally a miniature boat-ax was fashioned in amber, apparently for ceremonial purposes. The progression of pottery and implements of the Single-grave people show that they were contemporaneous with the surrounding Megalithic groups but distinct from them. Phase III of this culture coincides with the end of the Passage-grave period on the Baltic Islands.

In the central Polish area, the Globe-amphora stone-cist graves impinged upon the Kujavian type of Megalithic barrow. The typical Kujavian burial barrow was a triangular mound with simple burials under the larger end. In Globe-amphora versions of the Kujavian, the stone cist was added as a burial chamber and then the mound built over the whole. The Globe-amphora movement from the eastern steppes of Russia became closely associated with the Corded people of Saxo-Thuringia.

In Poland proper, these same ingredients gave rise to the *Złota culture*. The Złota culture was a combination of Megalithic, Corded, and Globe-amphora elements. In burial form, pottery, implements, and tools there were indications of all three traditions. Złota pottery, for example, showed typical Megalithic forms and decoration. Corded beakers, and beaker-like types are also present, and the Globe-amphora tradition was manifested in rounded pottery shapes.

Still farther to the east, the *Fatyanovo culture* of the upper Volga in central Russia was of the Battle-ax and Globe-amphora tradition. This was a type of Neolithic life established in European Russia perhaps first by Globe-amphora migrants moving from the south. There were indications also of the Kamkeramik or comb-marked tradition in the make-up of the Fatyanovo. The Fatyanovo development also was typified by special burials with battle-axes, another trait from the south. Because of its isolated position, the Fatyanovo was little influenced by the Megalithic or other western European manifestations.

In extreme southeastern Europe, also, there were movements at the end of the Neolithic period. In the Painted Pottery area, a wave of eastern invaders pushed into the terrain. These newcomers brought with them a Corded pottery tradition. It will be remembered that the original cord-decorated pottery area extended all the way from the Caucasus in the southeast to northern Germany in the northwest. The graves of the Caucasus Corded were shaft graves. In the Black Earth region, these shaft graves were marked on the surface by tumuli. The Neolithic people who buried their dead in these shaft graves and who manufactured the Corded pottery that they placed within them pushed into the Painted Pottery domain. The Painted Pottery people seemed temporarily overawed. The result of this infusion was the distinctive *Schneckenberg culture,* while farther westward a west Rumanian Painted Pottery and Corded combined in the *Coţofeni culture*. Schneckenberg material had elements of both the Painted Pottery and the south Russian Corded in its makeup.

Some of the major Painted Pottery sites survived to establish a renaissance of their original culture, following this invasion. *Cucuteni B,* for example, and *Schipenitz B* were both manifestations established after the movement of the Corded people. The main strength of the Painted Pottery tradition, however, had already spent itself.

The westward movement of the south Russian Corded and the Schneckenberg culture, which was the result of this intrusion, moved even farther westward than the Painted Pottery area. This curious combination extended well into the Theiss valley in Hungary. In the Theiss, or Tisza area, the Schneckenberg combined with the local Neolithic Tisza cultures already there. This combination produced the distinctive *Bodrogkeresztur,* which was distinguished by considerable quantities of copper.

The Painted Pottery people were finally overcome by a wave of warrior invaders, again from the east. These newcomers brought little, but destroyed much. The history of Europe, from this time on, became punctuated by periodic movements of warrior peoples moving out of the steppe lands into the peninsular area of the continent.

The Neolithic period of prehistoric Europe was, then, a welter of differing cultures that varied among themselves in such details as pottery, axes, and funerary customs. The underlying mode of life was, however, remarkably similar among all of these variants. The stimuli which changed Europe from Mesolithic hunting to the Neolithic agriculture originated from Mesopotamian and Anatolian centers. By land and sea routes these ideas moved into Europe in several streams. Farms and herds became the basis of life in all of those regions of Europe where these practices were feasible. With the different movements which brought in the Neolithic idea, came such differences as pottery traditions and religious rites connected with burial. It is only by these differences that we may trace the Neolithic tide as it swept into various corners of Europe and mark the ebb and flow of peoples. By the end of Neolithic times the linguistic areas of Europe as we now know them had taken form. Most of the racial types of modern Europe had already made their appearance. It was in the Neolithic period that the civilization of Europe came into being.

CHAPTER 9

The Dawn of Metal

THE INTRODUCTION of metal into Neolithic Europe did not occur at one time or at one place. There were many occurrences extending over a considerable period of time. Many early students of European pre-history supposed that there was a sudden break when all of Europe simultaneously adopted the use of metal and discontinued the use of flint and stone. We now know that this was not so. The Age of Metal materialized gradually, and the dates of the acceptance of metal were vastly different in various parts of Europe.

The first metal to be used in any quantities in European economy was copper. The name *Chalcolithic* is applied to any culture which used copper extensively. This term is consistent with the nomenclature which describes eras of human progress by the tools used in each. However, the Chalcolithic period was not a Pan-European phenomenon by any means. In fact, we can spot only a few isolated cultures in Europe which definitely show a Chalcolithic phase in their advancement. There is no such thing as a European Copper Age.

Whatever the development of the uses of metals within Europe, there is no doubt that the source of the idea itself was foreign to that continent. The smelting and manufacturing of copper objects undoubtedly reached Europe from Anatolia and Hither Asia through the Aegean area. Copper was early used in Egypt. The *Badarian culture* of the upper Nile valley showed a knowledge of the working of cold copper before the beginning of the fourth millennium. Smelting of copper ores appears to have been known as early as the beginning of the fifth millennium in Chaldea in Mesopotamia, although conclusive evidence of the very first metallurgy is difficult to determine. The ancient site of Susa in northern Mesopotamia has also yielded evidences of an early use of copper. From other indications of copper smelting in Anatolia and Hither Asia, it would seem that the use of metals began in the Near East almost as early as the Neolithic idea itself. This was a part of the same revolution in which man began to be a shaper of the products of the world around him rather than a quiescent user of such natural bounties as nature provided.

The first beginnings of copper were complicated by factors which were not present in other aspects of Neolithic life. Although trinkets and small weapons may be traded from place to place, the smelting of copper ores depends upon available deposits of these ores. In areas where no copper deposits exist metal working could find no foothold. So it was that the knowledge of the manufacture of metal moved from place to place in the ancient world as deposits of workable ores were discovered.

Although copper was undoubtedly the first metal to be used in any quantities in ancient times, there were two other substances which appeared almost as early—silver and gold. Both of these metals occur in a pure form in nature, although not always so. Both are relatively easily worked by cold-hammering methods. As such, they were undoubtedly regarded as malleable stone by the first artisans. Gold and silver trinkets and even small tools such as chisels were found at the Mesopotamian site of Ur. Gold and silver in small quantities occur over the same areas and during the same periods as the use of copper.

A fourth substance, a metal alloy, also appeared in the repertory of metallic items. This was electrum, a mixture of gold and silver.

This substance was very rare in ancient times, although it became more popular in the later Classical period.

The first implements manufactured from copper were hammered cold. Nuggets of pure, or almost pure, copper could thus be manipulated as a malleable stone. In the cold-hammering of copper, however, the object being formed must be heated from time to time to prevent its becoming brittle and splitting under the repeated blows of the shaping process. This treatment is known as annealing. Cold-hammering and annealing probably preceded the actual smelting of copper by at least a millennium. It was, however, only with smelting that any great quantity of copper could be made available to ancient craftsmen. The smelting of copper ores requires special furnaces to create heat of sufficient intensity to extract the copper from the various chemical combinations in which it is found in nature. The smelting of copper was, then, a series of discoveries and improvements rather than a single innovation. The dawning of the Metal Age in Europe was, in reality, the story of the discovery of local ore bodies and improvement in methods of smelting ores.

Ideas of the use of copper very early reached the Mediterranean from Mesopotamia or Egypt or both. The island of Cyprus shows abundant evidence of the early use of copper as do the other islands of the eastern Mediterranean. The most important of all of the island centers was Crete. It may be demonstrated that most of the knowledge of copper use in the Mediterranean area was sea-borne. At first, traders introduced copper items of foreign manufacture, undoubtedly creating a desire for the material. Then, as additional deposits of copper ore were discovered, the knowledge of the smelting of these ores became implanted in localities farther and farther from the original source of the idea.

At the same time that the usage and smelting of copper was spreading throughout the Mediterranean, similar knowledge was moving overland to the north out of Hither Asia. The spread of these ideas from Anatolia to the Balkan area and to Neolithic groups of European Russia was accomplished slowly, but was a fact as early as the third millennium. Because the overland expansion moved more deliberately, metal appeared in eastern and northern Europe later than in the southern reaches of the continent which had access to the sea-borne trade of the Mediterranean.

A Beakers

Irish
Bronze

Scandinavian Bronz

A Beakers
British Bronze
Urnfields
B Beakers
Wessex
Culture
Beakers
Armorican

Urnfields
Zoned Beakers
Urnfields

Tumulus

Lausit

Urnfields

Urnfields

Aunjetitz

Bell Beakers

Tószeg

Bronze Age
Lake Dwellings
Bell Beakers
Terremare
Remedello

Beakers

Bell Beakers

Urnfields

Bell
Beakers

El Argar
Almerian

Trade from Eastern
Mediterranean

Siculian

Mycenae

**THE INTRODUCTION OF METALS
AND THE BRONZE AGE**
Major routes and directions
of dispersal are shown.
0   100   200   300   400   500 miles

Late
Kamkeramic

rnfields

drogkeresztur
ungarian
onze
Urnfields

Steppe Warrior
Cultures

Kuban

Hittites
(with iron)

Anatolia

Mesopotamia

Knossos

Cypriot

Trade
Routes

Egypt

From all of these sources, the dawn of the European Chalcolithic began in several major centers where these ideas became implanted. Foremost, perhaps, was the area of southeastern Europe and the Aegean where the use of copper was derived early from Crete. In northern Italy, also, there was a distinct Chalcolithic development centering around the copper-using site of Remedello. A separate, or southern Italian, Chalcolithic existed in the southern Italian peninsula. The Hungarian copper development depended upon the Aegean for its original inspiration and flourished because of the deposits of ores in the Slovakian and Transylvanian mountains. The copper development of the eastern Alpine region was derived from Hungary. In the western Mediterranean copper smelting appeared as early as the Neolithic idea itself, gaining a foothold there because of the rich ores of Spain. The site of El Garcel in Almeria, where the western Neolithic established itself, shows copper slag from Neolithic smelters there. The western Neolithic as it moved northward did not at first carry with it the use of copper because of the lack of ores.

From southern Russia, also, some metal objects found their way into Europe. Metal working in this area was derived from Anatolia and was centered chiefly around a distinctive weapon, the adze-ax. This type of copper battle-ax appeared sporadically well into central and even northern Europe. Warriors bringing with them copper adze-axes swept across the Ukraine to enter Rumania and the Hungarian Plain. Thus the invaders contributed to the formation of the Hungarian Copper Age which is also known as the *Bodrogkeresztur*.

At first the Neolithic Europeans who could not manufacture their own copper axes or trade for them made duplicates in stone. It was at this same time that the stone battle-ax became the typical weapon of the Corded or Battle-ax people of the Saxo-Thuringian area and also appeared among other northern Neolithic cultures. Thin-butted axes of northern Europe were flint copies of copper celts. Even flint daggers were imitations of the same weapons in copper.

The Hungarian Copper Age is often cited and is well described. Especially in the valley of the Tisza River, there was an outstanding metal development. In that area, by the period known as Tisza II, copper trinkets were fairly common. These tricklings of metal came into the Hungarian area from the Aegean. A typical weapon which appeared in the Hungarian Copper Age was the Cypriote dagger. This is a simple weapon with a lanceolate-shaped blade and a hooked tang. The Cypriote dagger was a widespread trade item in the Mediterranean world, first named because of its prevalence on the island of Cyprus. From Anatolia and Cyprus it reached Spain and Hungary during this same period.

Because of deposits of native copper ores in the Hungarian area, a lively industry of metal smelting was begun there at the end of Tisza II. Period III in the Hungarian area is known as the *Bodrogkeresztur.*

Bodrogkeresztur was ethnically an outgrowth of Tisza II plus the foreign additions of the invaders from southern Russia, called the Schneckenberg culture. The Bodrogkeresztur is best known from cemeteries extending from the lower Drave and Save rivers of Yugoslavia and Hungary to the Tisza and Maros river valleys in central Hungary. It is divided into two phases. The first is a proto-copper phase in which the metal appears only as trade items, imported from smelting sources elsewhere. The second phase features the advent of the adze-ax and the local manufacture of weapons and implements of copper.

The full development of the Bodrogkeresztur was typified by flat copper celts, copper daggers, awls, and copper ornaments. Some gold in the form of rings and pins also appeared.

Most of the material occurs with graves of the culture. Male skeletons were flexed and placed in the graves on their right sides. Females were buried on their left sides. With the male burials were usually placed several long flint blades which are exaggerated versions of upper Palaeolithic blades of the same type and apparently made with a similar technique. Copper and pottery also accompanied the graves. Most of our knowledge of the Bodrogkeresztur is derived from the cemeteries of Bodrogkeresztur and Pusztaistvánháza.

Perhaps most distinctive of this copper period in the Hungarian area was the pottery. Bodrogkeresztur ceramics, although derived from Tisza II material, were exotic in form. Typical was a large amphora which was provided with a hollow pedestal or foot. The pedestal was often cut out to form an openwork stand of complicated designs. Other amphora forms were provided with a separate pedestal of clay.

Milk-pot forms and tall bottle shapes of extreme design were common. Open-shouldered jars, bowls, and cups with two thin handles are distinctive Bodrogkeresztur types.

An allied culture in Austria and western Hungary was the Baden or Badner previously mentioned in connection with the late Neolithic. Baden was a group of cultures centering in Carpathia and extending northwestward to the Elbe. This culture had many connections with the Balkans and especially Macedonia. It had some copper implements in its repertory of tools and may represent groups of people pushing northwestward from Anatolia or the Balkans in search of copper ores. The Badner in this area is evidenced by skeletal graves and cremations. The Badner in western Hungary, as revealed by the pottery with typical Badner graves, was a combination of northern forms and Bodrogkeresztur. Danordic pottery forms often show Bodrogkeresztur decoration. Tisza influence was also present in fruit-stand types with Tisza decoration.

Northern Italy, centered around the site of Remedello near Brescia, was a copper-working center of great importance. Northern Italy was apparently in direct contact with metal traders from the island of Crete and had trade relations with metal-working people from Spain through Sardinia. These stimuli, on a basis of the previous Neolithic cultures, produced a distinct Chalcolithic center. Sardinian pottery occurs in northern Italy. Copper daggers and other forms of metal were brought from as far away as Spain and traded in the northern Italian region. Apparently the influences which created the copper culture at Remedello spread from the eastern Mediterranean without any of the Megalithic aspects which occurred in Spain, Portugal, and farther west. We may only surmise that those influences which gave rise to Remedello reached northern Italy earlier than the tomb-building fervor which initiated the Megalithic in the central and western Mediterranean. No Megalithic tombs accompany the Remedello copper culture, although the complex of building large stone graves was associated with metal-working farther west. To the north, the Chalcolithic of Remedello borrowed the stone battle-ax form apparently from the Corded Ware people by contacts through the Brenner Pass. Nomadic Corded folk left graves embellished with cord-marked pottery and battle-axes as far south as central Italy.

Perhaps these influences passed north in the opposite direction.

The Spanish Chalcolithic began in Almeria, notably at the site of El Garcel. It was here that the western Neolithic and metal smelting appeared together. At first the rich ore deposits in the Spanish area were little exploited. However, the smelting of copper was already understood in the Neolithic and practiced on a limited scale. Continued trade with the eastern Mediterranean stimulated this Spanish metal center with new ideas and trade goods. There also was trade in the reverse direction, for Spanish copper dagger forms, amulets, and copper trinkets appear in Sardinia and in northern Italy, apparently from a Spanish source.

The site of Los Millares on the Andarax River became a great trade center of the Spanish Chalcolithic. Los Millares, as well as the neighboring copper-smelting center of Almizaraque, became trading towns which dealt in copper and also in exotic items such as gold and silver and ostrich-egg shells and ivory from Africa. At Los Millares and Almizaraque are groups of impressive rock tombs. These tombs, which seem to carry on mortuary rituals of the central Mediterranean, or perhaps Cretan traditions, indicate the influences of Megalithic tomb building which spread northward from the Mediterranean to northwestern Europe, Britain, and the Baltic.

While the introduction of the Neolithic way of life and the knowledge of metal smelting was simultaneous at some points in southern Europe, the disparity between the two horizons was very great in northern Europe. Among many northern cultures, no copper period appears at all, because of their remoteness from the centers of manufacture or the scarcity of local ores from which they might derive their own copper implements. In these northern regions, many of the late Neolithic people copied in flint the copper implements of their more fortunate southern neighbors. There is no doubt that all of the Neolithic cultures, when opportunity presented itself, were anxious to acquire metal. At first they used the novel substance for ornamentation and later for weapons and tools.

A catalog of copper items from Neolithic Europe is quite impressive in its scope. It is apparent that agriculture and animal husbandry spread into Europe faster than a knowledge of the working of copper. The knowledge of smelting overtook the Neolithic idea later and at different times in different places. However, even during the time of the pure Neolithic there were occasional trinkets traded into Neolithic Europe from southern sources where metallurgy was already known.

The introduction of copper and metal smelting into the central and northerly regions of Europe has long been credited to a group of traders called the Bell Beaker people. The name is derived from the peculiar shape of their pottery, which is typically a flaring-mouthed beaker similar to a bell. Since Bell Beaker materials cut across and are superimposed upon graves of Corded Ware and First Northern types, the Bell Beaker period obviously occurred at the end of the Neolithic, or about 1900 B.C.

The Bell Beaker episode appeared fully developed with no antecedents. However, certain suggestive finds in northwestern Spain and northern Italy may give a clue to its origins. In the Iberian Peninsula, the descendants of previous Neolithic Capsian peoples were still inhabiting caves and painting on the rock walls the peculiar figure drawings which were the characteristic form of Capsian art. With the incoming of the Neolithic idea, these people began to make pottery. At first, these pottery forms were splayed-mouthed, pointed-bottomed vessels, occasionally decorated with the same animal forms as those on their rock shelters. Soon, however, these Spanish pottery vessels developed into the typical Bell Beaker shape. The decoration became stylized in a horizontal banded treatment. The bands were embellished with incised zigzags and punctuate repetitive designs. From this it would seem that the origin of the famous Bell Beaker people was in this north central Spanish Mesolithic area.

Whether this is true or not, the Bell Beaker people soon began to move northward, leaving behind as they traveled the graves of their dead accompanied by their typical pottery vessels. Since their homeland had been in the interior, they were not a seafaring people, but moved overland. The Bell Beaker movement is, for the most part, a tradition which was carried across the land trade routes of Neolithic Europe.

Curiously enough, bell beakers also appear in northern Italy. The Italian bell beakers were apparently not derived from a land route across southern France. The only alternative is that some of the

Beaker people moved by sea to Sardinia and thus into the northern Italian area. So difficult is this transition to demonstrate that some authorities are of the opinion that the whole Bell Beaker complex began in northern Italy in the region of Remedello, which was a commercial center of considerable importance. Northern Italian bell beakers are, however, of degenerate form, and none at all appear at Remedello itself.

Whether the original Bell Beaker impetus began in Spain or elsewhere, there is no doubt that it pressed northward into the body of Europe. The most easily traceable paths of Bell Beaker movements are northward from southern Europe. From the south they spread throughout most of the former Danubian regions. The Bell Beaker nomads moved and traded their wares among all of the mixed Neolithic elements of northern Europe. The period of the Bell Beaker newcomers serves as an easily recognizable terminus to the previous Neolithic combinations. Bell Beaker groups ranged from the Strait of Gibraltar to the North Sea and from the Vistula River west to the British Isles.

The Beaker folk were developing their singular pottery and culture in inland Spain around 2300 B.C., at the same time that the Megalithic religion was distinguishing western Europe. A century or two later, Bell Beaker immigrants had established themselves in southern France and northern Spain. By 2000 B.C. a Bell Beaker center, formed by migrant traders from southern France, appeared on the middle Rhine. From this center a number of subsequent movements took place. Another Bell Beaker concentration grew up on the upper Elbe in Bohemia, receiving its inspiration from Beaker movements from the south. This Bell Beaker focus had much to do with later events in that region. It was the potent Bell Beaker influences which contributed most to the formation of the coming Age of Bronze.

Evidences of the Bell Beaker traders are almost entirely in the form of graves. Few definite Bell Beaker settlements are known, although a few houses and pits in the Saale valley have been identified as Bell Beaker habitations. Graves of these trader people were typically dug into the earth and contain a single, contracted skeleton. Occasionally the burials are in groups or cemeteries.

The typical Bell Beaker grave contained the bell beaker and other pottery forms. Bell beakers varied in color from red to black or dark gray in different localities of Europe. Decoration was incised or comb-stamped in horizontal bands. Occasionally, white paint was rubbed into the incisions. Accompanying the distinctive bell beakers in the graves were broad-rimmed bowls, decorated in the same manner as the bell beakers and usually furnished with teatlike feet.

In the usual Bell Beaker grave there was a bundle of tanged and barbed arrowheads of finely worked flint and a bow-guard or brassard of stone which was strapped on the wrist of the archer to protect his arm against the slap of the bowstring. Bell Beaker graves also contained conical buttons of stone or amber with a V-shaped perforation. Flint blades, drilled animal teeth, and shell beads were found. Many graves also were accompanied by flat, straight-tanged copper daggers similar to the type first used in Spain. Copper awls and occasional other implements were also interred. Gold was present in a few trinkets, and a single brassard made of gold was recovered from the Bohemian region. Silver earrings have also been found in a few Bell Beaker graves in Moravia.

These Bell Beaker traders, carrying with them their copper daggers and other bits of metal, are given credit for introducing the knowledge of metal usage into many parts of Europe. Most of the Neolithic peoples there already had some acquaintance with the new material. The Bell Beaker nomads, however, traveled widely and profoundly affected the pre-existing Neolithic cultures. So uniform was the culture that the Bell Beaker pottery and other grave accompaniments varied little over the whole range of Beaker expansion. Fragments of Beaker pottery from Bohemia, Spain, the Rhineland, or Britain were often indistinguishable when placed together. A religious motive which held the Beaker culture together so tenaciously is strongly suggested. It must have required a powerful impetus to account for the wide and forceful spread of the Beaker folk.

The skeletal type found in most Bell Beaker graves is an individual of stocky build with a short, round skull. Many enthusiasts have described the Beaker folk as particularly strong and powerful in direct contrast to the longheaded and more lightly muscled Neolithic groups. This was not true in every instance. In northern Europe Bell

Beaker traders mingled with indigenous populations and produced mixtures of both physical types and pottery forms.

Perhaps the most significant of the mixtures resulting from the advent of the Bell Beaker people was that which occurred in western and northwestern Europe, in those areas where the Megalithic complex was the strongest. Just following the turn of the second millennium, the Megalithic fervor had reached its peak. Megalithic contacts were almost entirely by sea, and sea trade undoubtedly augmented the highest development of Megalithic religious ideas on these coasts. It was at this same time that the Bell Beaker people arrived in western and northwestern Europe from an inland direction. On the middle Rhine and in adjacent regions, the Battle-ax cultures or Corded Ware people were strongly entrenched. The fusion of people and ideas with these previous cultures produced a series of developments known collectively as the *Beaker cultures.*

The first result of the fusion of the Bell Beaker with the Corded development was the Zoned beaker. The pottery of the two forms coalesced just as the cultures fused. The zoned beaker was a pot with the general form of the bell beaker, but somewhat elongated. The zoned decoration was reminiscent of Bell Beaker horizontal banding but was coarsened and was made by cord marking. Burials, too, were affected, and were often made under round mounds in the Corded manner. Elements of the Single-grave culture also mixed with the Beaker elements in this area.

It is significant that the Bell Beaker folk were little affected by the Megalithic religion although in contact with it at a number of places. Presumably their own religious ideas were contrary to Megalithic ritual or contemptuous of it.

The bell beakers which have given these traders their name were probably used for some intoxicating beer brewed and traded as distinctive of their culture. The invariable presence of the bell beakers in graves suggests that beer drinking was ceremonial in aspect and probably a part of religious ritual. It will be remembered that Corded graves also featured a beaker form of vessel which may have been used for that same purpose. The Bell Beaker folk, with their intoxicating brew, may have been welcomed by Neolithic groups more on that account than because of the small amounts of copper which they carried. In most cases the making of beakers and undoubtedly the drinking of beer were eagerly taken over by various groups. Some curious mixtures of cultures and beakers resulted from these introductions.

The Beaker cultures are chiefly manifested in the British Isles by the Beaker invasion. These were migrations of groups of people from the low countries of the continent. Each wave of emigrants was marked by characteristic types of pottery beakers, which may be distinguished one from the other. There were two definite Beaker invasions of the British Isles, each originating from a different portion of the European coast. These waves of Beaker movements are known respectively as the B Beaker migration and the A Beaker movement.

Migrations to the British Isles across the Channel sea lane had already been made by preceding groups. There had been earlier Neolithic movements; for example, those of Windmill Hill and Peterborough people of earlier times. As the delayed subsidence of the Channel coasts was still continuing during Neolithic times, it is possible to date, by submerged evidence of earlier Neolithic camps, the exact time of the arrival of the Beaker peoples. Megalithic seafarers had also touched upon these coasts, but the religious fervor which they had engendered was dwindling. The subsequent Beaker folk provided a sharp break with preceding times.

The first or B Beaker invasion has been divided into three or more subclasses on the basis of pottery. Several distinct bands of Beaker folk may be distinguished from each other in both the B and the A movements. However, all the Beaker people were physically broadheaded and of a racial type close to that called Dinaric on the continent. They were armed with bows and flint-tipped arrows and they carried small daggers of copper.

The B type of Beaker was brought by the first migrants, who apparently came from Brittany. They landed in Britain near the mouths of the Stour and the Avon and overran southwestern England from Dartmoor to western Sussex leaving their typical graves and grave goods behind to mark their presence. The B beaker is one of typical shape with incised horizontal bands or hyphenated bands sometimes made with a toothed comb. This type of beaker is found in both Brittany and the Rhineland.

The B Beaker newcomers brought with them a Megalithic trait which had developed in Brittany. In spite of the fact that the Beaker folk were generally little affected by the Megalithic collective-burial practices, they had absorbed the Breton practice of building stone circles and alignments. Some of the most spectacular prehistoric monuments in Europe are the result of Beaker industry in constructing religious monuments of standing stones and stone-lined avenues. Such monuments were raised at Stanton Drew near Bristol, at Stonehenge, or at the even more impressive ceremonial structure of Avebury.

The typical Beaker B–1 grave contained a crouched body in an earth-dug pit with a round barrow superimposed over the interment. The grave usually contained well-made flint arrowheads with tangs and barbs and a stone bow-guard. Copper blades and copper daggers also accompany these B–1 Beaker round-barrow graves. They may have brought some copper with them from the continent but they soon began to trade with the metalsmiths of the Highlands and Ireland for these objects. They also derived some gold from Ireland.

B–2 Beaker or Zoned Beaker migrants came from farther north on continental Europe in the region of Holland and the lower Rhine. Here, Bell Beaker people had mingled with the Corded or Battle-ax cultures. The result was the Zoned beaker. Zoned beakers, as they appeared in the British Isles, were squat, coarse, and more poorly ornamented than those of B–1. Usually they were placed with burials in flat graves unaccompanied by other burial offerings.

The B–2 people moved across the narrow seas separating Holland and the lower Rhine from the British coasts. They landed their boats at several points in Kent and along the coast of Essex and Suffolk. Moving farther inland, the B–2 Beaker people superseded indigenous Neolithic communities in Kent and Sussex. Spreading along the coasts as well as inland, the movement reached as far northeast as Scotland. From the evidence of submerged B–2 sites along the British coasts, it is possible to date this invasion of Beaker folk soon after 2000 B.C.

B–2 graves are difficult to distinguish except by the presence or absence of zoned beakers. They also seem to have had little metal, perhaps because they were farther from the source of its manufacture. In general, however, the B–2 Beaker immigrants were roughly contemporaneous with the B–1, or only slightly later, B–1 and B–2 Beaker movements overlap in several places.

Another variant of the B beakers is the B–3 type. This vessel is usually a beaker decorated with zones of cord impressions. Some of these Beaker folk occupied the Yorkshire coast and Scotland.

The B–3 Beaker folk, just as the other varieties of beaker makers, replaced the indigenous populations or imposed themselves as overlords among them. They apparently deliberately besieged strategic areas. They managed to institute their own rite of single burial in contrast to the Megalithic collective-burial customs. However, Beaker sherds are sometimes found in the typical graves of the Megalithic builders. Beaker pottery also has been found at Windmill Hill and at other Neolithic sites indicating that the Beaker people dispossessed and displaced those previous groups.

A second invasion from the continent was that of the A Beaker people. This was definitely a later movement than the preceding B Beaker invasions and occurred after the continuing subsidence of the North Sea coasts had inundated the coastal camps of earlier cultures, or about 1800 B.C.

The A Beaker was typically a tall vessel with a middle constriction and elongated neck. The A Beaker was derived from the Bell urn or Veluwe beaker form as it was found in Holland. The Veluwe beaker was a form of pottery arising from a native grooved ware in the Dutch area intermixed with Bell Beaker influences. A Beaker ornament was more varied than that of the B Beaker and includes vertical as well as horizontal patterns. The straight-necked Corded Ware pot also suggests the A Beaker form. Connections with the Corded Ware development of continental Europe are also strongly suggested by the fact that A Beaker graves are often accompanied by stone battle-axes. It is obvious that the A Beaker folk absorbed more of the Corded and Battle-ax element from the continent than did earlier Beaker people who migrated to Britain.

The A Beaker people landed on the British coasts in the region of the Wash. They penetrated inland to the Wessex chalk region eventually reaching southeastern Scotland and Wales. Further seaborne movements of A Beaker people touched at other points along the British coasts as far as western Scotland. Northern A Beaker people were distinguished by a further variant of the beaker pot, the C beaker. The C beaker was a degeneration of the A beaker, or in some cases, a mixture of A and B types of beaker. Occasional C forms are evidences of fresh migrations of C Beaker folk from the continent. C Beaker folk arriving on British shores late, but in large numbers, pushed even farther than their B Beaker precursors. C Beaker colonists reached as far as Ireland, Man, Orkney, and the Hebrides.

A Beaker dead were flexed and placed in earth-dug pits with a superimposed round barrow. The mounds above the graves were further elaborated by stone or wood enclosures simulating a hut or dwelling. In addition to graves, A Beaker folk built ceremonial circles of earth or stone surrounded by a ditch. These may have represented a circular hut open to the sky.

A Beaker graves contain flint arrowheads and V-bored buttons but lack the archers' bracer or wrist guard of other Beaker interments. Copper daggers also appear but in a different form. The typical metal daggers with A Beaker graves are triangular-bladed knives with two rivets to which the handle was attached. This is a form similar to those from Hungarian copper sources rather than to the classic Bell Beaker daggers which were Spanish inspired. But perhaps even in A Beaker times trade copper was not yet plentiful, for flint daggers were also made. These flint forms were obvious imitations of the desirable metal daggers and were chipped with great skill. In central Europe flint daggers simulating scarce metal forms were in wide use at this time. In addition to flint daggers, the A Beaker immigrants also reverted to the use of stone battle-axes in the tradition of the Corded Ware warriors on the continent. A Beaker battle-axes were rudimentary copies of Corded types and were actually hammer-axes blunted on one end.

It is significant that Beaker settlements are practically unknown. Beaker folk were apparently pastoral nomads depending upon cattle, pigs, and sheep and upon hunting for subsistence. They were familiar with wheat and barley but evidently practiced little agriculture. The several waves of Beaker invaders ruthlessly overran the previous Neolithic inhabitants of Britain. The Windmill Hill people virtually disappeared as a culture, although they maintained themselves as an ethnic element in later British mixtures. The Peterborough people, living upon terrain not so coveted by the Beaker invaders, survived to reassert themselves after the force of the Beaker invasions was spent.

Perhaps the outstanding achievements of the Beaker folk were the great religious monuments which were left behind in Britain. The erection of these impressive ceremonial centers reflected a degree of organization greater than any of previous periods. The co-ordinated efforts of hundreds, if not thousands, of individuals of southern England and Wales were necessary for the completion of these ambitious projects.

The two largest sanctuaries which are commonly attributed to the industry of the Beaker folk are Avebury and Stonehenge. In addition, there are a number of other, smaller religious monuments spread over a wide area.

Avebury, in North Wiltshire near Marlborough, is the largest of the temples of the Beaker folk, if not the most impressive prehistoric monument in Europe. There were two periods of building at Avebury. In the first period, a row of three sets of concentric circles of standing stones was connected to the Kennet River by a zigzag avenue of upright stones leading southward. From there the avenue led to a distant sanctuary of two more concentric rings of stones on Overton Hill. The stones lining the avenue consisted of sarsen blocks with alternating tall narrow stones and shorter lozenge-shaped pieces to represent male and female properties of nature. At a later time, Avebury was remodeled on a more ambitious plan. The northern circle of the main group was eliminated. The two remaining circles were surrounded by a colossal ditch 30 feet deep in places and interrupted by causeways. The excavated earth from the ditch was piled outside to form an earthen wall whose crest is some 55 feet above the bottom of the fosse. The diameter of the final Avebury ditch was some 1,400 feet. An intermittent line of upright stones was placed around the inner edge of the ditch.

Less than a mile from Avebury is Silbury Hill, which is an artificial mound 130 feet high surrounded by a ditch 20 feet deep. This tumulus lies in a natural hollow which sets off its great bulk. It may have been a large burial mound of the Beaker folk, but tunneled excavations have not revealed any interment within the mound.

Stonehenge, to the west of Avebury in Wessex, is the most famous of the sanctuaries attributed to the Beaker people. Successive excavations at Stonehenge show several stages of remodeling and change. Originally, Stonehenge was a circular ditch with one entrance and the earth piled inside. A ring of posts stood within the circle. This circle of uprights is known as the Aubrey Circle after John Aubrey, who discovered the filled-in sockets for these posts in 1666. Later, a more impressive circle of standing stones was erected inside the previous structure. The center of this later, or Sarsen Circle, was fixed by relation to four station-stones. The center of the Sarsen Circle differs from that of the earlier Aubrey Circle by two feet. Within the Sarsen Circle a horseshoe arrangement of five massive trilithons was later erected. Both in the Sarsen Circle and in the horseshoe the uprights are joined at the top by stone lintels, in the circle continuously and in the horseshoe by pairs. These stone uprights are fitted with tenons at their tops to fit into sockets in the superimposed lintel stones, a technique undoubtedly borrowed from similar work in wood.

After the horseshoe was erected at Stonehenge, a later circle of blue stones was added inside the Sarsen Circle. A similar horseshoe was also erected within the original arc of trilithons. The blue stones are remarkable because they are spotted dolerite and must have been brought from the Presley Mountains in southern Wales, some 145 miles away. Actually, the blue stones were probably transported by sea around Land's End, then by water, and finally overland to the Stonehenge site.

Within the final, inner horseshoe of blue stones lies a prostrate stone called the Altar Stone. A long avenue bordered by a ditch up the gentle slope from the River Avon leads to the sanctuary of Stonehenge. Perhaps it was up this avenue that the blue stones were dragged on rollers to make the final additions.

Since Beaker pottery has been found in association with both Avebury and Stonehenge, it seems most probable that both of these monuments were built by the industry and organization of the Beaker folk. Surrounding Stonehenge are Bronze Age barrows which indicate that these people buried their dead around this sacred spot. There are indications that these sanctuaries may have been religious centers earlier than the Beaker invasions and remained sanctified and venerated places long after the Beaker folk had been superseded by later people.

Whatever the exact history of the great sanctuaries of southern England might be, there is no doubt of the major role of the Beaker folk in European prehistory. The Bell Beaker movement on the continent and the various Beaker invasions into Britain had a pronounced unifying influence. The Beaker cultures remained remarkably uniform and unchanged over great distances of ancient Europe and over a considerable span of time. It was from this uniform background that the Bronze Ages of Europe emerged.

CHAPTER 10

The Era of Bronze

THE DISCOVERY of copper had not solved all the problems for the making of tools. Indeed, for many uses, the earlier material—flint—was superior. Copper daggers, for example, had to be so constantly resharpened that the blades were soon narrowed. Copper axes were too soft for the cutting of hard wood. The manipulation of this new substance was a problem as pure copper has a high melting temperature and pure metal is difficult to cast in molds. Copper in the casting process tends to bubble, giving an imperfect reproduction.

Early metal workers had discovered that certain varieties of copper ores had different properties. Some of these made harder axes and daggers and, when molten, cast better. These superior properties were due, for the most part, to the presence of tin in natural copper ores. Even small percentages of tin resulted in better products. Any combination of copper and tin is called bronze.

Although there is no doubt that bronze was first used as a natural alloy in the Near East, it was not long before early metallurgists recognized that they were dealing with two substances. By extracting metallic copper and adding tin to it in desirable quantities, artificially alloyed bronze was produced. Bronze was deliberately mixed in the region of Mesopotamia and Hither Asia well before the second millennium b.c.

Coincidental with the development of the alloying of bronze was the discovery that different percentages of tin made a great difference in the final product. Generally speaking, the larger the percentage of tin, the more brittle the mixture. Eight per cent of tin produces a very brittle bronze but one that will cast well and is satisfactorily fusible. Two or 3 per cent of tin forms a harder bronze but is difficult to cast. Bronze with the smaller amounts of tin made excellent cutting implements such as swords, daggers, and knives. The greater amounts of tin produced a bronze which could be cast into intricate ornaments where brittleness was no problem. It was very much later that metallurgists learned to mix copper, tin, and zinc to make brass.

The new discovery of the alloying of copper and tin quickly spread to the eastern Mediterranean and the Aegean region. The early settlers of Troy worked with bronze. The knowledge of this metal appeared soon in the islands of Cyprus and Crete and spread along the same trade routes as those previously followed by Neolithic ideas and the use of copper. There was, however, a greater limitation in the manufacture of bronze, as its formation was necessarily limited to those places where tin could be found. Deposits of tin were discovered in Etruria, not far from the copper center of Remedello in Italy. Tin was also found in northwestern Spain, where it was soon utilized by early bronze workers. Tin deposits were found conveniently close to copper ores in Brittany. Especially important were the tin-producing streams of Cornwall in Britain, which were extensively worked in these early times.

Perhaps the most important of the metal deposits on the mainland of Europe was the combination of the copper ores of central Hungary and the tin deposits of Bohemia. In this region of central Europe, metal workers of the time found abundant quantities of both materials, sometimes in natural combination. It was from these lodes that the real European Bronze Age evolved.

The period following the Bell Beaker epoch on the continent and the Beaker invasions in the British Isles was not one of abrupt change. Bell Beaker elements merged with Neolithic foundations in various parts of Europe. Copper and copper-working became better known and finally the new material, bronze, followed copper over the trade routes. The period of this transition to the full knowledge of bronze is usually called the *Amalgamation period*. Occasionally these times are referred to as *Proto-Aunjetitz*, indicating that the period lay before the first of the European Bronze Ages.

The Amalgamation period was a blending of most of the other previous elements of Europe into a more or less cosmopolitan culture. The economy continued without great change from earlier times and might be called a "barnyard" type of life. Trade moved briskly over well-established routes throughout the body of Europe. Amber and flint forms were traded from the north. New metals were derived from the south. Ideas introduced into one part of Europe became known in other places much more quickly than before.

Pottery-making, always sensitive to cultural change, showed that this period of formation was a true amalgam. Footed bowls and pots with broad handles were degenerate Bell Beaker forms of the Amalgamation period. Pouched jugs and amphora were scarcely recognizable First Northern and Michelsberger forms. Corded elements, beakers, and pitchers were still present. Decoration on the pottery of the Amalgamation period varied from the incisions and stamping of Bell Beaker to the cord-impression technique of true Corded.

Tools and weapons, also, were a combination of previous elements. Flat copper celts and copper daggers mixed with Megalithic flint tools chipped in obvious imitations of metal forms. Hammer-axes and boat-axes of Megalithic derivation occurred with shaft-hole axes from Hungarian centers. Metal, in the form of copper tools and a few of bronze, was becoming better known and more widely distributed.

The Amalgamation period in central Europe was terminated by a series of developments such as that called *Marschwitz,* from the type site in Silesia. At Marschwitz occurred the first beginnings of the true Bronze Age near the tin regions of central Europe. The Marschwitz seems to be a derivation of Corded and Bell Beaker elements with an added Neolithic Danubian tradition. Most of the Marschwitz material has been recovered from graves at the Marschwitz site which are remarkably like those of the Bell Beaker. The metal catalog of the Marschwitz—predominantly pins and trinkets—indicated the growing knowledge of the new material. Indeed, the first true bronze objects in the region of central Europe are in the form of round-headed pins, Near Eastern inspired and apparently used for the fastening of flowing garments. These elongated pins were the first of a long series of developments in the manufacture of pins and clothing fasteners.

The early beginnings of bronze in Europe were scattered, and their derivation is difficult to ascertain. Perhaps groups of smiths first began to manufacture the new metal in areas where tin was available and where trade routes made distribution of their products possible. These smiths may well have been descendants of the Baden people who perhaps first prospected for metal in Europe; or new groups of immigrants may have introduced the new knowledge. The inspiration for bronze certainly was Near Eastern.

Bronze-working centers arose at the Town of Tószeg on the Tisza River in Hungary, and this first development is called *Tószeg A.* Another center began at Perjámos on the Maros River and at Mad'-arouce in Slovakia. The unusual feature of all these centers was their relative permanence as compared with most Neolithic communities. Cemeteries at Perjámos and Tószeg show that these towns were occupied by many generations. Perhaps this stability was made possible by the use of plow agriculture.

An interesting bronze development in western Europe was that called the *Armorican Bronze Age* from the old Celtic name for Bretagne or Brittany. Early in the history of metal usage in Europe, a group from Spain came to Brittany, presumably by sea. These sea-going chieftains, however, did not settle in those areas already occupied by Megalithic settlements. The Armoricans were warriors who left a record of their early Bronze Age life in the form of elaborate graves under cairns. These graves were furnished with well-made bronze daggers and other war gear. Curiously, the surrounding peoples of northern France had little metal and no bronze at this time. The Armoricans later carried bronze and bronze-working to England.

Although bronze smelting was obviously earlier at several points in southernmost Europe, the first significant bronze period in the main body of Europe was that called Bronze Age A, or the Aunjetitz. The name is derived from a small village in Czechoslovakia, twelve kilometers from Prague, where a large hoard of typical bronze implements of this date was discovered. The graves in the great cemetery there were usually accompanied by bronze objects, evidence that the alloying of bronze was actually practiced in the region. Forms and molds in which bronze implements were cast and the slag and other by-products of the smelting process were typical of Aunjetitz sites. In this region of central Europe, with the copper deposits of Hungary and the tin ores of Bohemia, the first and most significant of European bronze developments evolved.

There was no distinct break from the preceding Amalgamation period or Marschwitz type of culture. The general economy of the Aunjetitz period was still based upon agriculture. There is considerably more evidence for a division of labor as contrasted with previous periods, as the smiths and traders apparently did not plant fields of their own. All grains grown in modern times were known to Aunjetitz farmers. Most crafts were also practiced by them. Loom-weights and spindle whorls indicated the continuing use of textiles of several varieties.

Aunjetitz villages were built on hill sites as well as in the valleys. Their log houses were rectangular with peaked roofs. The bodies in the Aunjetitz cemetery were placed on their right sides, facing north, and in some instances were interred in cists, a form derived from Neolithic levels in northern Europe. Others were placed in large earthen jars with another pot forming the lid. Relatively few bronze pieces were placed in the graves. It is obvious from these significant items that the Aunjetitz Bronze period was not an intrusive element. Most Aunjetitz features may be accounted for by various combinations of preceding Neolithic traits.

Many of the Aunjetitz cultural items are known, not from habitation sites, but from hoards. These were deposits of bronze and other objects presumably buried by traders for safekeeping and then never recovered. The hoards discovered at Aunjetitz and at Altenburg contained large collections of bronze objects buried in Aunjetitz times.

A plot of the distribution of hoards and settlements shows the range of the Aunjetitz people to extend north and south through central Europe. There was obviously a concentration of Aunjetitz activity in the Prague basin, and Aunjetitz material is found in its purest form in Bohemia. From this center, it radiated out into Silesia, Saxony, the Rhineland, Bavaria, and Austria as far as the Danube. Eastward, the Aunjetitz extended into Poland. To the south, trade connections were maintained with the increasingly important Bronze Age site at Tószeg on the Tisza. This extensive diffusion of the Aunjetitz was obviously stimulated by the general uniformity of the pre-Aunjetitz Amalgamation period. In spite of this, however, the Aunjetitz Bronze Age never notably reached such outlying areas as western Europe, Scandinavia, Russian Europe, and the British Isles. Bronze developments in those places came from other sources.

In the southeast, some of the Painted Pottery settlements continued their Neolithic tradition undisturbed. Tripolye, which was flourishing during this time, was little affected by the Aunjetitz development. The Altheim of the upper Danube and the Beaker folk of western Europe were at first little influenced by the new metal manufactured in the Bohemian area.

Aunjetitz pottery continued Amalgamation forms, with some significant changes. The pouched jug shifted into a carinated mug with a small round handle placed on its lower edge. This, because of its peculiar outline, is often called the "Turkish pipe" mug. Jars with ledge lugs and bowls persisted from the previous period. Large storage vessels were also typical Aunjetitz forms, one of which was a heritage from the First Northern Neolithic. The other, a big-bellied, flaring-rimmed vessel with a barbotine surface treatment, was a new Aunjetitz form. It was in these large vessels that burials were sometimes made. Pedestaled jars in the Aunjetitz recall Hungarian shapes, as much of the ceramic tradition was derived from this area to the south. Some of the pottery forms are Aegean. There were northern elements as well, but Aunjetitz pottery did not change radically from preceding forms.

Stone materials were not abandoned with the advent of the Bronze Age. Flint blades were made and triangular flint arrowheads were widely used. Presumably bronze was still too valuable to use for arrow points. For the first time, the saddle-ax or grooved-ax appeared, made of hard, igneous rock. Most of these were blunted and were used for hammering and shaping bronze forms. Amber, in many forms such as pendants and beads, was widely traded and was carried as far as Mycenae in Greece. *Cardium* shells, for ornamentation, were typical of the Aunjetitz period.

Particularly illustrative of the Aunjetitz era were the bronze tools and weapons which were manufactured at the time, the most outstanding of which was the flanged celt. This was a bronze ax with a flat cross section. The body of the flanged celt was narrow with a flaring, convex cutting edge. The butt was rounded, often with a notch. Along the sides of the celt a thickening, or low flange, was developed for hafting purposes. The flanged celt of Aunjetitz times was simply an improvement on the flat copper celt typical of the preceding Chalcolithic of southern Europe. The Aunjetitz flanged celt was, of course, made of the superior bronze and showed an improvement in its outline and in the hafting flanges.

Aunjetitz daggers were typically made with a round-headed, triangular blade fitted with rivets at the base for the accommodation of the hilt. These daggers showed some influence from the bronze forms of the Aegean area. Occasionally gold and even amber was inlaid into the surface of the bronze dagger blades in elaborate designs. This technique was also Aegean in derivation.

Perhaps the greatest elaboration in the Aunjetitz period occurred in the fashioning of pins. The knot-headed pins of the Marschwitz period had now been varied in a number of details with influences from distant points. The Cypriote type was a long, straight, bronze pin with the upper end looped over and wrapped around itself. There were flat-topped pins with eyelets and others had circular rings as heads. A still more elaborate form was topped by three rings forming a trilobate pattern. Another pin had a racket head with a flattened top. There were many other variations on these basic themes.

Bracelets were also common in the Aunjetitz period. The earliest type was a simple spiral of heavy bronze wire or a bronze rod which was wound around the wrist. There was also the plain bar type, cast in a mold and then bent to the contours of the arm. A later version was the manchet, a type of bracelet made of several bar bracelets fused together or wound in a series.

One of the most interesting of the early Bronze Age jewelry forms was the ingot torque. This was a bronze bar, either plain or ornamented, which was worn around the neck as a large ring. For aesthetic reasons, these often were twisted and thus were given the name of torque. Ingot torques were usually plain, with the ends turned back to form a pair of loops. Torques were a Near Eastern form found at Byblos and also in Egypt. They appear in Hungary and at Perjámos and later in the Aunjetitz region.

The torque, as used in Bronze Age times, was more than a simple ornament. Apparently these neck rings were used as a medium of exchange and a unit of value. Torques have often been found in large hoards such as that at Altenburg, which contained over a thousand of these ornaments in one deposit. From such circumstances it would appear that torques, and probably other bronze pieces as well, were used as a medium of exchange in trading. This was quite clear in some hoards where the torques were not finished. Plain bronze rings were cast in roughed-out shape, obviously never intended to be worn, or plain bronze bars, only slightly curved, were cast and otherwise unworked. These latter curved bars are called ribs or talents and are presumed to be unfinished torques. These were the standard monetary units in early Bronze Age times.

Earrings and finger rings were also made of bronze in the Aunjetitz period. Earrings were typically formed of a loop of bronze wire in the shape of a small basket. Finger rings were formed of plain, coiled bronze wire and were worn on the base of the finger or over a knuckle.

These simple bronze forms characterized the Aunjetitz period, or the first Bronze Age of central Europe. The entire Aunjetitz development was stimulated by the introduction of metallurgy from the south, notably from the Mediterranean. From these connections it seems that the Aunjetitz center appeared slightly after the turn of the second millennium, or about 1900 B.C. For perhaps three centuries the Prague basin, with its adjacent deposits of copper and tin, remained the center of bronze-making in central Europe. Following these beginnings, the emphasis shifted to the westward, where a new center appeared.

In the mountainous area south of the upper Danube, the cultures of Laibach Moor and Mondsee continued into early Bronze Age times. In upper Austria and the hill region of Bohemia, Corded elements had not given up their typical round-barrow burials. In western Slovakia, where the Aunjetitz did not penetrate, the *Veselé culture* showed a strong Corded influence. In western Hungary the *Wieselburg culture* was a variation of the Aunjetitz with close connections from Perjámos. In lower Austria the *Böheimkirchen culture,* like the Veselé of Slovakia, differed from classic Aunjetitz. At Tószeg a special development grew from earlier Hungarian precedents of the Danubian tradition and was analogous to the Aunjetitz of Bohemia.

It was the Aunjetitz with its centralized position, however, which essentially introduced bronze into northern and western Europe.

About the turn of the fifteenth century B.C., several ethnic groups or cultures to the west of the Aunjetitz learned to work bronze. This change of events ushered in the period of Bronze II, which, from its grave type, is often referred to as the *Tumulus* period. Generally, the Tumulus bronze workers were people of the hills and forests rather than the valley-dwellers of the Aunjetitz. The Tumulus period did not succeed the Aunjetitz or Bronze I in most of the lowland area. At Aunjetitz itself, as well as in Hungary, the two were developing simultaneously. Bronzes of both types are often found in the same hoards. Generally, the Tumulus folk left their mound-dotted cemeteries in such forested areas as Haguenau and the Hercynian Forest, later spreading to the north of France and Luxemburg.

The Tumulus people of the forested hills were probably hunters and herdsmen rather than farmers. They were also warriors. Gradually they overawed many of the Aunjetitz lowland villages and moved into the Danube valley. In the west, in Brittany, the Armorican bronze-working warrior chieftains were already established.

The ethnic element of the Tumulus may well have been those original western Neolithic warrior groups which had entered this same area some centuries earlier. The mode of burial of these people suggests that they were the descendants of the Corded folk. The bronze working which accompanied the Tumulus development also took a new turn, inspired likewise from a western direction. There were, however, many Aunjetitz elements in the Tumulus period. By the sixteenth century B.C., the trade routes and the traders who traveled them had bound Europe together so that there were few isolated portions of the continent.

Very few settlements of the Tumulus development are known. Most of the information from the Bronze II period comes from large numbers of Tumulus burials. These were simple pit burials with a superimposed earth mound or tumulus to mark the grave.

There was little social distinction in burial, as the mounds are much the same for all individuals. These tumuli were often found in groups or mound fields. Occasionally Bronze II graves were marked by mounds of rock. In a few instances, these people practiced cremation of their dead.

The Tumulus influence was obviously a diffusion from west to east. This spread of a new idea, as well as new types of bronze tools in late Bronze II times, engulfed south and south central Germany and proceeded eastward at least into western Hungary. Below the Danube, there is little Tumulus influence. Late Tumulus influences are, however, found as far east as western Slovakia and across the Carpathians into Galicia. Western Europe itself was profoundly affected by the Tumulus period. Most of the Bronze Age developments in outlying regions of western Europe stem from Tumulus influences rather than from the earlier Aunjetitz.

Typical Tumulus pottery included stand forms and ring feet. There were also pitchers, bowls, and amphora. A considerable number of local variations may be distinguished in Tumulus pottery, as well as a chronological sequence. Indeed, Tumulus or Bronze II cultural traits, including pottery, tend to divide the culture into a number of distinctive variations including the *Hercynian, Bavarian, Swabian,* upper, middle, and lower *Rhenish,* and *Thuringian.* For example, Bavarian Tumulus pottery showed a typical lattice-like decoration, for the most part in zigzags and alternate triangles. Bohemian types featured linear decorations, with some incised floral designs. A late Tumulus decorative motif was the pendant triangle filled with incised lines. None of these forms may be described as inspired or particularly beautiful, and certainly Tumulus pottery is not one of the great ceramic traditions of Europe.

Toward the end of the Tumulus period, pottery vessels tended to be more sophisticated in shape, and pedestals were fewer. Gored bodies became popular along with a type of decoration which simulated the human breast or, in some instances, metal rivets. This type of buckle decoration was extensively used in the succeeding period of Bronze III.

Tumulus bronze workers, obtaining tin from western sources, had learned to make a variety of metallic forms. Some of these were based upon preceding Aunjetitz bronzes, but many of them were new. Pins were still a common item of bronze manufacture in the Tumulus period. A typical ornament was the seal-headed pin which was a straight pin of bronze with a flat, seal head. Other Tumulus pins featured openwork, wheel-like heads, and another type with a flat, mushroom-like top was bent to the side so that the face could be seen.

Perhaps the greatest development was that of weapons. Daggers and poignards were made by Tumulus craftsmen with elongated and differentiated blades. Some of these daggers were inlaid, and most were provided with four rivets for the accommodation of the hilt. Bronze swords also had appeared. These were long rapiers with evenly tapering blades, with a mid-rib for added strength. Sword handles were usually riveted on. Occasional Tumulus swords, however, were provided with bronze hilts, some of them cast in one piece with the sword blade and decorated with ornamental pseudo-rivets as an atavistic characteristic.

Additional weapons in the Tumulus repertory included bows and arrows with socketed arrowheads of bronze and spearheads of the same material. Both of these were made with mid-ribs to strengthen the penetrating point and with a hollow socket at the base to accommodate the shaft. Bronze mace heads of several forms were also used by Tumulus warriors and were likewise provided with a socket for hafting.

Bronze ornamentation in Tumulus times was extremely varied and an occasional gold form appeared. Bronze bracelets of plain and manchet form were common. Often the bracelets were ornamented with incision or with extra spirals and finials of bronze at their terminations. In late Tumulus times, bronze workers exhibited their skill by manufacturing the ribbed bracelet. This was a heavy affair, ornamented around its periphery with lobes or ribs.

In addition to bracelets, pendants were popular. These, made of flat pieces of bronze with cut-out designs, were utilized in a number of forms to ornament belts and clothing. In addition to pendants, Tumulus peoples made wide use of the tutulus, a small round boss usually of bronze. These were fastened in series on leather or cloth, perhaps as rudimentary protection against a sword thrust as well as for decoration. Tutuli bosses were embellished by raised knobs, concentric ridges, and the like. Often gold tutuli were shaped and ornamented in the same manner as the bronze examples.

The craftsmen of the Tumulus period also used bronze for large numbers of practical implements. The flanged ax of previous times had now developed to the stop-ridge celt. This was an obvious improvement over the Aunjetitz flanged method of hafting but was not revolutionary. The stop-ridge celt was provided with an open socket-like hafting arrangement at its basal end. The handle of such an ax would still, of necessity, have to be elbow-shaped. How much easier it would have been simply to provide a perforation through the body of the ax and haft it in the manner which had already been discovered by the stone battle-ax makers of the Neolithic, several centuries before!

The Tumulus craftsmen may have been poor ax-makers, but they were proficient in the manufacture of knives and razors. Bronze knives, usually with curved blades, were skillfully made in a number of forms. Usually a thickened rib was provided at the base of the blade to give it rigidity. In many cases an openwork handle was cast in one piece with the knife blade. Bronze razors and tweezers were also made in quantity. The razors usually were large, by modern standards, with a broad, flat blade sharpened at the end. Handles were of openwork bronze and cast in one piece with the blade.

From these few outstanding examples, it may be seen that bronze working had progressed a long way since the first beginnings in the Hungarian area. The Tumulus bronze development continued its dominance for more than two centuries in western and central Europe. Following this period, a new bronze center in northeastern Europe appeared. This new focus of metal working ushers in the period of Bronze III.

There is considerable evidence that a new ethnic element moved into eastern Europe at the end of the Tumulus period, but it is difficult to guess what this new group might have been. Settlements of these newcomers were sometimes fortified, apparently against the indigenous peoples into whose lands they had intruded. Some scholars see only a movement of smiths and metal-ore miners who brought in new techniques of mining and bronze-working. Bronze became available to all who wanted bronze swords and spears. Perhaps it was because of this availability of weapons that warfare became prevalent and fortified towns necessary.

Whether Bronze III was inspired by smiths with new manufacturing techniques or by an actual invasion of new peoples from the east, the late Bronze Age was a time of crisis. Just as in the late Neolithic in Europe, a number of distinct cultures appeared, each evolving different characteristics. These different peoples engaged in warfare on a large scale. Population pressures alone were enough to spark invasions and counterinvasions. The resulting variety of towns, cemeteries, and burial hoards of traveling traders, as well as the evidences of bronze and pottery types, is sometimes confusing and always difficult to interpret.

The most readily recognizable changes of the Bronze III or Bronze C period occurred in eastern Europe in Silesia. Soon these developments were apparent in the Danube valley and as far west as the Rhine. The crisis of Bronze III is dated about 1400 B.C. although some students, by comparing Italian Bronze Age history with that of central Europe, would place the late European Bronze Age as late as 1000 B.C. Trade with central European bronze-producing areas was carried on with Greece and probably with Italy. These Classic centers are more easily dated.

Bronze III methods of bronze working and modes of burial spread over the old Aunjetitz centers and finally reached the former Tumulus areas in the west. Late Bronze or Bronze III, concentrated around German Silesia, is often called the *Lausitz period* or *Lusatian,* from the name of the large cemetery in Silesia where material of this age was found in great quantities.

Many settlements of the Lausitz development are known. These are both open towns such as those in Moravia, fortified crannog sites such as Buchau and Württemberg, or fortified hill sites such as that called Römerschantze near Berlin. Most of the Lausitz material has been derived from large cemeteries. The graves in these cemeteries usually contained cremated remains placed in pottery vessels. The pots were then buried at set intervals and in rows, generally with no surface indication of the location of the burial. This type of cemetery is often referred to as an urn field. For this reason, the Lausitz period of Bronze III is often alluded to as the *Urnfield period*.

Many Urnfield cultures have been distinguished in different areas, most on a basis of pottery. The Lausitz proper was centered generally from the Carpathians north to the Elbe River. Another group of Urnfield folk developed in the upper Danube and the northern Alpine area. A separate group of Urnfield cultures is sometimes recognized in the upper Rhine and Main valleys. Hungarian Urnfield people developed several variations on the Hungarian Plain, in Slovakia, and in western Hungary. Another group appeared in the lower Danube. There were, in late Bronze Age times groups even farther to the west who were affected by Urnfield customs. Pottery is used by archaeologists to distinguish different groups of the Urnfield, primarily because bronze tools and weapons were less sensitive to change. Often archaic types of bronzes persisted in certain regions. Many urn fields do not have bronzes with the burials at all.

The Lausitz was a center of emphasis, but it was not the only manifestation of Bronze III. There were radiating lines of influence in all directions. The Lausitz grew from an Aunjetitz base, and Neolithic elements were still present in the Oder such as the Warrior cultures of earlier times.

In central Europe, the Bronze III continued in the Aunjetitz tradition. In its spread, the Lausitz culture extended from the Saale to the Vistula River and south to the Austrian Danube and the mountains of Slovakia. To this extent, the Lausitz is suggestive of the later grouping of Germanic peoples and may be identified with them. The ethnic grouping of the Teutonic tribes may thus begin with the Bronze Age. But analogous Urnfield cultures expanded over an area reaching from the Balkans and Troy in the southeast to Spain and the British Isles in the west. The Lausitz people have been identified with the Dorian invaders in Greek lands and the Illyrian peoples who appeared during the Iron Age in Illyria at the head of the Adriatic. Lausitz people have also been identified with the Slavs to the east and with the Celts who became the dominant ethnic element in western Europe during the late Iron Age. It is almost certain the Urnfield folk west of the Alps spoke Celtic. It is difficult to equate the Lausitz with any one people or group, but there is no questioning their great influence upon Europe in the late Bronze Age.

The Lausitz continued its ceramic tradition with the usual European progression of vessel forms and decoration. Lausitz pottery was generally dark-colored, and the forms were outgrowths of what had already begun earlier in the Bronze Age. The one innovation was a burial urn shaped like two cones placed together at their bases. Many Lausitz urns were decorated with human-breast forms. In late Lausitz times this type of decoration degenerated into concentric circles. On a basis of the pottery, the Lausitz is usually divided into two phases, Lausitz A and B, but in some parts of Europe, scholars profess to see three separate phases of Lausitz progression.

As far as bronzes are concerned, the Lausitz craftsmen in most parts of Europe had an abundance of metal. Trade routes, well established from earlier times, carried ideas to most parts of the continent. There were military movements which mixed and spread culture. Cremation and burial in urn fields became the hallmark of the times.

In early Lausitz or Phase A, the cemetery was typically accompanied by a square crematory area surrounded by a low wall. The burial urns themselves were usually biconical. Also in the early Lausitz, the vessels are quite dark-colored—black or very dark gray. Usually a dish or shallow pot cover was placed over the urn. In the early part of the Lausitz, some burials under barrows persisted from earlier Tumulus times.

In Phase B of the Lausitz, pottery was covered with warts, nipples, and breasts. It was even darker in color, sometimes rubbed with graphite, and the angles were flattened to give circular contours. At the very last, the typical Lausitz nipples and breasts degenerated into circular forms which can scarcely be recognized. There was also a type of late Lausitz vessel with gores in an angular, spiral pattern.

The late Lausitz development seems to have concentrated more and more to the south of the original centers. There are late Lausitz sites in Bohemia, Moravia, and Slovakia. The villages were unprotected, for the most part, and marked by rows of log cabins of the megaron type. The appearance of the megaron indicates that the Aegean tradition of this type of porched house had not died out since Painted Pottery times. The megaron was originally, of course, inspired from Troy II and the Balkan area and appeared at Erösd in the Painted Pottery area.

The push of the Lausitz people from their original centers in the Silesian area of eastern Europe had much to do with subsequent events in Europe. The more widespread Urnfield type of culture spread farther and persisted in many places throughout the subsequent Iron Age.

Lausitz bronzes were generally continued on a basis of preceding Aunjetitz metallurgy. There were, however, a number of new elements. Bronze was common in the Lausitz and the tools tended to be more massive than those of the previous periods. The Lausitz smiths also utilized bronze for cultivating implements. Evidences of metallurgy in the form of slag and smiths' hoards are known from a number of places in the Lausitz area. Few bronzes were placed with the cremated burials.

Bronze pins were still one of the most common Lausitz items of manufacture. They used seal-headed pins, round-headed varieties with twisted stems, and other ornamented models. In the late Lausitz, the two-membered pin or fibula became common.

The fibula, although possibly not actually developed in the Lausitz area, became a common and typical ornament from Bronze III times on. The original fibula may have been developed in Italy, Greece, or the northern portion of Europe. All types of straight bronze pins were impractical in that they tended to pull out of the clothing in which they were fastened. To prevent this, a small bronze cap was provided to slip over the point of the pin and a short length of bronze wire was attached to the cap to hold it in place. Thus when the straight pin had been threaded through the cloth or garment, the cap, with its holding wire, was placed on the point and the contrivance was secure. This arrangement is essentially the same as the modern safety pin. The northern, or two-membered fibula, has been often referred to as the Nordic fibula.

In the southern regions of the Bronze Age, a fibula was developed in which the pin, the guard for its point, and the connecting pieces, were all manufactured of a single bronze wire. This is known as the Mediterranean or Italian type. Fibulae of both northern, Italian, and southern varieties became extremely popular following Bronze III times, and appeared subsequently in some hundreds of variations. Many of these variations of fibulae were extremely significant as indicating tribal connections, trade contacts, and other influences.

Early Lausitz celts or axes were of the high-winged variety, a development of the flanged celt and the stop-ridge celt of earlier bronze times. In the later Lausitz, the ax became a socketed celt. This was a hafting contrivance with the high flanges to enclose a socket at the base of the implement. The socketed celt was probably a development of the Lausitz center. The bronze workers of central Europe were very late in devising axes and adzes with a socket or shaft hole for better hafting.

Bronze sickles, hoes, and knives occurred frequently in Lausitz collections. Swords and poignards were manufactured in a number of forms, with rapiers and slashing swords combined in one form. During the late Lausitz extension over Europe, many of the Lausitz weapon forms were affected by local variations, thus producing real differences and types. Socketed spears and arrowheads were made in quantities; apparently the principal weapon was the bow. Mace heads and a few pieces of bronze which were sewed on the clothing as rudimentary armor were also present. Horse bits and trappings of bronze began to appear. The chariot as a weapon of war undoubtedly added to the strength of invading armies and very greatly increased their range of activities.

Especially interesting in the Lausitz repertory of bronze manufacture is the fibula with the spiral catchplate which developed into the spectacle brooch that appeared late in Lausitz times. The spectacle brooch was an elaborate two-membered fibula, although of a special variety. A single piece of heavy bronze wire was spiraled to produce two reverse coils. The pin portion of the brooch extended from the center of one of these to the other. Spectacle brooches in later times became more elaborate with local variation.

Bronze cups of Italian manufacture, as well as gold wire, amber, glass beads, and other foreign items are evidences of the influences of the far-flung Lausitz trade connections.

213

In the area of old Aunjetitz development surrounding the Prague basin, the Bronze III is not called Lausitz, but is known as the *Knoviz culture*. The Knoviz combined the fading Aunjetitz tradition with incoming Tumulus elements. The Knoviz was not an original culture but a new combination of existing features and, in its purest form, is found only in central Bohemia.

Knoviz burials indicate the mixed aspect of the culture. Normally these people buried their dead in a flexed position in plain pits. There were, however, some cremations from the Urnfield influence. Many dismembered human skeletons have been found in connection with the Knoviz, indicative of cannibalism to some authorities.

Knoviz pottery is especially distinctive, featuring a number of long-necked, cylindrical vessel forms. Some jars were made in the double *étage* shape, as though two vessels had been stacked and joined. Some Painted Pottery decoration appeared in the Knoviz as it did in the Lausitz. Black on red was typical. Occasional Knoviz potters decorated their wares with black graphite streaks rubbed into the surface of the pottery. Painted geometric designs appeared frequently on wall plaster in house pits. Knoviz potters were also interested in statuary. Animal figurines of several recognizable species are present; certain of these are unmistakably horses.

Bone work was utilized in the Knoviz culture for projectile points, harpoons, and spears. Antler hammer-axes provided with square holes for hafting were also used, as were sled runners made from the long bones of deer.

Knoviz bronzes were predominantly influenced by Lausitz forms. Immense pins with segmented heads, the spectacle brooch, bracelets, and other ornaments show little variation from Lausitz patterns. Socketed celts, sickles, and other tools and weapons were similar.

Knoviz artisans also worked in gold, and more of these ornaments have occurred with the Knoviz material than with most other bronze-working centers.

Extremely late Lausitz material in the center of its original development is often called *Silesian*. The Silesian culture was essentially a continuation of the Lausitz Urnfield. Typical Silesian remains have been found in urn fields and cremated graves. Individual burials were made in ossuary urns covered with bowls. Often, other pottery vessels surrounded the original cremation, and sometimes small auxiliary pots were actually formed on the shoulder of the ossuary urn itself. The cremated, urn-contained burials were, in a few instances, placed in stone-lined cists. The burials were aligned in rows and spaced. Urn fields of the Silesian culture often contained hundreds of cremated burials with the cremation pits located near by in much the same manner as the preceding Lausitz. Occasional skeletal burials, especially in the southern Silesian area as it intruded into Moravia, may be indications that slaves or other persons of low rank were not cremated.

The general economy of the Silesian was obviously a continuation of the Lausitz, as was the ethnic element. Silesian pottery differed to some extent from earlier forms. Round-shouldered pottery vessels and squat forms, with widely flaring and inverted rims, began to appear.

Silesian bronzes were essentially the same as Lausitz forms. Most of the bronze material from the Silesian has been recovered from hoards and not from grave depositions. Most remarkable in the Silesian catalog was the appearance of iron pins. This was the first indication of iron in central Europe. A few iron pins from the more southerly Knoviz culture indicate that traders from the south were bringing in this new material.

The Silesian is often included within the Iron Age as a preliminary period. The extremely late Bronze development such as the Silesian is sometimes called Bronze D. Bronze Age materials of those times when the manufacture of iron had already appeared in southern Europe are called Bronze Age E.

While the metalsmiths in central Europe were learning the secrets of the new metal, iron, there were many cultures on the peripheries of Europe which were fast developing new traditions based upon bronze tools, weapons, and ornaments. The major progression of the Era of Bronze took place in central regions. The variations of European Bronze Age life which took place in other areas of the continent did not exactly coincide in time with the central developments, nor did the culture patterns closely duplicate the Aunjetitz, Tumulus, Lausitz sequence.

CHAPTER II

Variations in Bronze

WHILE the central European development of the Aunjetitiz-Tumulus-Lausitz is a convenient sequence for following the trend of Bronze Age times for most of Europe, these centers were not the only bronze-working areas. Nor indeed were the central European bronze cultures the earliest. The alloying of copper and tin to make bronze had already been initiated at a number of points along the Mediterranean coast of Europe even earlier than the Aunjetitz development in central Europe.

Perhaps the most outstanding of the southern bronze areas was that of Hungary. This center initiated metallurgy earlier than the Aunjetitz farther to the north, and it is evident that the Aunjetitz received its inspiration largely from Hungarian sources. The Hungarian Bronze Age was centered for the most part around the one great site of Tószeg on the middle Tisza in eastern Hungary, an enormous settlement mound with marginal palisading for protection. The houses were rectangular and built of timber on the megaron plan. A number of minor sites in the vicinity of Tószeg were built in much the same way. However, it is from the site of Tószeg itself that most of the sequence of the Hungarian bronze progression has been worked out.

On a basis of house types, pottery, and bronzes, many authorities have divided the Hungarian Bronze Age into four Tószeg periods— I, II, III, and IV. More modern research has tended to reduce this number of Hungarian periods. The four Hungarian bronze periods correspond roughly to the bronze succession in Europe with which there was interchange of ideas. However, the Hungarian Bronze Age shows many differences and is usually treated as a separate entity.

The Bell Beaker period was well represented in Hungary, especially in the northwestern portion of the area. Bell Beaker material found with graves of these trader-wanderers is amazingly consistent. Presumably also during this time, metal became known over trade routes from the Mediterranean and from northern Italy. Of the Amalgamation period, which affected the bulk of Europe, there appears little evidence in Hungary. The Bronze Era began immediately following the Bell Beaker period.

Tószeg I or Tószeg A is roughly contemporaneous with the Marschwitz or pre-Aunjetitz development farther north. Tószeg I is based almost entirely on the Tószeg site, but is found also at the adjacent site of Nagy Rev and at Perjámos in Rumania. Most of the material has been recovered from the dwelling areas. Tószeg graves and other graves of the early Hungarian Bronze Age were almost entirely skeletal and seldom accompanied by bronze grave offerings. Tószeg I pottery was similar to early Aunjetitz ware. Long-necked jars and mugs were typical. Open pedestals were in some cases carry-overs of the Bodrogkeresztur period of the Hungarian area. Large storage jars with straw-brushed decoration were similar in form to Aunjetitz vessels.

It is evident that early Tószeg was a continuation of the previous Hungarian Copper Age. Metal forms indicate that early smiths, familiar with new techniques in the Aegean area, were moving into the Hungarian copper-working centers and even penetrating beyond to the Bohemian tin and copper deposits. It was the working of these deposits which brought the first bronze to Europe.

Bronze work was scarce and scattered in the period of Tószeg I. Many metal pieces from the earliest Hungarian Bronze Age are not from Tószeg at all, but have been recovered from other Hungarian sites. Knot-headed pins, Cypriote pins, trilobate- and racket-headed pins have been identified from this early period. The flat celt was present, as was the halberd, a pointed weapon which was hafted at right angles to the handle. The halberd may have developed from antler picks of ancient form. Finger rings and bronze wire ornaments make up the sketchy repertory of the first Hungarian Bronze Age.

In Tószeg II or Bronze B, the influence from Aunjetitz appears more strongly, constituting an interchange of pottery forms and bronze types. In the Aunjetitz area there was also evidence of Hungarian influences at this same time. Skeletal graves of Tószeg II have yielded some bronzes, but the bulk of the material is from the habitation areas of Tószeg and adjacent sites. The pottery of Tószeg II was of rather exotic outlines with vessels of double *étage* or long-necked pottery pieces. These were characteristically decorated with incised lines into which white paint was rubbed for an incrustation effect. The motifs were parallel lines with curls or tendrils at their ends.

Tószeg II bronzes include flanged celts and even stop-ridge celts. Narrow-bodied celts with high flanges were also present. Some of these forms show the influence of Tumulus bronze work. Dangles and bronze bosses also are suggestive of Tószeg connections with Tumulus centers to the westward. The Aunjetitz rivet-hilted sword was present in Tószeg II, as was the triangular dagger. Large squarish razors and knives were similar to examples from central Europe. Beginning with Tószeg II, Hungarian metal workers had an abundance of bronze at their disposal, as well as skillful methods of working it.

Bronze III in the Hungarian area is sometimes called the *Panonian* Bronze Age. Actually the Panonian was a group of middle Bronze Age sites and cemeteries extending from the Austrian border into central Hungary. There were other groups of Hungarian Bronze Age sites at the same time which are distinguishable by their pottery and bronzes. The Panonian often includes Bronze II and III in this area, and the period is roughly contemporaneous with the Lausitz farther north. It was also the contemporary of the Mycenaean Age in the Aegean area. Some Panonian and middle Bronze Age pottery was decorated with buckles and nipples. Cremation burials occurred as further indication of customs imported from the Urnfield people. In northern Hungary a tumulus-building people persisted from earlier times. In Slavonia inhumation was practiced.

Panonian pottery ware is often referred to as the finest fabric of the Bronze Age. The pottery itself was slipped in orange and black, a very colorful innovation as contrasted to the usual relatively drab European pottery. Furrowing, incision, and stamping, with abundant use of incrustation in white paint, made the Panonian ware further distinctive. The tendrils and curves initiated in Tószeg II reached their full fruition in the curvilinear art of the Panonian. An especially interesting variation is a type of pottery handle which appeared in the Panonian period. This is the *ansa lunata* handle with two widely flaring wings giving the tip of the handle the appearance of a half-moon. This distinctive type of handle appeared also in the Italian Bronze Age.

Panonian bronzes occurred in great profusion. A large variety of straight and early fibula pins appeared. Hungarian hammer-axes and pole-axes were present. Rivet-handled swords and daggers, as well as swords with the handles cast in one piece, were manufactured, and bronze girdle strips and dangles were popular. Large coils of flat bronze rods were apparently used as ornamental breast plates. Manchets, or multiple bracelets, rings, and anklets were also supplied by the Panonian bronze workers.

Tószeg IV, or Bronze IV is, in reality, a period which bridged the Bronze and Iron epochs in the Hungarian area. All burials of this time were cremations with many Lausitz and Knoviz features. The pottery of Tószeg IV was quite similar to Lausitz with buckles and breasts accentuated into points and spikes. Many of these may have imitated metal forms, as the pottery was dark-colored and, in some instances, had a metallic appearance.

The bronzes of Tószeg IV were perhaps the most exotic and plentiful of all of the European forms. Huge spitlike straight pins show the ultimate development of that ornament. Italian one-piece fibulae were found in a number of variations. The spectacle brooch had, in Tószeg IV, achieved spectacular dimensions, with multiple convolutions of heavy bronze wire that would cover the whole breast of the wearer. Bracelets and anklets had increased at this time to enormous puttee-like bands of bronze which were wrapped around legs and arms. These terminated in large spirals. These band leg and arm ornaments were so cumbersome that the wearer must have, in many instances, been rendered almost immobile.

Socketed celts and axes, chisels, and gouges indicated that the late Hungarian bronze craftsmen were influenced by the Lausitz and Knoviz groups. Slashing swords of bronze show the influence from the emerging European Iron Age. Bronze daggers were made with the handle cast in a single piece with the blade. Indigenous Bronze Age groups mixed with Urnfield folk and with Tumulus groups to produce the later, barrow-building Iron Age cultures around the Adriatic, such as that at Glasinač. In Hungary itself the Lausitz invaders mingled with the local groups in Northern Hungary and produced a series of flourishing cultures marked by extensive urn fields.

Perhaps the most interesting of the Bronze IV weapons were the elaborate Hungarian axes. These were pole-axes, for the most part, with a perforated sleeve ornamented with a series of ferrules in the midst of the instrument to accommodate the handle. The axes varied from long, thin, cutting blades to wide battle-ax forms with double blades. Some of the Hungarian ax types contained a spike on either end instead of a cutting edge. Hungarian archaeologists have arranged these ax types into a series to show their development from the simplest ax form to the most complex and highly elaborated variation.

The Hungarian Bronze Age may be seen from these developments to have been one of the most outstanding of all the European centers. Certainly with the abundance of bronze and the skillful techniques, the metalsmiths of Tószeg were dominant. Because of their central geographical position, the Hungarian areas exerted great influence upon bronze centers in surrounding regions.

In addition to the most important Bronze Age development in

Hungary, a parallel progression took place in Italy, especially northern Italy. This northern Italian bronze industry was undoubtedly stimulated by some of the same influences which had initiated the Hungarian centers. There were, however, a number of differences.

The Italian Chalcolithic culture, centered around the site of Remedello in northern Italy, had already established a groundwork of metallurgy. The manufacture of bronze was, then, correspondingly early. The first bronze implements appeared in the northern Italian area possibly as the result of an influx of new colonists who settled in the Po valley. But there were other groups as well who contributed to the Italian Bronze Age.

The use of bronze became implanted among four culture areas or groups of early peoples in northern Italy. First, there were the town cultures of the Po valley and other northern river valleys established by newcomers, possibly from the eastern Mediterranean. These people knew bronze working or received it from Adriatic traders. To the north, on the Alpine slopes, were a number of lake-dwelling peoples, as a lingering remnant of that type of Neolithic culture. These also readily adapted the new art of bronze-making into their cultural structure. Throughout the old lake-dwelling area, many of these settlements extended into the Bronze period. The third group in Italy at the beginning of the Bronze Age consisted of a number of cave-dwellers. These cave-dwelling peoples in the Apennines, Liguria, and elsewhere in the Italian peninsula were Neolithic groups who had persisted in their cave-dwelling habits from earlier periods. These also soon became affected by the use of bronze. The fourth Italian bronze manifestation was that evolving from indigenous Neolithic villages of peasants who had settled in the major river valleys mostly in northern Italy.

The most important of the Italian Bronze Age settlements are the *Terremare*. The name Terremare was derived from the current Italian peasant name for black earth from their long-established habit of deriving fertilizer from these piles. Our chief knowledge of the Terremare culture is derived from the inadequate excavations of Professor Pigorini in the last part of the nineteenth century, especially at the Terremare of Castellazzo di Fontanellato. Professor Pigorini's diggings at this initial site led to the widespread belief that all Terremare were similar to Castellazzo. Subsequent excavations have indicated that this is not the case and that the Terremare of Castellazzo was unique.

Considerable numbers of Terremare occur in the lower Po valley. Other sites of this nature are scattered to the south of the Po. All the classic Terremare are confined to northern Italy, although there are indications that Terremare were established along the eastern coasts of Italy as far as Taranto.

The more formalized Terremare such as Castellazzo were artificial lake dwellings on dry land. These were built in the form of trapezoids, parallelograms, and other geometric shapes. There are indications that most Terremare were not as formalized in plan as at first supposed. Castellazzo was surrounded by an artificial moat in the form of a trapezoid, fronted by an earthen rampart backed by timbers and catwalks. The settlement itself was divided into quarters by bisecting roads or avenues which ran through the center of the settlement at right angles to each other. The dwellings of the Terremare were built on piles erected in the formalized lake maintained by the surrounding moat. At the east portion of the Terremare was a separate area consisting of an earthen terrace surrounded by its own moat. This presumably was the temple area set apart for religious ceremonies. To the southeast were additional separate areas also moated and sustained on piles. On these areas were large wooden buildings used for burial of the dead. The bodies were cremated and placed in funerary urns stacked within the charnel structure.

From this layout, many classical scholars have postulated the beginnings of the formalized Roman camp. It was even suggested that a Terremare existed beneath the Forum Romanum. The Roman camp as described by Caesar many centuries later did bear a remarkable resemblance to the oriented arrangement of Castellazzo. However, other Terremare do not uphold this theory. There are Terremare sites in the Po valley which are irregular in plan, circular, or oval. Most of the other examples also presented little attempt at orientation.

The abundant remains on the Terremare mounds indicated that the inhabitants were farmers and stock raisers. Some of the Terremare were provided with central enclosures for the corralling of stock. Bones from the fertilizer mounds show that the Terremare of the Bronze Age knew and used oxen, sheep, goats, horses, asses, pigs, cats, ducks, and other fowl. Most of these features were derived from foregoing Neolithic people in this same area. There were, however, a number of indications that the Terremare dwellers were intrusive in the Po valley. Professor Pigorini believed that they were derived from some lake-dwelling groups as evidenced by their insistence on moating and pile foundations. Other authorities are of the opinion that the Terremare were offshoots of Tószeg in Hungary from the presence of *ansa lunata,* or moon-shaped handles, on pottery. This feature was also found in Apulia and Greece as well as at Tószeg. Bone and horn cheek pieces from horse bridle-bits indicate the Terremare knew and used the horse and probably the war chariot. The bridle-bit is a European invention which occurred also in the second mound at Tószeg, or Tószeg B, where a series of palisades around the settlement mound is suggestive of the Terremare arrangement. However, the burials at Tószeg were not the cremations typical of the Terremare. Thus Tószeg may have contributed to Terremare developments, but the latter certainly is not a colony spawned by Tószeg.

Other Terremare pottery consisted for the most part of large numbers of hemispherical or ovoid ossuary urns. Ordinary pottery was ornamented with incision, furrowing, and appliqué. Terremare potters produced large numbers of clay models and figurines.

Perhaps the greatest clue as to the origin of the Terremare people was their habit of cremating their dead. This practice was foreign to Neolithic Italy, arising in more northerly Bronze Age regions and culminating in the Urnfield practices at the last of the Bronze period. Following this clue, the Terremare may well have been some northern group who entered Italy through the Alpine passes, absorbing lake-dwelling characteristics as they progressed. With influences from Tószeg and additional stimuli from Adriatic contacts, the brilliant Terremare culture was probably a combination of backgrounds, rather than a single one.

All of the Italian Bronze cultures shared a common bronze heritage. The hut-dwelling cultures of the Po region interchanged materials and ideas with their neighbors, the Terremare. Apennine cave dwellers and Alpine lake-dwelling cultures also traded bronze work. For these reasons, generally, the Italian Bronze Age may be divided into a number of convenient periods. Some authorities recognize two, and others three, phases of Italian progression. Most of the evidence seems to indicate an introductory bronze phase or Phase I. This was a period in which bronzes were being introduced and local alloying developed. The second phase was the fully developed Italian Bronze Age. This paralleled Tumulus and Lausitz developments to the north and the Hungarian development which culminated in the Panonian period and Tószeg. It was to this second phase of the Italian Bronze Age that the Terremare development belonged.

Local metallurgy of the fully developed Italian Bronze Age produced a wide variety of artifacts. Most of these have been recovered from hoards, some of which appear to have been votive in nature rather than simply depositions made by merchants for safekeeping.

A large part of Italian hoards consisted of winged and flanged celts. The socketed celt was rare and very late in Italy. The triangular dagger, especially a round-heeled variety, was made throughout peninsular Italy. Examples with the handle cast in one piece with the blade in the Mycenaean manner were also common. The halberd appeared in several simple forms, apparently an import from western Europe. Swords, short and broad, with spiked tangs, knives with concavo-convex cutting edges, also were part of the Italian Bronze Age tradition. Sickles, razors, combs, and tweezers of bronze were used. Horse bits, chisels, and pieces of bronze used for plowshares indicated a growing tendency of the smiths to use bronze for utilitarian purposes. Fibulae appeared at the very end of the Italian progression. The commonest form of Italian fibula is the so-called "violin bow" type which was made in one piece according to the southern fibula tradition.

In addition to bronze objects, the hoards and occasional graves also contained amber beads and amber disks. A few glass beads show Mediterranean connections with Egypt. Thus the Terremare and other bronze peoples of fully developed Italian Bronze Age traded for their amber with the Baltic coasts on the one hand and the eastern Mediterranean on the other.

From these elements, it may be seen that the Italian Bronze Age was progressive in its development. Farming and stock-raising methods were particularly advanced at this time, with a wide range of grains and domestic animals. These developments formed a firm basis for the subsequent Iron Age in Italy and the later Roman civilization which drew all of these elements together.

The Bronze Age of the Iberian Peninsula was, in general, an isolated one. Although in previous times there had been considerable interrelation between Spain and Italy by way of Sardinia, this liaison had weakened by Bronze Age times. Even the sea routes through the Mediterranean seem to have lessened in importance during the middle and last of the second millennium. The Megalithic, with its dominating religion and burial cult, lost its importance. The development which had started at Los Millares and spread over most of the Iberian Peninsula around the turn of the third millennium also lost its force.

The Bronze Age apparently started in Spain not far from the original inception of the Los Millares development in Almeria. The site usually associated with the Spanish Bronze period is the great fortified town of El Argar which evidently was flourishing about the middle of the second millennium before Christ. El Argar was a fortified settlement built on top of a hill by invaders who overcame the local inhabitants of Los Millares tradition. Other Bronze Age sites in the vicinity of Almeria include El Oficio and Fuente Alamo. The *Argaric* culture center extended from Almeria to Valencia. The inspiration for all of these appears to have been a sea-borne invasion. In spite of these tenuous trade connections by sea, however, the Spanish Bronze Age as characterized at El Argar was relatively late when compared with other European bronze-working centers.

Earlier, sophisticated traditions of architecture continued at El Argar. Quadrate stone houses were predominant, and cut stone was handled with considerable skill. This tradition in stone architecture was, of course, in sharp contrast to the relatively crude wooden and log buildings of more northerly European Bronze cultures. Graves at El Argar were made in cists, often formed in the house walls themselves. Cremations were infrequent but were practiced on occasion, no doubt an influence from northerly regions where this practice was the rule.

Over the rest of Spain, the Bronze Age was marked by various degenerate combinations of Megalithic traditions and El Argar influence. In places in the north and west of the Iberian Peninsula, the Megalithic cult maintained itself. In these regions also, the Bell Beaker tradition continued into Bronze Age times.

The pottery of El Argar was possibly stimulated by the Aunjetitz from some distant overland trade-route connections. The forms are for the most part simple and pleasing in outline. Carinated bowls and jars with sharply splayed shoulders, pedestal forms, and egg cup types were typical of El Argar wares. These vessels were polished but otherwise undecorated. The color was universally dark with the polished surface and classic outlines. El Argar ceramic ware ranks high among European traditions.

The bronze working of El Argar, although showing little direct connection with other bronze centers in Europe, roughly paralleled the major European trends. Generally the El Argar bronze industries, in spite of the fact that large quantities of metal were available in the Spanish area, were retarded in technique and form. The flat celt, for example, continued to be used, especially in an El Argar form with a wide-bitted blade. Only occasionally did El Argar craftsmen manufacture celts provided with flanges which other European bronze workers had already recognized as a superior form. Late in the Bronze Age the socketed celt was finally developed in the Catalonian area of Spain.

The other forms of El Argar bronze work, although late in actual date, reflected early developments in the rest of Europe. Pins, bracelets, awls, chisels, and arrowheads were of conventional types of early manufacture. Triangular daggers, and stunted flat swords were also made. The halberd appeared in the El Argar bronze work as it did in Italy. The Spanish halberd was a simple type with a long triangular blade strengthened by a mid-rib.

Silver and gold were commonly used by El Argar craftsmen. Ornaments of rings, diadems, bracelets, and anklets in these rare metals were often placed with the dead in El Argar graves. Beads of many kinds of stone and shell were also common, and those of imported callais, a turquoise-like stone, were often placed with the

El Argar dead. In one instance, blue faïence Egyptian beads accompanied an El Argar burial.

Connections with the eastern Mediterranean, although tenuous, were indubitably present in the Argaric culture. In addition to the Egyptian faïence, the inhabitants of El Argar used palettes of schist such as those common in the Aegean. Clay altars at El Argar, with hornlike projections on their sides, were inspired by Cretan altars of the same general design.

With the dwindling of the sea routes which had carried the Megalithic complex widely throughout the Mediterranean area and along the Atlantic coasts, trade by land increased. Of those routes in western Europe, none was more important than that in the Rhone valley. Up the Rhone ran a natural corridor of movement by which influences from northern Italy on the one hand and northern Spain on the other might make contact with Tumulus and Aunjetitz centers farther to the north. In the valley of the Rhone there developed, during the late Bronze Age, a distinctive province of metal working. This has been called by many authorities the *Rhone culture*.

The Rhone culture was, in general, an outgrowth of the Aunjetitz with a large number of north Italian features. Spanish influence was slight. Especially outstanding in the Rhone culture was a dagger with a bronze hilt. The skill of the Rhone craftsmen in casting bronze-hilted daggers was indicative of the high level of their metal work. Many kinds of straight pins, torques, and bracelets are reminiscent of Aunjetitz types. Money torques, or talents, were common in the Rhone culture.

In Brittany, the Armorican culture was established apparently from northern Italy on the one hand and from Iberian sources from northern Spain on the other. The Armorican Bronze Age was already present in Brittany when the Tumulus development began in those areas. The Armorican was the major inspiration for the *British Wessex culture* of Bronze Age date.

The influence of the Bronze Age also profoundly affected the Alpine region where, in Neolithic times, the lake-dwelling cultures had arisen in a number of variations. Aunjetitz influences pervaded the Alpine regions from the east and north. On the west, Bronze Age movements along the same routes which had been traveled by the western Neolithic peoples brought metal usage into the areas of the western Alps. The Italian Alps to the south also paralleled the other areas in Bronze Age development. Such sites as the lake-dwelling of Morges on Lake Geneva was a Bronze Age manifestation, closely connected with the Rhone culture. Typical of late Bronze Age lake-dwelling or crannog sites is Wasserburg-bei-Buchau, near the Federsee Moor at Buchau, which was a crannog town built in a marsh. At Buchau were two large settlements, both of them late Bronze Age in date, consisting of a palisaded town built on an earthen platform in a shallow lake or marsh. Houses were rectangular and scattered in plan. One central house divided into two rooms seemed to be the hall of a petty king. Pottery of Buchau showed flowerpot forms, amphora, and even degenerate bell breakers, suggesting a dozen crosscurrents and connections from earlier times.

One of the most significant Bronze Age developments of western Europe was that which took place in Brittany. Armorican Bronze Age Bretons had continued a different form of culture somewhat reminiscent of the Single-grave type which appeared in northern Europe in the late Neolithic. The Bretons buried their dead in large stone cairns with a corbeled vault in the interior. These were essentially different from the Megalithic tradition. Large numbers of bronze and flint grave goods were placed in the cairns. Flint arrowheads of beautiful manufacture were very common offerings. Long knives, especially those of the honey-colored flint from Grand Pressigny were also used. Bronze was made into axes with low flanges and triangular daggers with a small nib or projection on the butt of the blade for the accommodation of the hilt.

The pottery which occurred in the Breton Bronze Age was generally made in tall forms with high shoulders with a special form for ritualistic purposes. Band handles for decorations were usual.

A distinctive feature of the Armorican Bronze Age was the presence of gold in the ornamentation of dagger sheaths and dagger hilts. The gold, in the form of tiny nails, was studded in a pointillé technique of great beauty. Such ornament indicated the great skill of these people in the handling of metal.

The bronze development in the region of Brittany was influenced by the inland Tumulus centers. The Tumulus people, with an ethnic background derived from the Corded warrior folk of earlier Neolithic times, had become dominant throughout this whole area. These warrior people with their barrow type of burial moved westward and entered the previously Megalithic region of Brittany. The later Breton Bronze Age as we now know it was undoubtedly a result of this fusion.

Brittany was a major route by which Bronze Age ideas entered the British Isles. Barrow-building people with a knowledge of bronze moved across the intervening water and landed in the British Isles near the mouths of the Stouer and the Avon. From here they spread through Wessex, leaving behind their distinctive Tumulus burials and indications of their metal work.

It was the Beaker folk who were the first carriers of metal to the British Isles and the British Bronze Age properly opens with the several Beaker invasions. One group of Beaker folk, originating presumably in Spain, made their way along the Atlantic coasts to Brittany and the Channel Islands and from there on to Britain. Other Beaker adventurers mingled with the Battle-ax people in central Europe and with this mixture occupied the lowlands in northwest Europe. From these shores the mixed Beaker adventurers sailed across the Channel and the North Sea to land in Britain along the coast from Sussex and Kent to northern Scotland. A few Beaker colonists even reached as far as Ireland and the Orkneys. These Beaker newcomers ruthlessly dispossessed the original inhabitants of Britain or drove them to less favorable terrain. Thus the earlier Windmill Hill people were largely overawed by the Beaker invaders. The Peterborough people, living in less attractive territory, did not compete with the incoming Beaker folk and so survived.

The combination of Beaker folk with the Peterborough Neolithic produced the *Food Vessel culture,* so called from distinctive pottery vessels which differed radically from the earlier beaker forms. The Food Vessel culture became established in the north including Scotland, Wales, and Ireland.

In southern Britain, another combination with earlier Neolithic folk produced the *Urn culture,* again named from a distinguishable pottery urn. The Urn culture also spread to include much of the areas of the Food Vessel people and was well established by the middle of the second millennium before Christ.

About 1400 B.C. a group of bronze-using warriors came across the Channel from Brittany bringing with them the knowledge of the Armorican Bronze Age already so well established there. These invaders had wide trade connections and soon established more in Ireland and the Baltic. The Bronze Age Armoricans in southern Britain became the *Wessex* culture, Wessex being their first foothold in England. Other centers were established along England's southern coasts as far as Cornwall. The Wessex culture was chiefly known for the barrow graves of important chieftains of this group.

Barrow and cairn building, as practiced in Brittany, was carried over into the Wessex area in the form of the bell barrow. This form of mound burial was a tumulus surrounded by a ditch with an intervening shoulder or berm. The cross section of this special type of monument appears somewhat like a bell. Furthermore, funerary deposits made with these barrow burials were similar to the Breton work. Triangular bronze daggers, particularly a few examples with hilts studded by tiny gold nails, were remarkably parallel to certain Breton examples. Two types of ceremonial pottery also appeared in the British Isles as a carry-over from Breton ceramic ware. A small type of vessel known as the grape cup from the appliquéd knobs of clay on its surface, as well as another diminutive form with white inlaid decoration, indicated that the Breton ritual was carried over into the British Isles. In addition to exact parallels with those of Brittany, these new Bronze Age invaders had a wealth of grave goods. Flat and flanged bronze axes, as well as gold and amber items, appeared with their burials in considerable quantity.

The climax of the southern British Bronze Age was reached in the great ceremonial structures such as Stonehenge in Wessex. The religious fervor represented by this monument was a combination of Megalithic, Beaker, and other Neolithic elements, augmented by the infusion of new ideas from Brittany brought by the Wessex people. This hybrid combination produced a vigor which resulted in the awesome monuments of prehistoric Britain. Most of the rough stone structures such as that at Stonehenge were actually begun in Megalithic or Beaker times. There are evidences of previous and earlier building at Stonehenge with later remodeling and changes. Apparently the earlier building of this great monument was at least as early as the Beaker period, but in its final form it was a great center of Bronze Age activity. Large numbers of Bronze Age barrows surround Stonehenge to indicate that it was a funerary center of great importance in later times.

In its final form Stonehenge was perhaps originally consecrated in Pembrokeshire and then transported bodily to Salisbury Plain. The technique of this gigantic monument appears Megalithic. In time, its greatest use certainly occurred in the Bronze Age.

While these events were transpiring in the south, the northern British Bronze Age was already developing. In these regions also, the Megalithic laid the foundation for Bronze Age culture. The knowledge of the metal itself apparently came by sea. The original invasion of bronze-using and barrow-building people from Brittany did not reach into northern Britain and Scotland as there were many groups of intervening Neolithic peoples. Rather, the northern bronze cultures seem to have received their own stimuli and followed their own course of development. The village of Skara Brae in the Orkneys survived until Bronze Age times, although these people used no metal. The inhabitants of this remarkable site were not Beaker folk but were probably displaced by the Beaker invasions and forced to move out to the distant and inhospitable Orkneys. From Skara Brae an extraordinarily complete picture of the secular life of the times has been reconstructed from the excavations in the drifting sands which finally overwhelmed the site and preserved it.

In northern Britain, the fusion of Peterborough Neolithic and Beaker folk with some Passage-grave people produced the Food Vessel culture in middle Bronze Age times. The Food Vessel people were largely nomadic, although they traded in Irish bronze and gold, and some of them settled along the trade routes. Ireland had become, during middle Bronze Age times, one of the centers of mining and the manufacture of metal articles. It was this hardware which the Food Vessel people traded and used.

Perhaps most interesting of the contents of the burials of these people, which were usually made within a stone circle, are their food vessels. These food vessels occurred in two types. The most common is known as the Yorkshire vase or Food Vessel B. This was a flat-based cylindrical type of pot with a short shoulder. Apparently it was a carry-over from one of the northern Beaker types and was evolved earlier than the Bronze period in Britain. Another type of food vessel was a variety found in Ireland and called the Irish or A type, a round-bottomed bowl with incised and stamped ornament over sides and bottom. Food vessels of many other variations occurred as combinations of these fundamental types. There seemed to be considerable influence from preceding Beaker types as well as an incipient wood-carving tradition. Pots of the food-vessel family occurred in many Bronze Age and stone ring graves. These were commonest in the north, especially in Scotland. Indeed, there is considerable evidence that Scotland was the point of origin of the food-vessel forms of pottery.

Ireland was, during these times, a most important center of metal working. Ireland also provided cultural crosscurrents and trade which affected the British Isles as well as the Atlantic coast of Europe. Megalithic sea routes between the Iberian Peninsula and Ireland and between Ireland and Baltic areas were apparently still used during the time of the spread of metal. Ireland became a center of bronze working and gold working in its own right. The tin for the manufacture of bronze apparently came from Cornwall.

Irish Bronze Age monuments were usually in the form of degenerate megaliths and passage-graves. Stone-ring burial was common during these times, with the interment made singly as opposed to the collective burials of the preceding Megalithic ritual. Pottery accompanying the Irish Bronze Age burials was essentially of two types. The first of these persisted from a preceding Passage-grave period. The second major type, apparently flourishing during the middle Bronze Age, was the Irish type of food vessel or Type A. The Type A food vessel, with its characteristic round-bottomed outline, occurred also in southwestern Scotland, indicating trade connections in this direction. It is difficult to ascertain whether this type of food vessel was an Irish innovation or a borrowed form.

One of the most distinctive of the Irish metal forms was the copper flat-ax which was later manufactured in bronze with the addition of Cornish tin. This peculiar type of flat-ax was most common

Statuette of Minoan Snake Goddess in ivory and gold, 16th century B.C.

Etruscan terracotta, 6th to 5th century B.C. statue of warrior, probably votive.

Tarquinia: Tomba del Triclinio. Etruscan painting of a dancer, early 5th century B.C.

A GROUP OF VESSELS

Top left: Vase, three handles, decoration of scrolls in palace style, said to be from Knossos, Late Minoan period (ca. 1500–1400 B.C.).
Courtesy The Metropolitan Museum of Art, Rogers Fund, 1922

Top right: Stirrup jar, octopi and other fish, terracotta, Mycenaean, 1230–1135 B.C.
Courtesy The Metropolitan Museum of Art, Louisa Eldridge McBurney Gift Fund, 1953

Below, left: Amphora, IV Cypriote Mycenaean ware, later Bronze Age II, pottery.
Courtesy Museum of Fine Arts, Boston

Below, right: Bucket of bronze with scenes from life, found in Watch.
Courtesy Bettmann Archive

in Ireland but extended into Scotland and appeared at several points in England. This same flat-ax was also traded into Sweden and Denmark.

This trend of trade may also be traced through a number of other Irish metallic items, notably the halberd. The evidence seems strong that the halberd actually originated in Ireland and from there was traded or copied throughout many parts of Europe. The preponderance and variation of the halberd type of weapon was greatest in Ireland, perhaps being derived there from flint or wooden prototypes. Irish types of halberds were traded into Scotland and at several points in Great Britain. These same forms also occurred in the Baltic area, whence they were apparently carried from Irish sources. Irish halberd forms, occurring in such widely diverse areas as Italy, Spain, and central Germany, are more difficult to explain. It may be, however, that by devious trade routes the halberd idea reached even these remote areas.

Gold work from Ireland, perhaps because of its spectacular nature, has received more attention. Bronze Age Irish workers made a number of gold forms which may be associated with a religious complex, perhaps derived from the Iberian Peninsula. Plaques from Iberian Megalithic tombs are remarkably similar to some Irish gold work.

Gold was beaten into sheets and made into lunulae, or flat gold collars, lozenge- and rectangular-shaped plaques, and into gold mountings for amber beads and cone-shaped pieces of stone. Small objects were often coated with sheet gold, and occasionally utensils were beaten from gold, such as the famous cordoned cup from Rillaton. The lunulae and the plaques were perhaps the most distinctive and were usually ornamented with parallel lines in simple geometric arrangements.

Lunulae and plaques of the Irish type have been found in France, Denmark, and at several other spots along the Baltic coasts. These were essentially the same trade connections along which other Irish influences moved. Perhaps Irish gold was traded in one direction for Baltic amber in the other.

In addition to the spectacular Irish gold work were some peculiar necklaces which occurred in the same complex. These were made of amber in some instances, but in many graves these multiple neck-laces were made of lignite or jet, apparently as a substitute for amber. These multiple-necklace types also occurred in Scottish graves and farther northeastward in the Baltic region.

The Bronze Age movement of people from Brittany into the British Isles showed strong contacts with these Irish centers of trade. Their barrow burials were often enriched with typically Irish gold work. These Breton invaders also had large amounts of amber traded from the Baltic. Generally speaking, the Bronze Age of southern Britain and that of Ireland accomplished the most. Eastern regions of the British Isles, in many instances, had little metal or traded for less valuable flint items of preceding times. The northern portion of the British Isles, stimulated by the crosscurrents of foreign trade from the Irish metal-working centers on the one hand and the Baltic amber-producing areas on the other, was more prominent. None of the Bronze Age developments in the British Isles, however, were other than peripheral manifestations of earlier happenings on continental Europe. For this reason, most of the British Bronze Age was comparatively late. Bronze developments in the British Isles lingered perhaps two hundred years behind the succession of events on the mainland of Europe. The Bronze Age continued in Britain long after the use of iron appeared on the continent.

The Bronze Age in Scandinavia and the Baltic was also late. Up to this time these northern regions had maintained a Neolithic economy. Actually, the Scandinavian Bronze Age did not begin until Bronze Age III and the Urnfield period in central Europe. In spite of its late date, however, the Scandinavian Bronze Age was distinguished by rich burials and hoards with many types of Bronze Age objects. Scandinavian chronologists have divided the Bronze Age in the Baltic area into a number of periods. Even in Period I, however, forms developed which were late in Britain and Europe.

In spite of its late inception, the Scandinavian Bronze Age may be described as brilliant. A plethora of tools, weapons, and ornaments were deposited with rich burials in this area as an indication of the new wealth of the owners of these sepulchers. Undoubtedly these newly rich chieftains of the Scandinavian area were the descendants of the Megalithic builders who had earlier expended much energy in building rough stone tombs. Now they turned these energies to the working of metal. Tombs were large barrows and bronze items were liberally interred with the dead.

At the very last of the Bronze Age in Scandinavia, the influence of the Urnfield folk initiated a change to cremation burial in urns. Cremation had become dominant by Period III in Scandinavia and Denmark. The Urnfield method of burial had also reached most other areas of western Europe by this time. These northern and western regions of Europe were evolving their Bronze Age during the centuries when iron was already changing the course of history and the lives of other peoples in southern Europe.

CHAPTER 12

Iron

Dᴜʀɪɴɢ ᴛʜᴇ ᴄᴇɴᴛᴜʀɪᴇꜱ in which a knowledge of the manufacture and use of bronze was spreading to all parts of Europe, other developments were taking place in the Near East. Chief among these was the discovery of a new kind of metal—iron.

Actually, iron in its natural form had been used in very ancient times, certainly as early as the Neolithic. Fragments of meteoric iron had occasionally been found by early peoples searching for new stony materials. Metallic meteorites, with their characteristic heavy weight, had attracted early man, but he saw in them only a new and intriguing material for the manufacture of celts, axes, chisels, or ornaments. The early use of meteoric iron in no sense initiated a metallic age.

Even the early use of copper and subsequently bronze was not in itself introductory to the use of iron. Furnaces and equipment for the reduction of copper and tin from their respective ores were relatively simple, and the metallurgy of these processes uncomplicated.

Iron, on the other hand, is difficult to reduce to a metallic state from its normal compounds as found in nature.

Copper ores were discovered by early Europeans in only a few areas where these substances could be successfully mined and the copper extracted. Tin was even scarcer. The location of these ores had determined the centers of manufacture of the Bronze Age in early Europe. Iron ores, on the other hand, are relatively abundant and occur in many localities where copper is scarce or absent.

In spite of the abundance of iron ore, however, the smelting of iron was not easy nor was it discovered simply because of this abundance. Even with good grades of iron ore, which occurs in nature usually in the form of iron oxides, a very high temperature is necessary to separate the oxygen from the iron. A temperature of 1,535 degrees Centigrade is necessary to reduce iron ore to its metallic state. Even with this process successfully completed, the elements recombine as soon as the mixture is cool. It is necessary to introduce into the furnace with the iron ore a new substance called a flux. The flux combines with the molten impurities during the smelting process and is poured off in the form of slag. It is only in this way that the molten iron can be isolated.

In order to achieve the high temperatures for the successful smelting of iron, a more complicated furnace and forge was necessary than in the case of bronze. Enough oxygen had to be supplied to raise the temperature sufficiently to melt a mixture of iron ore and flux. The usual flux used was limestone. The molten and very impure iron produced by this process was shaped into the desired forms by subsequent hammering. The hammering process produced a form of iron called wrought iron. This method of working the iron makes a tough, somewhat soft iron product which collects on its surface a black scale. Since this blacksmiths' scale is resistant to oxidation, wrought iron is more readily rust-resistant than other forms of iron and thus is usually better preserved in archaeological deposits. Cast iron was a product of much later times and is a brittle substance unsuitable for weapons or tools.

The smelting of iron from its ores was, then, a very complicated process. It involved a series of discoveries or developments rather than a single invention. The development of iron was probably not the work of any single individual. The first smelting apparently took place on the periphery of Mesopotamia. Iron deposits in the Taurus and anti-Taurus region were of sufficiently high quality to supply the background for these beginnings. Sporadic pieces of wrought iron were being manufactured in and around Mesopotamia by 2500 B.C. A few pieces of Mesopotamian iron work may go back as far as the third millennium. In these few instances, however, the new metal was obviously of great value and was treated as a precious commodity rather than a workable metal. Iron appears in the Dynasty XVIII in Egypt, apparently as an import from Mesopotamia. It was the Hittites of Asia Minor who began to work iron on a large scale and who spread the practice to other peoples of the eastern Mediterranean. Its use, especially for swords and rapiers, was adopted in the Aegean area, Crete, and the mainland of Greece. Greeks were familiar with the use of iron by the end of the second millennium before Christ.

It must not be supposed that iron immediately replaced bronze in all of these regions. Iron was an ugly material and hence not in demand for the manufacture of ornaments. Bronze, on the other hand, especially when patinated green with time and perspiration, was far more beautiful for bracelets, rings, torques, and other items of personal adornment. Bronze continued to be used in large quantities even in those areas where iron was introduced and the process of smelting was learned. Iron was superior for swords and cutting weapons. An iron sword could cleave through a helmet made of bronze or cut away large pieces of a bronze shield, whereas a bronze weapon would have been ineffective against these defenses. The superiority of iron for the manufacture of weapons and ultimately for helmets, shields, and protection against weapons was a primary reason for the rapid spread of this new material. Peoples of the eastern Mediterranean, who first armed themselves with iron swords, were more powerful than those of cultures farther to the west and north who still used only bronze weapons.

The Hittites of Asia Minor certainly had worked out smelting techniques and transformed the metal into wrought iron swords. These swords probably accounted for the great power and spread of the Hittite Empire, which remained great so long as its people held a monopoly on iron weapons. When the Hittite Empire fell, the knowledge of iron working was spread to surrounding regions. The secret of iron smelting had been learned by several peoples in the Near East by the middle of the second millennium before Christ.

An even more cogent reason for the spread of iron was the abundance of the ore. Iron deposits occurred almost everywhere in Europe, so that no tribe or small merchant group had a monopoly on its manufacture or trade, and the tribes of Europe were eager to learn the process by which they could make their own iron.

Following the introduction of iron into Greece and the island of Crete, the mainland of Europe received a knowledge of the new material from the Greeks and the Classic peoples of Italy. The introduction of iron was accomplished in this way around the year 1000 B.C., although most areas of Europe were not able to make their own iron weapons until much later.

Iron developments in the region at the head of the Adriatic are usually connected with the Illyrians. These people were a group of mixed ancestry who have left abundant evidence of their iron handiwork as mortuary deposits in their cemeteries. Illyrian mound-field cemeteries contained some thousands of tumuli under which the dead were buried. Most of the Illyrian tumuli cemeteries are located on or near the Istrian Peninsula near modern Trieste.

Excavations at Santa Lucia, the mound field of Istria, Glasinač, and at other points in Illyrian territory have shown the general nature of early European iron work.

The first European Iron period has been named after a discovery which was made in the upper Austrian Alps. Near the small village of Hallstatt, in a hanging valley, a large cemetery was accidentally discovered in 1894. In this peculiar location, peasants, digging drainage ditches in a marshy hay field, came across a number of burials. Excavations in the valley of Hallstatt over a period of years have revealed that these burials were of several types. Because many of the bodies were accompanied by long iron swords and other articles of iron, the cemetery of Hallstatt was accepted as typical of the earliest European Iron Age development, which has been termed the *Hallstatt period*.

Actually, the designation of Hallstatt for the period of the first

Iron Age is unfortunate because it implies that Europe was at this time united in a single variety of culture, the outstanding feature of which was iron. This was not the case. Equally misleading is the use of the name Hallstatt by some authorities to designate certain late Bronze Age cultures which had no iron at all.

Part of the burials in the little Hallstat valley were of cremated remains, and some were only partially cremated. This was obviously a mixture of burial customs, and the graves appeared to have been made over a considerable period of time. A difficult point to determine at Hallstatt was the provenience of the population involved. No town site or other center was found near the Hallstatt cemetery. The most likely explanation is that the persons buried at Hallstatt represented a garrison guarding the trade routes that led through the Alpine passes. It was over these routes that such items as salt, and later iron weapons, were traded.

The original Hallstatt collection recovered by excavator Ramsauer, the manager of the near-by salt mines, consisted of large numbers of bronze and iron swords, iron poignards, lances, arrows, axes, utensils, helmets, and armor. Ornaments included girdles with stamped bronze plates, fibulae, pins, bracelets, pendant chains and beads. A number of gold pieces and ornaments of amber and glass were also present. An exceptionally fine series of bronze vases, situlae, cups, and plates were also recovered from the Hallstatt cemetery. Among these were some bronze pieces of Italian workmanship.

Several later excavations at the cemetery at Hallstatt have verified the mixed nature of this culture. Examination of the Hallstatt civilization as it was found in various parts of Europe indicated that the Urnfield cultures of the late Bronze Age paved the way for the Hallstatt. In peripheral areas, the precedents of the Hallstatt are missing. Essentially it was a central European development, centering more specifically in the southeastern Alpine region. The inspiration for the Hallstatt was supplied from the Iron Ages of Greece and Italy. During the *Geometric period* or the so-called Dark Ages of Greece, this type of culture became well known in the Italian area. During the formation of the Hallstatt, fresh inspiration was derived from these same sources.

The late Bronze Age, as well as the antecedents of the First Iron

Age, were marked by the movements of the Urnfield folk with their typical bronze types and cremations. The mixed nature of the Hallstatt reflects the expansion of the Urnfield people and their mixture with a variety of cultures. Urnfield folk moved into western Europe and mingled with several Tumulus groups there. Other Urnfield tribes moved south and southwestward to carry their culture across the Pyrenees into Spanish Catalonia. Other groups with Urnfield types of burial moved down the Rhine to the North Sea. Many of the cemeteries of these mixed times featured cremated burials in urns, with a tumulus over the grave. Urnfield people who crossed the Channel to settle in southern England are known as the *Deverel-Rimbury cultures* in Britain.

To the south also, Urnfield peoples moved in a series of migrations. To the southeast, Urnfield influences mixed with the old Painted Pottery and Warrior elements who did not cremate their dead. The Illyrians around the head of the Adriatic were affected by Urnfield customs and indeed may have arisen from an actual Urnfield tribe that settled there. In Italy, Urnfield folk contributed to the final phases of the Terremare towns, and there is evidence that Urnfield invaders may actually have overcome the Terremare. These same invaders lingered to form the centers which left large cemeteries at Bologna and Este in northern Italy. The Villanovans, the name given to the people who left their urn fields around Bologna, had much to do with the following Iron Age.

Villanovans from the centers around Bologna crossed the Apennines into Latium and into Etruria, a region named for the Etruscans. In these centers of later Roman culture, these newcomers, called Southern Villanovans, contributed to classical cultures. Indeed, the Southern Villanovans were probably identical with the tribe later called Latins who spoke an early form of the Latin language. The Villanovans then were an Indo-European-speaking group who derived their knowledge of iron from Greek sources. The Villanovans' main remains are in large cemeteries in central and upper Italy which marked the course of their culture. Based upon excavations at these cemeteries, a chronology has been worked out. In the very earliest of the Villanovan remains, iron was still rare. Soon, however, it gained in popularity and became common by the period called *Benacci III*.

Benacci is one of these late Bronze Age and early Iron Age cemeteries.

Even during the course of the Villanovan development, however, bronze was still the commonest metal. The early Iron Age was actually a Bronze Age if considered by percentages. The most distinctive Villanovan pieces were beautifully decorated bronze buckets or situlae ornamented with registers of raised figures. Italian work of this sort was traded northward and became a part of Hallstatt beginnings. Bronze urns of Italian manufacture were found in late Bronze Age hoards and sites of central Europe. This would place the whole Villanovan development somewhat earlier. Some authorities doubt that the Hallstatt Iron Age was inspired entirely from Italy and point out that the trade and influences might have traveled in the other direction.

Iron smelting was at this time known in Greece and Macedonia. From these areas the knowledge may have passed to the Illyrians or by sea to the Villanovan centers. But whether directly from traveling smiths or indirectly from culture to culture, a knowledge of iron and iron smelting reached the area north and west of the Danube about 900 B.C.

If the Hallstatt was inspired from the Italian Iron Age, it soon achieved its own individuality. In addition to Hallstatt pottery, which, like that of most other European cultures, was distinctive, the iron swords and fibulae were also indicative of the spread of the culture. Fibulae, although a development of the late Bronze Age, were far more typical of Iron Age times. It has been suggested that Hallstatt be confined only to those peoples using the Hallstatt long sword made of either iron or bronze. Professor Childe has pointed out that the Hallstatt sword, with a long blade differentiated for thrusting and slashing, is really a cavalry weapon. The real Hallstatt was then a culture of mounted knights armed with these swords, and Hallstatt pottery occasionally depicts warriors on horseback. Hallstatt chieftains were often buried with horses or with horses hitched to chariots. The true Hallstatt culture was probably carried by mounted warriors rather than by traveling ironsmiths or traders.

From the type site of Hallstatt, in the Saltzkammergut, these mounted and armed men spread the knowledge of iron in Europe. It has been usual to recognize several regional variations of the Hallstatt culture. A southeastern Adriatic group, including the Dinaric Alps, Bosnia, Croatia, and other portions of Yugoslavia, was a variation based upon the Illyrian Iron Age development, obviously closely allied to the Hallstatt proper. A central or Danubian Hallstatt included western Hungary, Bohemia, and Austria. Actually, there was little iron influence in the middle Danube basin before the Second Iron Age around 400 B.C. A northeastern Hallstatt centering in the Elbe-Oder region developed some variations. The western spread of the Hallstatt in eastern France, Switzerland, and southern Germany may be recognized. There were Hallstatt movements into the British Isles, and differences developed there. There was also a very late Hallstatt development in the Iberian Peninsula.

In such peripheral areas as Spain, Britain, and Scandinavia, the coming of iron was considerably later than its development in central Europe. Much of the peripheral Hallstatt was not true Hallstatt in the sense that it was carried by mounted knights armed with typical Hallstatt swords.

The Hallstatt development proper was smelting and using iron weapons by 800 B.C. The spread of the new knowledge over Europe occupied the next three or four centuries. There were the usual peripheral developments of bronze weapons made in imitation of iron forms, and the increasing use and cheapness of iron accounts for the almost complete abandonment of stone tools. The superiority of iron swords caused the rapid dispersal of a knowledge of iron over the trade routes of Europe. Iron-using people began to move into the British Isles by the sixth century B.C. and were well established there by the fifth century B.C. It was in these late times also that the knowledge of iron reached Spain and Scandinavia.

In spite of the chronological variations and certain cultural differences in the Hallstatt in various parts of Europe, the use of iron produced a number of universal changes. Hallstatt peoples organized in a feudal manner, ruled over by small groups of aristocrats. Some of these were actually royal families of rulers. Although the economic basis of life was much the same as in preceding times and cultures, it was more stabilized and integrated by the time of the Hallstatt period. The economy was primarily agricultural, supplemented by animal husbandry. All cereals and animals derived from Near Eastern sources were known to the Hallstatt peasants. There is no doubt that the abundance of iron, making tools and utensils available to all instead of only to a few, made life easier and the production of an adequate food supply more certain. As is usual among human groups, when the food supply was sure, the populations increased and warfare became more common.

Hallstatt metal forms include the socketed celt which was a belated improvement over earlier Bronze Age winged celts. Bronze razors in lunuli form, bronze pins, buckles, tutuli, and studs were typical of the Hallstatt. Plain bracelets of hollow or boat types were often engraved. Torques were usually engraved rather than twisted. A variation of bracelet used by Tumulus Hallstatt was the "turban bracelet," a large hollow form. The spectacle brooch of the late Bronze Age was widespread in Hallstatt times.

Iron knives in both arched and machete-like shapes, as well as iron swords, were common Hallstatt types. The typical Hallstatt sword had a heavy bell-shaped knob on the hilt for balance when using the weapon from horseback. The blade was truncated near the tip. The scabbard terminated at the bottom end with a two-winged chape. There were many types of Hallstatt swords that departed from these forms in one or more particulars, and some were made of bronze. Iron was also used for socketed lance heads and sometimes for horse bits and chariot fittings, although bronze usually served better for the latter. Rough iron plowshares, billhooks, and iron sickles made farm work easier.

In the Hallstatt period, weaving and textile-making made great progress. Spindle whorls and loom-weights became more common. Apparently animal as well as vegetable fibers were utilized.

Flint and bone were not completely abandoned by Hallstatt artisans, however. Stone sledges for ore working and even flint axes were still used in places. Bone awls, needles, and some bone arrowheads were made in the Hallstatt period.

Much Hallstatt material has been recovered from tumulus graves in northern France or from Alsace and Baden close to the original Hallstatt center. Tumuli of Hallstatt age in France are especially famous and comprised several types. Burials were made either at ground level or in a shaft excavated into the ground, both with a superimposed mound of earth. Some tumuli were surrounded by stones or roofed over by corbeled vaults of stone. Especially in the late Hallstatt certain of these tumulus burials were covered by very large mounds and furnished with rich funerary furniture. Chariot burials made in four-wheeled war carts or wagon hearses complete with horses and harness were the graves of Hallstatt aristocratic chieftains of importance. Tumulus Hallstatt burials occurred in Bavaria and Bohemia as well as in France.

In the development of the Hallstatt, two periods have been recognized, called respectively Hallstatt I and Hallstatt II. The differentiation between the two Hallstatt sub-periods is not clear in many parts of Europe. A pottery sequence and a development of Hallstatt iron swords does seem to indicate a certain cultural progression. The general Hallstatt period lasted in most parts of Europe for about four centuries.

In the early Hallstatt, weapons were still characteristically of bronze. Thrusting swords of bronze with a narrow blade and a simple handle were found. Also present, however, were thrusting swords of iron with swelled blades, engraved hilts, and the bell-shaped knob on the hilt. These typical Hallstatt swords had leather scabbards provided with iron chapes at the tips. These chapes had pronged terminations, or the fleur-de-lis form.

Also present in the early Hallstatt were engraved bronze razors, more ornamental than the earlier Bronze Age types. There were few fibulae from the early Hallstatt and ornaments were relatively rare. There were, however, some cordoned buckets and Italian cists in beaten bronze. A number of long pins, many with superimposed spheres forming their heads, were found in southern Germany and at Hallstatt.

Pottery of the early Hallstatt was generally plain, with several types of ware derived from earlier traditions in various parts of Europe. There was brown, black, red, and Bucchero pottery, many continuing earlier Urnfield types. Pottery shapes were generally squat, such as the bomb-shaped pot and another low, angular variation which was common in central Europe. The occasional ornamentation was incised, and some painting was used. Dull red paint in simple zigzags and spiral motifs decorated some Austrian Hallstatt ceramic forms. Occasionally designs were stamped.

245

The transition from the earlier Bronze Age and Urnfield cultures to the Hallstatt produced some variations known by different names in certain areas. For example, in the Prague region the *Bylany culture,* derived from the Knoviz in that region, was a transitional period to the Hallstatt. Bylany settlements, some of them fortified, and cemeteries are known. In the latter, skeletal burials show the continuation of that particular mortuary tradition. Bylany painted ware in black or dark brown was done in bands or triangles bordered by dots. Bronzes and iron pieces of the Bylany were much the same as early Hallstatt forms in other regions.

In the original Lausitz area of Bronze III the Urnfield type of life had given way to a specialization known as *Platenice.* In the Platenice, high-shouldered jars similar to those of the Hallstatt already were present. Plates with an umbo in their centers introduced a characteristic form which was developed in the Hallstatt. Platenice burials were cremations, following the Silesian tradition.

In the original Tumulus area of Bronze II, the Hallstatt followed the local traditions of Tumulus burial. Pottery also contributed to the subsequent Hallstatt forms. In much of peripheral Europe the widespread Urnfield variations of the late Bronze Age developed into the *Urnfield Hallstatt.* It is not unusual, then, that at the original type site of Hallstatt both cremation and inhumation burial customs were present.

A famous variation of Hallstatt life was revealed at the cemetery of Les Jogasses near Epernay in Champagne. The people there maintained a skeletal type of burial in Hallstatt times. Some of the Jogassian royalty were interred in elaborate graves with the deceased chieftain placed in his war chariot for a coffin. These war chariots or hearses were four-wheeled wagons with bronze fittings and ornamented harnesses for the horses. Bronze studs which decorated the wide harness straps showed an elaboration of equestrian gear indicative of the advanced civilization of the times.

The Hallstatt civilization as it entered the British Isles is indicative of the form of the culture as it was known on the western periphery of Europe. Hallstatt swordsmen, probably spreading their influence by military might had already established themselves along the western periphery of the continent. These same warrior groups bringing smiths and a knowledge of iron working soon crossed to the British Isles, taking with them a late version of the Hallstatt culture. Changes of climate on the continent and the increasing pressure of large population undoubtedly kept groups of Hallstatt peoples on the move searching for new and favorable lands for settlement. Hallstatt groups with a peripheral type of Hallstatt culture set out from the Low Countries and landed on the eastern coast of England. Hallstatt warriors from northern France made landings in southern Britain, following paths which had already been used by earlier Bronze Age migrants.

In Britain, as in other parts of Europe, the coming of iron did little to change the fundamental way of life, although the newcomers had a better integrated society and more highly developed farming methods. Perhaps it was only the merchants, who had long monopolized the lucrative bronze trade and its sources of supply, who were actually disturbed. Iron Age farms in Wessex show that the newcomers changed the fundamental economy little, if at all. Families lived in isolated farmsteads and plowed adjacent fields with an ironshod two-ox plow. They cut the grain by hand with iron sickles and, after threshing, ground the harvest into flour on crude stone querns.

Implements of iron on the peripheries of the Hallstatt area were at first used sparingly, and those of bronze still held numerical superiority. However, the use of bronze increased as more of the native populations learned the secret of smelting the new metal from its ores. As the increasing use of iron made their life easier, farmsteads sometimes were gathered into villages. There were also fortified settlements surrounded by wooden palisades often supplemented by ditches. Such strongholds appeared in many places on the chalk downs of southern England. Hallstatt forts like those common in southern and southwestern Germany were duplicated in the areas affected by the Hallstatt swordsmen. Such forts were the sites of Cissbury in Sussex and St. Catherines Hill, Winchester. Hallstatt forts of the early Iron Age in Britain were sometimes as large as sixty acres in size.

The first Iron Age immigrants into Britain were called the Iron Age A people, and replaced the Deverel-Rimbury culture of Urnfield inspiration. The first British Iron Age migration took place in the fifth century B.C. After a century or so of penetration and settlement, the Iron Age A folk were harried by more recent iron-using arrivals from the Marne valley of northern France. It was probably these chieftains from the Marne who carried a later version of iron culture that caused the outbreak of fortress-building among the already established Iron Age A communities. British authorities speak of an Iron Age A before the invasion of the Marnian newcomers. The Marnian chieftains who invaded Britain later brought with them the second variety of European Iron Age culture, that called the *La Tène*. Iron Age B in Britain is not necessarily chronological but indicates the dominance of the La Tène culture. An Iron Age C is also recognized and is distinguished by Belgic invaders and their characteristics.

Hallstatt pottery from the British Isles was different from that of the continent, although it followed the same general tradition. There was a distinction between utilitarian ware and vessels for ceremonial usage. Fine crockery was often made in imitation of bronze situla types with thin walls. Such ware was frequently decorated by the addition of a red slip of hematite cut with geometric designs. Even the crude utilitarian ware made of coarse clay seemed to follow more sophisticated shapes copied from metal forms.

Incoming Hallstatt people in the British Isles had brought with them also the central European pin or fibula. In the preceding times of the Beaker folk, western Europe had followed the Mediterranean and Atlantic custom of fastening garments with conical buttons made of various materials. The pin, in its final complicated fibula form, was carried by the Hallstatt newcomers. Present also in the British Isles were several types of straight pins either derived from more northern Hallstatt peoples or locally made. The swan's neck pin was popular among Hallstatt groups of Germany, Switzerland, and northeastern France. The ring-headed pin was also a common Hallstatt type.

In the British Isles, Hallstatt newcomers completely overwhelmed earlier Bronze Age peoples in southern England. With new customs and ideas, as well as with the introduction of iron, they changed the previous culture and replaced it with their own. In eastern England, however, the Hallstatt colonists from the Low Countries represented a much more diluted form of the Hallstatt culture. Hallstatt communities on the lower Rhine, for example, still continued to cremate their dead and bury them in urns in the old Urnfield tradition of the Bronze Age. Bronze Age ceramic forms were also carried over. Hallstatt immigrants with this strong Bronze Age tradition more readily mixed with British Bronze Age groups with little break in culture.

Even Highland Britain was affected to some extent by the Hallstatt movement. Iron Age fortifications were built in Wales and Scotland.

Hallstatt or perhaps later Iron Age people also were responsible for the *Glastonbury* culture. Glastonbury in Somerset represents a type of settlement called a crannog, which was an artificial island in a swampy place or lake; crannogs may date from this period. The crannog settlements of Ireland and the British Isles probably developed from a western Neolithic lake-dwelling tradition or from elements such as that at Buchau in Württemberg.

Late Hallstatt times on the continent may be distinguished by certain changes in cultural items. Swords of the second Hallstatt period were shorter and in the form of poignards. Some long, thrusting swords were also still made. Late Hallstatt swords of both long and short types, however, characteristically were embellished on the hilt by two curled antennae. Especially indicative of late Hallstatt times were classic imports of the Hallstatt area which may be dated. Attic, black-figured vases and comparable wares of the same period from Magna Graecia in Italy found their way north over the trade routes. Metal situlae, many of them actually made in Classical areas, also furnish reliable criteria for dating. Fibulae in a number of forms become more numerous in the late Hallstatt. Boat, leach, kettle-shaped, and serpentiform types of fibulae appeared in various parts of the Hallstatt area. Many kinds of fibulae were of regional importance indicative of a certain area or tribe. Pins of bronze, especially with the swan's neck curve still continued. Sets of toilet articles, including ear pickers, ear spoons, toothpicks, and the like, were usual possessions of late Hallstatt dandies. Large girdles of beaten bronze with stamped decorations were typical, as were bronze bracelets with raised decorations, some of them hinged to facilitate donning and removal.

Pottery of the late Hallstatt usually continued the plain-ware tradition of earlier times, with many local types appearing in different parts of Europe. Hallstatt potters in central and western Europe often tried to copy situla shapes and metal outlines. Footed vases copied from the Este center in Italy and various Classical shapes of Italian and Greek derivation indicated the increasing influence of the higher civilizations to the south. Classic egg and dart motifs were occasionally used to decorate pottery.

It was during late Hallstatt times that two significant influences began to mold the course of events in central and western Europe. The Etruscans, who had established themselves in the eighth century on the coast of Italy and built up their characteristic culture there, began to affect profoundly the Hallstatt people to the north. Etruscan types of chariots, helmets, and weapons were adopted by the Europeans. Also the Greek colonists of Marseilles sent trade goods northward.

In addition to the Etruscan and Classic centers, a new people had appeared in southeastern Europe—the Scyths. These wild, horse nomads, although contributing little to the total of European culture, nonetheless possessed a distinctive style of ornamentation. The Scyths, from their own drawings, were non-Mongoloid people with heavy beards and deep-sunk eyes. However, they lived in felt houses and practiced Shamanism of the Mongol type. The Scyths were probably a mixed people with a Near Eastern culture. The Scythian style consisted chiefly of horse motifs and animal forms depicting fighting and hunts usually done in groups on metal objects. This animal style originated by these virile and warlike people also affected the late Hallstatt groups of central Europe. Scythian types of cauldrons, triangular-shaped arrowheads, and other fragments of Scythian culture were adopted.

It was these foreign influences, as they began to affect the central and western Europeans, that heralded the second of the European Iron Ages—La Tène. The name is derived from a site in Switzerland at the outflow of Lake Neuchâtel by the ancient bed of the Thielle. The original La Tène site, although probably late La Tène in date, was apparently a toll station where fighting had taken place. As in the case of the Hallstatt type site, La Tène was not a permanent settlement but a garrison post commanding the route from the Rhone to the Rhine and also that which connected the valleys of the Rhone and the Danube.

The La Tène civilization presented no break with the preceding Hallstatt. It was forming at the same time that the people carrying with them a late Hallstatt type of culture were occupying southern and eastern England in the fifth century b.c. It was in the fifth century b.c. also that the civilization of Greece had reached its climax in the *Periclean Age.* During this same century, Rome, compounded from motley elements of Italy and drawing heavily upon the Etruscan culture, was forming from these various ingredients. In the west, the Greek colony of Masilia (modern Marseilles) made these urban civilizations, with all of their superior culture, known to the western Europeans. Etruscan trade found its way north through the Alpine passes and Scythian elements entered the Danube valley. From all of these stimuli the La Tène culture was born.

The rise and spread of the La Tène was chiefly connected with the name of the Celtic peoples. The Celts, although not a race in themselves as is often alleged, were a group of tribes centering originally around the Rhine and the Alpine region. They spoke dialects of the Indo-European linguistic system. Such languages as Irish, Gaelic of Scotland, Manx of the Isle of Man, and Welsh, including Cornish and Breton, are survivals of Celtic tongues and indications of Celtic penetrations. Most of the Celts apparently were dark- or red-haired and had blue eyes. The men were large and characteristically warlike. It was these sword-wielding Celtic chieftains who had spread much of the late Hallstatt culture in western Europe. Armed with a knowledge of iron and iron weapons, the Celts in the fourth and third centuries b.c. spread over much of Europe. They crossed the Alps, moved down over northern Italy and sacked Rome, which at that time was struggling to achieve the status of a major center. They invaded southern France and Spain. In the third century, adventurous Celts battled their way even farther, pushing into Greece against the Macedonians and even crossing into Asia Minor. There, Saint Paul spoke of them in later times as the "foolish Galatians."

Hellenistic centers such as Pergamon battled against "Gauls" in Asia Minor. Other groups of Celtic fighting men crossed the Channel into Britain and enthusiastically attacked the followers of the Hallstatt culture who had preceded them to England.

The Celtic culture in Europe and in the British Isles was stimulated by wealth which had come from a spirited home trade which the Celtic people had carried on with the great Classic cultures to the south. The Celts sent over the trade routes slaves, furs, amber, metals, gold, and such raw materials as they could derive from their primitive economy. In return, the major import was wine, usually contained in pottery vessels of Greek or Etruscan manufacture or in metal containers from the same source. In this way, Classic ornament and a wide variety of Classical cultural items were made known to the Celtic barbarians.

Even though the Celtic people may have simply adopted many tools and weapons from their more advanced Classical neighbors to the south, they nonetheless welded these into a cultural whole which we call La Tène. Worthy of note was a stylistic method of ornamentation typical of La Tène times. Possibly stimulated by the Scythian animal style as well as by Classical ornament, the Celts developed a linear, abstract type of art characteristically their own. Depictions of animals, domestic or wild, were highly abstracted, and the prototype, if any, of much Celtic ornament is unrecognizable. The Celtic style may have been barbaric in contrast to the soberer and more lucid traditions of the Classical region, but it developed into one of the most tenacious and satisfying abstract arts to come out of the European region.

While the Celtic people were forming the La Tène culture from such ideas and items as they could derive from their Classic neighbors, the urban centers of the south were in their turn becoming more familiar with the barbarian Celts. It was this familiarity which later led Julius Caesar, at the head of his legions, to conquer these same Celtic people and thus usher in the next cultural epoch, the *Roman period*. However, the La Tène itself was to leave a decided imprint on the bulk of European culture before it was obliterated by the Roman legions.

The characteristic La Tène weapon was a long sword. A type of

La Tène sword was later adopted by the Romans. Celtic tactics were the same as those used so successfully by their Roman conquerors. Chariots and cavalry were employed in fighting, and flights of javelins and arrows usually preceded close combat.

The Second European Iron Age has been divided into three subdivisions on a basis of changes of the La Tène sword and La Tène pottery. Generally, in early La Tène times the sword was a pointed thrusting weapon with a relatively simple hilt and a trefoil or circular chape at the tip of the scabbard. In later La Tène times, the sword became longer with a blunt or obtuse point and a double cutting edge. The hilt became more complicated with a cross piece to protect the hands. The chape in the late La Tène sword was rectilinear and reinforced by transverse bars.

To a certain extent, La Tène pottery followed the threefold separation of La Tène swords. In La Tène I, a high-shouldered form of vessel was usual. La Tène II was characterized by bottle types with narrow necks. In La Tène III, a widemouthed jar with a roll rim and combed surface was typical. Most La Tène pottery was characterized by the use of the potter's wheel. This contrivance, introduced into La Tène Europe at this time, gave far greater symmetry of outline in much less time than was possible by old hand methods. Decoration on La Tène forms was characteristically the ribbed and outlined effect that could be achieved on a potter's wheel. Many Hallstatt traditions were continued, however, in burnishing, combing, and incising. Painting appeared in late La Tène in the form of geometric decorations.

Many other items of La Tène manufacture followed a progression from early to late La Tène. Some authorities, however, regard these three segregated divisions as too artificial. In many peripheral areas of Europe and in the Germanic region, the La Tène period was marked by modifications of this progression.

The spread of the La Tène was probably connected with the military use of the light war chariot, such as that made by the Etruscans. Just as the mounted knights of Hallstatt were supreme with their long cavalry swords, so were the La Tène warriors with their war chariots. The previous four-wheeled Hallstatt wagons were clumsy and perhaps not used for chariots at all. Light, swift chariots used by Greeks and Etruscans to the south were invincible.

In addition to the La Tène swords, many items of material culture were continued from the Hallstatt or borrowed from Classical people. Many La Tène swords were hilted with double antennae above and below the hand grip, an anthropomorphic form. Shields were usually rectangular or elongated, decorated on their surfaces with the Celtic abstract style embellished with enamel work. The La Tène warrior chieftains were very colorful figures with their richly ornamented helmets of varying shapes and other decorated articles of martial gear.

La Tène lance heads of iron were wider and shorter than previous forms. Arrowheads were also made of iron, some of them perhaps manufactured for use as crossbow bolts. Horse bits and horse trimmings were iron, as were socketed axes and mattocks. Some perforated axes were also made. Iron fibulae appeared in the La Tène. Varieties of knives were manufactured, and shears appeared for the first time.

Bronze was not abandoned entirely in the La Tène Iron Age. Elaborate bronze bracelets with thickened ends or series of segmented hollow knobs were worn. Fibulae of many forms were skillfully formed of bronze. Especially common was the Certosa type of fibula based upon an Italian prototype. Another form with a broadened bow and a foot which turned back on itself was developed. The crossbow fibula was also typical of La Tène times.

Wine pitchers and bronze vessels with Roman shapes were made by La Tène craftsmen or traded from the south. Fluted cists were manufactured of bronze or iron.

Breastplates of bronze with chains appended were made by the more skillful La Tène craftsmen. Fine chainwork covering a wide range of trinkets and gadgets was typical. The baldric, an over-the-shoulder type of sword belt, was a La Tène innovation. Keys and spurs appeared, as well as human and animal figurines in metal. Especially diagnostic are the coins which were found in La Tène deposits. Many of these were Roman pieces brought into La Tène territory in the normal trend of commerce. There were some Celtic copies of them, although the earliest Celtic coinage on the continent seems to date only from the second century B.C. Hoards of coins are occasionally found which may be dated from the most recent coin of the lot.

Glass, usually in the form of glass paste, although it appeared earlier than La Tène times on the mainland of Europe, was used with marked effect by Celtic craftsmen. Glass provided ornamentation on bracelets and fibulae. Large beads of glass paste were trade items among the Celtic peoples. Glass paste in the form of enamel adorned metal objects such as shields, helmets, and sword hilts. This paste, crudely colored in many vivid hues, was placed in small cloisonnés on the metal surfaces to produce spots of contrasting color. In addition to glass, lignite was often used for bracelets and other ornaments.

It was in the La Tène period that flint, which had long been used in the course of European prehistory, was finally abandoned. Stone was still used for honing and polishing pieces or for crude mauls for crushing ores. Bone, however, reached new heights of popularity. Hemp-working tools of bone, sled runners, spatulae, spoons, and bone pins were used by La Tène people. Combs, some of them made of three pieces of bone cleverly fastened together illustrated the skill of the La Tène craftsmen.

La Tène sites were varied in nature. In the early La Tène, settlements were few and scattered. Many of these were the farmsteads of La Tène peasants, following the Hallstatt pattern. Graves constitute many of the early La Tène remains. Tumuli, covering incinerations or mounds over shaft graves, indicate that the La Tène period followed mixed traditions of burial, as had the Hallstatt. Some very elaborate multiple burials in tumuli are known from the early La Tène.

In the period known as La Tène II, small camps are known from a number of places in Europe from southern Bohemia to the Atlantic coast. It was in La Tène II that the site of La Tène itself was occupied by garrison forces that battled there. Tumuli and cemeteries with skeletal remains constitute the bulk of La Tène II remains. Classical coins and abundant trade items derived from southern Classical sources provide ample criteria for dating.

It was only in late La Tène, or La Tène III, that large settled areas appeared. Fortified towns such as Stradoniče and Mount Beuvray date from this period. Military architecture of elaborate plan and large scale was derived from Roman contacts. Regular ashlar masonry also following Roman models was adopted by many of the southern Celtic people. Large cities developed as far north as central Europe. Caesar stormed walled strongholds of this type in southern Germany only a short time later.

Burials of the late La Tène still showed a mixed tradition. Cremation was still dominant in some areas. Flat graves were placed in cemeteries near town centers, and multiple burials were occasionally made, possibly as a result of battles. Chariot burials, especially in La Tène centers of northern France, reached new heights of elaboration. Northern France in the vicinity of the Seine was the stronghold of the tribe of Celts known as the *Parisii* who have left their name in the capital city of Paris.

Throughout the Celtic world of these times there was a notable social stratification. Celtic chieftains amassed large collections of military gear and jewelry. An important person could boast of a complete set of wine bowls, wine service for mixing drinks, and drinking goblets, all imported from some Classical trader to the south. He adorned himself with jeweled brooches. His military accoutrements usually consisted of an ornamental helmet with a plume at its crest and a shield decorated with typical Celtic art work and enamel. His sword was carried in a baldric over his shoulders. The baldric was skillfully made of iron chains and embossed plates decorated with bronze work, also in the Celtic manner. The ordinary people of these Celtic tribes, however, lived amid a squalor and simplicity that was little different from that of the preceding Bronze Age population. Even the chieftains or upper classes lived in primitive huts or log structures. It was this crudity which caused the Romans and the Greeks to despise these "Gauls" and look down upon them as barbarians. Only in late La Tène times did the Celts, and to a lesser extent the Germans, begin to absorb Roman patterns of luxurious living.

Although the development of the Iron Age took place for the most part in central and western Europe, it found its way into other areas as well. In the Iberian Pensinsula, the Iron Age was relatively late and obviously derived from other centers. In southern Spain, Phoenician influence, particularly from Carthage, was present in a limited degree; the Punic Wars prevented the further development of Phoenician influence in the western Mediterranean. During the

Iron Age, Spain was also in close contact with Italy, continuing those influences which had begun in the early portion of the Bronze Age.

The closest contacts in the Spanish Iron Age were with southern France. The first real Iron Age to appear in Spain was a late and peripheral Hallstatt form. Large cemeteries such as that of Aguilar de Auguita show late Hallstatt affiliations. Usually Spanish Iron Age remains are found as large groups of tumuli, usually covering cremations. Rows of plain graves with urns, each containing a cremation, were reminiscent of Urnfield practices of late Bronze Age time. In Spain a tombstone was set above each burial urn.

Typical Spanish Iron Age materials included late Hallstatt swords with antennae hilts. The long bell-hilted Hallstatt sword did not reach Spain or other peripheral areas. Iron-socketed lances, knives, javelins, and arrowheads followed late Hallstatt models. Some piece armor and casques appear.

Ornaments and implements of the Spanish Iron Age included a number of Iberian versions of late Hallstatt forms. Brooches with a perpendicular foot and a button, ring fibulae, and an Italian form with a horse, often with a rider, worked into the metal are Spanish forms. Horse trappings in iron and bronze, some of them highly ornamented, were skillfully made.

In Andalusia, Phoenician influence was manifest in tablets of ivory, alabaster figurines and vases, and some amphora in Classic Greek and Libyan forms with Classic ornamentation.

Hallstatt forms lingered long in Spain, but were finally replaced by the La Tène. The La Tène in the Iberian Peninsula was a generalized type. The long straight La Tène swords and shields were adopted. Diluted Celtic ornamentation vied with more Classic Roman motifs. Such La Tène material was recently discovered at the site of Cabrera de Mataró near Barcelona. In La Tène times, burial of bodies under tumuli was the usual type in Spain.

Spanish Iron Age pottery varied from Lausitz-like ware, with the archaic appearance of the Bronze Age, to indigenous pieces copying Greek shapes and ornamentation. In the latter Spanish Iron Age, a geometric type of pottery was made following that tradition of the Classical area. There were, however, many other types, including earthenware copies of metal cists and some red-painted ware. Unlike her position in earlier ages, Spain during the Iron Ages was a recipient of culture and not an exporter of ideas.

Among the major movements of the La Tène people was that of their several migrations into the British Isles. The preceding Hallstatt sword-wielding warriors had already paved the way, as well as many earlier people before them.

As early as 250 B.C., warrior folk carrying the La Tène culture began to cross into the British Isles. They provoked a number of changes on the islands, and by displacing or mixing with various peoples there, produced a number of distinguishable cultures.

A considerable group of Celtic invaders landed in Scotland in the vicinity of the Firth of Tay and northward to the Moray Firth. From these places, they soon spread across to the Atlantic coast and possibly as far as northern Wales. The indigenous inhabitants of Scotland had been little affected by the preceding Hallstatt culture and were still in a Bronze Age state of development. The La Tène newcomers easily overcame them and consolidated their holdings with a series of powerful fortresses. These they built in a manner which was described by Julius Caesar when he told of the military works built by the Gauls. The main walls were built of stone blocks interspersed with large timbers at right angles to the face of the wall. The interior of the wall was filled with stone refuse and timber. When such a wall was burned either accidentally or by an attacking force, the heat generated was sufficient to fuse the stones. This produced the famous vitrified forts of Scotland that have been a puzzle to archaeologists for over a century. Forts built by La Tène invaders were those of Finavon in Angus and Castle Law near Abernethy. From the latter, the term *Abernethy culture* is derived. Material accompanying the Abernethy sites indicated that the warriors who built the vitrified forts brought a La Tène type of culture with them.

Another group of La Tène chiefs emanating from the Parisii tribe of the Seine region of northern France landed in eastern Yorkshire and Lincolnshire. Ptolemy, writing of this region four centuries later, stated that the Parisii still held the Yorkshire coast in his time. In Yorkshire the newcomers left elaborate graves similar to those in the Marnian cemeteries in Champagne, their original homeland.

Nobles and chieftains were buried in their war chariots or four-wheeled hearses complete with the richly ornamented possessions and weapons of their high station in La Tène society. The cemetery near Arras contained modest graves of the lower-class La Tène people and a few very elaborate ones of the rich, ruling families of La Tène Yorkshire.

The artistic work of the Yorkshire La Tène was especially notable. Apparently attracted there by the relative prosperity, wheel-wrights, carpenters, sword-makers, and other metal workers founded a flourishing center of manufacturing and decoration. Some of the finest pieces of La Tène workmanship comes from the Arras culture.

Marnian chieftains of the La Tène culture also pressed into southern England. It was at this time that the Iron Age A or Hallstatt peoples who had already occupied this territory built large numbers of forts to stand against them. The La Tène Iron Age in Britain is usually called Iron Age B.

The people of Iron Age B, however, gained only a scant foothold in southern England. Apparently the Iron Age A inhabitants, with their hastily constructed fortresses, kept them out. In spite of this, small parties of La Tène invaders conquered portions of the Hallstatt area and ruled as overlords in these regions. Even those areas which were not overcome were affected by La Tène culture and copied some of their ways.

Still another group of La Tène invaders, emanating from western France, landed in several waves in southwestern England. Seemingly they came purposely to seize the sources of tin in western Cornwall. Even in advanced La Tène times, bronze was of such importance that the tin necessary for its manufacture was a major economic item.

The invaders in the southwest left behind them cemeteries and stone fortresses very different from anything that the preceding Iron Age A people had built. Such a stone fort built by the incoming La Tène people is Chun Castle. This, like other ring forts of the same sort, is a circular fortification with a wall fourteen to fifteen feet thick surrounded by a ditch. It protected a series of house clusters in which the inhabitants lived. Hill forts like this were the citadels of chieftains who looked after their followers and protected their lucrative tin trade. A fragment of recorded history was left by Pytheas, a

Greek explorer who visited Cornwall about 325 B.C. He described how the people there mined and refined the tin and shipped it to the continent, where it was taken overland to the mouth of the Rhone.

An interesting variation of life attributed to the La Tène invaders in the south of England was the *Glastonbury culture* from a village in the valley of the Brue close to the modern town of Glastonbury in Somerset. Glastonbury, originally used in Hallstatt times, illustrated that the La Tène settlers used natural bodies of water as well as massive circular forts to protect themselves and their new trade. Glastonbury covered an area of about two acres in the midst of a crannog or swamp. The marsh was firmed by platforms of logs supplemented by other fill laid down upon the spongy peat. This area, surrounded by a palisade, formed the base for the village. As many as ninety buildings were constructed on this artificial island. It was amply protected by its water surroundings and yet commanded a position controlling the tin trade as well as other movements in the region.

Many objects recovered from Glastonbury show that the artisans there represented a later movement of La Tène peoples in the region. Glastonbury pottery was decorated with a local version of the curvilinear Celtic style. Versatile carpenters created works ranging from the heavy woodwork of the houses and dugout canoes to beautiful lathe-turned wooden bowls. Iron work followed the La Tène pattern, especially in the form of such utilitarian objects as sickles, billhooks, chisels, and gouges.

With iron sources probably in the forest of Dean, the Glastonbury smiths manufactured tools and weapons as well as currency bars. These long, flat iron bars, pinched into a handle-like form at one end, were probably originally blanks from which swords were to be made. They were manufactured by the Iron Age people in a number of standard units which could be used for currency. They were clumsy and difficult to carry, but were used as a medium of commerce over a wide area.

The Glastonbury culture, with its highly developed trade connections, was apparently ended by another invasion of people from the continent, the Belgae. This period and culture is sometimes known as Iron Age C. The Belgae overwhelmed the Glastonbury merchants with fire and sword and disrupted their trade. With the coming of the Belgae, coinage replaced the iron currency bars.

Perhaps as a further extension from the Gallic-dominated area of southwestern Britain was a distinct culture which appeared in northern Scotland. This, because of the characteristic small forts or brochs which it left behind, has been called the *Broch culture*.

Large numbers of brochs appear in northern Scotland, including Shetland, Orkney, Caithness, Sutherland, the Outer Hebrides, and Skye. These brochs were usually base-enclosed towers of massive masonry. The central structure was a circular castle with massive walls, especially in the lower portions. Within this mass were several oval or circular chambers, possibly serving as guard rooms. The upper portions of the typical broch rose forty feet in a cylindrical tower. The top was reached by a stairway within the thickness of the massive walls. The building of the brochs and the surrounding enclosures was an indication of well-integrated societies whose labor could be commandeered for a common cause. The chieftain, with the broch as his citadel, might protect the vulnerable huts of his tenants with this fortress.

The Broch culture itself was a weak version of the La Tène. The people did not practice fine metal work or use fibulae, as they were far from sources of supply. They often tried to copy familiar metal forms in stone or bone. Pottery was not of the Glastonbury type but was plain and crude. The broch builders had deviated far from the original Celtic inspiration.

During the spread of the Celtic La Tène peoples in most parts of Britain, Ireland was little affected. Most of the typical varieties of Iron Age forts, graves, and pottery are absent in Ireland. However, the demonstrable fact that the Irish language belongs to the Goidelic group of Celtic tongues has been taken as evidence that Celtic peoples also invaded Ireland.

There is, however, in Ireland no evidence of any La Tène invasion, at least on a large scale. A scattering of La Tène objects indicates that there was some contact and some penetration into Ireland by a few La Tène groups. For the most part, however, Urnfield folk of the preceding Bronze Age survived in Ireland comparatively untouched by Iron Age ideas and movements. Linguistically, these people may have been Celtic, and this variety of the Indo-European language may well have been introduced at that time. The Celtic group of languages and La Tène culture do not coincide in all parts of Europe by any means.

The stylistic traditions of the Marnian chieftains who invaded Yorkshire and left their evidences in the cemetery of Arras were representatives of early La Tène culture. Even the Marnian invaders of southern England carried early La Tène objects with them. It was another group, the Belgae, who carried a later version of La Tène culture.

Originally, Celtic-speaking peoples had occupied western Europe, including much of what was later Germanic territory. Several Celtic tribes were originally on the right bank of the Rhine.

Even in late Hallstatt times, Germanic tribes had begun to push against the Celtic peoples in the Lowlands and force them westward. This may have been one of the reasons for Celtic movements into Great Britain. The Celtic tribe of Helvetii, originally situated on the upper Rhine, migrated westward under this pressure. But not all of the movements of the Cimbric and Teutonic tribes to the westward were military. Numbers of Germanic peoples infiltrated and mixed with the Celts of the lowland countries. Such a mixed group was the tribe known as the Belgae, who originally occupied the country between the lower Rhine and the mouth of the Seine.

The Belgae civilization was late La Tène. These people overawed the earlier La Tène type of culture as exemplified on the Marne by the Parisii who previously had invaded Yorkshire in Britain.

The Belgae, from their position on the northwest coasts of Europe, overflowed into southeastern Britain. The Germanic movements beyond the Rhine had been taking place in the second half of the second century B.C. The movement of the Belgae across to England, however, did not occur until around 75 B.C. There were, perhaps, two Belgic invasions of Britain.

Although large groups of the Belgae migrated to Britain, a considerable contingent remained on the continent. Caesar records that the Belgae, whom he fought on the mainland, received help from their relatives across the Channel. This was one of the major reasons why Caesar concluded that his Gallic conquests on the continent could only be consolidated by the conquest of Britain itself.

Archaeologically, the Belgic invasion of England was recorded by the spread of cremation cemeteries, a Germanic Bronze Age mortuary custom never completely abandoned by the invaders. Wheel-made pottery, largely pedestal urns, also traced Belgic times in Britain. The pottery forms were taken over by the Belgae from earlier La Tène peoples on the continent. The potter's wheel also had been known there earlier. Its introduction into Britain at this time provides a recognizable archaeological change. Wheel-made pottery of both pedestal-urn types and a roll-rim form of jar without the pedestal were made in large quantities in Britain by ceramic specialists.

In addition to the mass production of pottery, the Belgic newcomers made great changes in the daily living. They established relatively large and organized kingdoms in contrast to the preceding small and fluid tribal groups. The Belgae also introduced a large, wheeled plow which could turn sod and cultivate new regions impossible to work with the previous two-ox plow that merely scratched a furrow in the earth. The high organization of the Belgae and their superior plowshares initiated an agricultural revolution.

Belgic invaders, including large numbers of peasants and artisans, moved into Great Britain, landing first on the Kentish coast, where the Aylesford cemetery on the Medway with its rich late La Tène funerary offerings has left abundant evidence of their presence. In two decades after their first landings on the Kentish coast, the Belgae had spread from Kent to the Thames and subsequently crossed the Thames into Hertfordshire. In all this territory they established a well-integrated kingdom allied with that of the Belgae who remained on the continent. Chief of the Belgae in this region was Cassivellaunus, who established a capital above Wheathampstead. It is clear that the non-Belgic peoples in Britain disliked the Belgae intruders. Such were the Trinovantes who lived in Essex and who sought Caesar's aid against Cassivellaunus and his Belgae.

European prehistory at this point becomes increasingly substantiated by fragments of written history. The Roman historian Strabo made illuminating comments upon these regions in these times. The major source is, of course, Caesar himself, who told with impersonal detail of his conquests of the Gallic peoples and the Belgae. Caesar conquered the Veneti, a people who inhabited the coastal portions of Brittany and who carried on most of the cross-Channel trade with southwestern Britain. In 56 B.C., Julius Caesar engaged the Veneti in a great sea battle and completely destroyed their fleet, as a prelude to his invasion of Britain. However, archaeological evidence of the Veneti and their famous fighting ships is largely absent.

In 55 B.C., Caesar crossed from Boulogne with ten thousand men to conquer Cassivellaunus and the Belgae. He reckoned correctly that the organized Belgic state of Britain was the only effective core of resistance which might oppose him. Although Caesar stormed and took the capital of Cassivellaunus at Wheathampstead, he suffered several reverses when storms destroyed the fleet which supported and supplied his army.

Classical sources also contain information concerning the non-Belgic tribes of Britain. These peoples, all apparently Celtic, were descendants of the Iron Age A and B peoples in various parts of the British Isles. Such Celtic people were the Britons who have given their name to Britain, and the Picts, a Latin term meaning the tatooed or painted ones, who were also probably Celtic. Much historical information may be found in Tacitus' *Agricola*, which contains abundant material on the tribes and peoples of Britain a hundred years later than the time of the Belgae and Caesar.

While the Belgae were building their integrated kingdom in Britain under the leadership of Cassivellaunus, Roman culture had already taken over southern France. Caesar's conquests, of course, completed the Romanization of Gaul. Caesar was appointed governor of the territory in 59 B.C., but his conquests lasted long after his time. After his invasion of Britain in 55 B.C., he returned to the continent to attempt new Gallic conquests. Archaeological evidence has not been produced for all of the peoples and happenings mentioned by Caesar, although most of his statements are no doubt substantially correct.

It is difficult also to distinguish many Celtic and Germanic tribes by direct archaeological evidence. Most of these carried late La Tène versions of culture. More detailed information on La Tène culture, especially the less material aspects of life, may be derived from Latin

descriptions than from actual discoveries. However, even at this time
—the first century B.C.—European prehistory was still almost completely unwritten.

There are almost no written records of the Germanic tribes who
were pushing westward against the Celtic-speaking people even before Caesar's time. The chief source of information is again Tacitus,
whose *Germania* was written in 98 A.D. Prior to this time, Teutonic
peoples had continued a diluted version of La Tène culture. Celtic
ornamentation and the typical Celtic linear style was largely absent
among the Germanic tribes. Other aspects of La Tène culture were,
however, possessed by most of these. In peripheral areas, far from
the Celtic center of La Tène development, the Hallstatt type of life
lingered on. In many outlying regions, the Bronze Age continued,
comparatively untouched by developments in central and western
Europe. However, the La Tène culture as a whole was remarkably
homogeneous from the Balkans to western Europe. It did not coincide exactly with the distribution of Celtic languages, but included
much of the Germanic and other linguistic areas.

The La Tène in western Europe and in Britain ended abruptly
as each tribe and region was conquered by the Roman legions. In
southern Europe, however, Roman culture had already asserted itself.
Even among the Teutonic tribes who were never actually conquered
by Rome, the Roman version of Classical culture was infiltrating.
Thus Rome, even as it began to weaken as a political entity and con-
quering force, still was the cultural power which colored the succeeding times.

CHAPTER 13

The Classical Cultures

WHILE THE MAIN COURSE of European prehistory was progressing on the mainland, parallel developments of great importance were taking place in the Aegean area and in Italy. The development of previous cultures had proved the importance of the eastern Mediterranean initiating or greatly influencing periods and progress on the continent of Europe. The most significant development was a series of cultures which arose in the eastern Mediterranean from the same stimuli which brought forth the European Neolithic. These cultures, inasmuch as they culminated in the outstanding civilizations of Greece and Rome, had a tremendous effect upon Western Civilization and later European events. Even during the centuries of their formation, the cultures of the Aegean islands, Crete, mainland Greece, and, later, Italy profoundly influenced the trend of events farther north on the European mainland.

Renaissance scholars and later antiquarians were primarily concerned with *Classical culture*. This concentration of study was first fostered by the church which had its own roots in Roman times and used Latin as its official language. The later Humanism, which was in part a revolt against the church, found examples in the Classical world. The cultures of Greece and Rome were regarded as the only essential studies in European antiquity. But the origins of Greek and Roman culture were neglected, and the relationship of the Classic civilizations to the rest of European culture was largely ignored. Even in the late nineteenth century, a tendency prevailed to regard the "Classics" as separate studies.

The separation between the Classical cultures and other early European civilization is accidental and demonstrably artificial. The earliest Neolithic on the European mainland found its first foothold in Greece. The Megalithic religion, which affected so many of the Neolithic peoples in Europe, had its origin in the Classical regions of the eastern Mediterranean. The western Neolithic, which established itself in Spain and from there moved northward into western Europe, came from the eastern Mediterranean. The first knowledge of the working of metals came into Europe from the Mediterranean trade routes.

However, in spite of the liaison between the Classic area and the bulk of Europe, there was a certain separation between the two which was quite distinct until the Iron Age. Classical culture reached a peak far in advance of the rest of Europe.

Perhaps the two best-known authorities on Classical archaeology are Sir Arthur Evans and Heinrich Schliemann. Both of these men based their researches on Classical myths or cycles of myths purporting to tell of events and places concerned with the origin of Greek civilization. Schliemann, following clues which he found in the Homeric stories of the *Iliad* and the *Odyssey*, located the ancient town of Troy, which was the focal point of the Homeric epics.

Sir Arthur Evans, following similar clues derived from a cycle of legends which evolved around the hero Theseus, pinpointed another city celebrated in Classical legend. This was the town of Knossos, which he located on the island of Crete. As the legends told of the Great King Minos who ruled in "broad Knossos," Sir Arthur called the civilization which he found there the *Minoan*. With the informa-

	Troy	*Crete*
4000 B.C.	Anatolian Neolithic	
3900		
3800		
3700		Earliest Neolithic
3600		
3500		
3400		
3300		
3200		
3100		
3000		
2900		
2800		
2700	Troy I	Early Minoan I
2600		
2500		Early Minoan II
2400		Early Minoan III
2300	Troy II (Bronze)	
2200	Troy III	
2100	Troy IV	Middle Minoan I
2000		(Bronze Age)
1900	Troy V	
1800	Troy VI	Middle Minoan II
1700		(Destruction of Knossos)
1600		Middle Minoan III
1500		Late Minoan I
1400		Late Minoan II
1300	Troy VI—Destroyed	(Destruction of Knossos)
1200		Late Minoan III
1100	Troy VII*a*	
1000		
900		
800		
700		
600		
500		
400		
300		
200		
150		
100		

Greece	Hungary	
Greece	*Hungary*	

Neolithic from Ana
↓
Sesklo

↓

Dimini
Minoan in Cyclades & Aegean
Early Helladic

(Minyan) Middle Helladic

Mycenaean—Late Helladic

Late Mycenaean
Proto—Geometric
Geometric Period (Iron)
  Dipylon
Orientalizing Hellenic (Archaic Greek)
Transitional
Periclean Greek Golden Age

Hellenistic

Roman

Körös
  Bükk
Tisza I

Lengyel
↓

Tisza Polgar

↓   Baden
Bodrogkeresztur   ↓
Bell Beaker

Bronze I—Tószeg A

Bronze II—Tószeg D

Bronze III (Panonian)

Bronze IV (Beginning of Iron)

Hallstatt (Iron)

La Tène II

La Tène III

	Danube–Central Europe	Southern Scandinavia – Northern Germany–Denmark
4000 B.C.		
3900		
3800		
3700		
3600		
3500	Barbotine—Introduction	Mesolithic—Ertebølle
3400	of Neolithic	
3300	Vínča	
3200		
3100		
3000	Danubian I*a*—(Linear ware)	
2900		
2800		
2700	Danubian 1*b* (Stroke ware)	
2600	Rössen	Neolithic (Danubian &
2500	Danubian II—Jordansmühl	Mesolithic mixture)
2400		
2300		
2200	Swiss Lakes—Aichbühl	Megalithic—Dolmens
		Passage Graves
2100	Swiss Lake Dwellers—	
2000	Corded ware	
1900	Bell Beaker	
1800	Bronze I—Aunjetizt—A–1—A–2	
1700		
1600	Bronze II—Tumulus B	
1500	(Western Europe)	
1400	Bronze C	Bronze I
1300	Bronze III—Lausitz D	
	Urnfields	
1200		Bronze II
1100		
1000	Hallstatt I–A	Bronze III
900	Hallstatt II–B	Bronze IV
800		
700		Bronze V
600	La Tène I	
500		
400		
300	La Tène II	First Iron
200	La Tène III	
100	Roman	

Britain	Rhineland–Belgium–Northern France

Mesolithic

Mesolithic

(Western Neolithic
(Danubian

Danubian 1*b*
Köln Lindenthal

⎧Neolithic A–1
⎱Neolithic B (Peterborough)
⎩Neolithic A–2
Neolithic A–B Megalithic
Passage Graves
  Gallery Graves

Neolithic A–B

Beakers
Beakers B–1 B–2
  Megalithic Survivals
Beakers & Food Vessels
Wessex Culture

Cortaillod—Swiss Lakes

Michelsberg—Horgen
Corded Ware
  Danordic—Altheim
Bell Beakers

Bronze II—Tumulus–B

Middle Bronze Age

Late Bronze

Bronze III–C   Urnfields
  Bronze D
  Bronze E

Hallstatt—Iron

La Tène I

First Iron

Iron Age

La Tène II
La Tène III
Roman

tion from the beginnings at Troy and at Knossos, the early history of the Classical development is now fairly well known.

Crete and the other islands of the eastern Mediterranean were of little importance during the early phases of European prehistory. During the Palaeolithic and Mesolithic eras of human accomplishment most of the events of major significance took place on the mainland of Europe, Asia Minor, or Africa, and in most cases at some distance from those areas which were to become important in Classical times.

With the advent of the Neolithic, however, many areas were occupied which had been inaccessible in earlier times or had been considered unfavorable because of a lack of game animals. By Neolithic times peoples with their new knowledge of agriculture and animal husbandry began to move by sea as well as by land. Boats, seaworthy enough for coastal navigation, were in use early in the Neolithic period. With these boats the Neolithic migrants from the area of the eastern Mediterranean quickly discovered the many islands of that region and soon occupied the largest and most favorable of them.

The impetus of the Neolithic as seen in the Danube valley and western Europe came from Mesopotamia and the Near East. Secondary centers appeared slightly later in Anatolia and Egypt and were the sources of the Neolithic which penetrated to the islands of the eastern Mediterranean. Even earlier than their arrival in the Danube farther north, Neolithic ideas from the general region of Anatolia and perhaps of Egypt had reached the islands of the Aegean. Neolithic peoples, carrying the new way of life with them, colonized Cyprus, Rhodes, Melos, and many of the smaller islands. Certainly the earliest extension of Neolithic culture on the larger island of Crete was of this Anatolian variety.

A significant stream of cultural influence from early Egypt came slightly later. These Neolithic ideas were of the variety that early developed in the Nile Delta. On the Rosetta branch of the Nile was a type of Neolithic culture called *Merimdian,* from the site of Merimde in that region. Merimdian influences were a powerful stimulus on early Crete and to a lesser extent on the other islands of the eastern Mediterranean. Merimdian Egyptians in the Nile Delta region grew emmer wheat quite early. They also had cattle, pigs, sheep, and goats. Perhaps it was this Merimdian influence that caused the Cretan Neolithic to appear quite different from the Neolithic that developed on the European mainland at Sesklo, Dimini, and Drakhmani.

Because of their position, the island cultures of the eastern Mediterranean soon took on seafaring characteristics. In the sea-borne trading which inevitably grew up between the islands and the mainland, Crete was the natural center. Perhaps it was these various stimuli as well as the relative immunity of Crete from attack or disruptive influences that explain the momentous cultural growth on that island.

Remains on the various islands point to the introduction of the Neolithic idea in this region as early as 4000 B.C. Thus the Neolithic began on the islands of the eastern Mediterranean some centuries earlier than its inception in the valley of the Danube or in western Europe.

The first evidences of Neolithic culture in Crete and on the other islands are similar to those in Anatolia, although different from the type of Neolithic which began in Thrace. Polished stone axes revealed the new Neolithic technique of stone working on Crete. Flint blades and knives of obsidian from Melos paralleled techniques from other Neolithic centers on the mainland. Especially diagnostic was the early Neolithic pottery in these regions. The earliest Cretan pottery was dark faced and decorated only with incision. The first of this was of simple manufacture and had rudimentary ornamentation. Bag and bowl shapes predominated. Some of the early types of black ware were decorated with incision filled with white paint. This white-incised tradition may well be an inspiration from Africa or Egypt.

Many authorities divide the early Neolithic ceramics of the eastern Mediterranean into three fundamental traditions. The first was a shape of pottery copied from animal skins which were probably used for receptacles before pottery was developed. Another pottery form imitated grass-woven baskets. The third type was apparently copied from containers made of gourds. Of the three, the gourd forms seemed to be the latest—many of the early Danubian forms of pottery were shaped like gourds. Much of the Anatolian ware continued the leather tradition, and Egyptian pottery copied leather or basket prototypes.

Physically the early Minoans of Crete were longheaded, longfaced Mediterraneans. Culturally, however, they derived their Neolithic tradition from the Anatolian mainland and supplemented it by continued additions from Egypt. There were also contacts with the Levantine coast.

The Neolithic streams of culture which began at several points in the eastern Mediterranean produced a number of roughly parallel maritime or trading cultures in these places. The island of Crete was certainly the most important of these. The maritime cultures which developed from the first Neolithic beginnings appeared in several places during the third millennium. Several maritime trading centers appeared on the Aegean islands and especially on that particular group known as the Cyclades. Although the *Cycladic culture* is usually recognized as a distinct culture, it closely paralleled developments on the island of Crete, with which it was in close contact. On the mainland of the Balkan Peninsula, another series of developments took place which have been grouped together as the *Helladic cultures*. A fourth series is known from the site of Hissarlik or Troy on the mainland of Asia Minor near the mouth of the Hellespont and from the neighboring site of Thermi in Lesbos. There were also simultaneous maritime centers on Rhodes and Cyprus, but these were of less importance to Europe.

The culture which evolved on the island of Crete had the greatest significance in the early phases of the Classic progression. On a basis of his excavations at the one great site of Knossos in Crete, Sir Arthur Evans has divided the culture there into three major periods which he calls Early, Middle, and Late Minoan. Each of these three periods he has further subdivided into three separate divisions—Early Minoan I, II, and III; Middle Minoan I, II, and III; and Late Minoan I, II, and III. In spite of the artificiality of these divisions, they rather closely approximate the natural breaks which occurred at Knossos. Subsequent excavations at various other ancient sites on the island of Crete have verified Evans' chronology. Phaestos and Hagia Triada are perhaps the most important of the lesser Cretan sites.

A vague pre-Minoan period at Knossos has been described from generalized indications of the first inception of Anatolian Neolithic colored by Egyptian parallels. Most of the earliest evidences and many of the later ones were found entirely in the eastern portion of Crete.

By Early Minoan I, the maritime culture was well formed with its own distinctive characteristics. Painted ceramics of the Early Minoan period may be paralleled closely with wares of the early Egyptian dynasties. A stone vase from the Early Minoan level of Knossos resembles a type which belonged to the Dynasty III of Egypt. This evidence indicates that the whole Minoan sequence did not begin before 2700 B.C. or thereabouts, somewhat later than the original conception of Sir Arthur Evans. Parallels with Egyptian chronology—which is supported by lists of kings and more exact designations of time—have been the best means for establishing the centuries in which various Minoan periods existed. In its beginnings, the Early Minoan period was still a rude maritime culture, although progressive and changing. Habitations were simple and the economy was one of rudimentary Neolithic agriculture, fishing, and animal husbandry. Only the seafaring character of the Early Minoans seems to have set them apart from other Neolithic developments of their day. Possibly it was this same sea trade which stimulated the later progression of Minoan culture. By the end of early Minoan I, metal objects from Egypt appeared and were soon augmented by native Cretan metallurgy.

Even in earliest Minoan times, settlements became sophisticated and city-like. Most were situated on the seacoasts where trade, rather than agriculture, was the determining factor. These urban areas became manufacturing centers for trade goods, and various craftsmen moved into these towns to ply their trades.

By Early Minoan II times, pottery, always an archaeological criterion sensitive to change, had developed spiral and curvilinear decorations. More sophisticated shapes, such as the long-spouted vases, appeared. *Vasiliki* ware with a varnished surface in red and black patterns became characteristic. Especially indicative, perhaps, was the appearance of rude figurines or idols, reflecting spiritual belief in anthropomorphic deities. An ossuary at the site of Hagia Triada dates from this period. This type of burial indicated a more complicated mortuary practice than that of earlier Neolithic peoples.

In Early Minoan II the tholos or beehive tomb evolved, possibly from the use of circular huts. The tholos was usually buried within a mound of earth or dug into a hillside, and may have been a continuation of the concept of cave interment. The tholos, later used in the Aegean islands and on the Grecian mainland, suggests one area of ideological union among all the early Classical peoples. The tholos tomb may have inspired the original Megalithic cult in the western Mediterranean.

Polychrome decoration evolved in Early Minoan III pottery. White designs on black paint and brown glazes suggested trade connections with distant centers. The increasing use of metals revealed the change in Minoan culture from simple, Neolithic maritime to a sophisticated complex. Leaf daggers of copper and flat copper axes were made. Gold ornaments in the forms of armlets and diadems were associated with the last part of the early Minoan period. Seals found with this material show that early Minoan III was roughly contemporaneous with the later part of the Old Kingdom of early Egypt. Minoan burials, perhaps influenced by the carefully made Egyptian tombs, evolved by middle Minoan times into well-constructed, cut-stone tholos tombs with an entranceway and a square forecourt. In Crete, burials were multiple rather than individual as in Egypt. In the Early Minoan period, cist graves, terracotta coffins, and charnel houses were all used. With the extensive use of metal and the beginning of cut-stone architecture, the Minoan civilization had already far outstripped its contemporaries on the mainland of Europe. At this same time, the Danubian Neolithic had scarcely begun, with little development of architecture and practically no metal.

Middle Minoan times mark the initiation of the Bronze Age in Crete. The first metal objects had been Egyptian imports. With the development of the Middle Minoan period, tin was imported from the region of Delphi on the mainland, and the alloying of copper and tin was practiced in Crete. Bronze beginnings in the Minoan sequence occurred a century or two earlier than the inception of bronze in the bulk of Europe.

Elongated daggers, bronze rapiers, and other weapons were manufactured of the new material. Bronze was also used for utilitarian tools and for receptacles. Gold and silver remained popular and were used in various combinations for ornaments and in some instances for masks and ceremonial vessels.

The greatest development of Middle Minoan times was in architecture. Inspired by the ashlar building methods of Egypt, Cretan architects began to erect large palaces at the sites of Knossos and Phaestos. These were, in reality, tremendous apartment houses containing dwelling space for the king, his retainers, and many of the lower-class people. The extensive site of Knossos at its height was covered with a colossal building of this type.

The lower parts of the typical Minoan building of the period were constructed of cut blocks of gypsum. Upperworks and superstructure were made of brick and wood timbers. Most of the buildings had several stories, with the upper levels reached by broad stairways. The unit of Cretan architecture was the *insula* or island. Each island or unit of rooms was grouped around a light well, which illuminated the interior rooms. The units were informally grouped together to produce an agglomeration which was called a palace. Cretan architects favored wooden columns with simple capitals. Rectangular piers, as well as columns, were arranged in porticos or colonnades. Open courtyards surrounded by flights of steplike seats for spectators were erected for ceremonial exhibitions. Sanitary facilities were provided by conduits for fresh water and drainage pipes. The palace of Knossos contained a throne room with a carved-stone throne and flanking stone benches, apparently for the king's councilors. The lowermost stories of the palace contained storage rooms with rows of huge jars or *pithoi* filled with olive oil.

Colorful frescoes decorated the walls of the various rooms. The chief subjects were marine, but other decorations were idyllic, mythological, or fanciful. The frescoes, done on the wall plaster in polychrome, were part of a definite Cretan style. This has been described as naturalistic, but it presents a certain decorative stylization. Frescoes in the palace at Knossos depict the attendants of the king, dancing girls, garden scenes, and in some instances vignettes of marine life such as a group of sea lions or fish. The subjects are painted with considerable spirit and great accuracy of outline and color. At the same time, there is an ornamental quality about them which adds to the decorative and aesthetic effect. There were some conventions, however, such as the drawing of a full-face eye in the profile of the human face.

The dress of the Cretan women shown in these paintings appears almost modern and is particularly reminiscent of European garb of the "Gay Nineties." Skirts were full and bodices very low; the waist was pulled in by a wide belt arrangement in an hourglass effect. Women also wore a peaked cap on the head. Men wore loincloths and boots and carried a dagger at the belt. The Cretans depicted themselves as brown-eyed and sallow-skinned. Their hair was dark and wavy, and they obviously adhered closely to the racial type which is usually called Mediterranean.

It is interesting to note that some splendid examples of Minoan art have been found in the palace of Ikhnaton at Tell-el-Amarna in central Egypt. Evidently the cultural currents which reached the island of Crete from Egypt were reciprocal.

The Middle Minoan cultures were distinguished by many other accomplishments in addition to the pronounced development of architecture. Linear script was developed, apparently by Cretan traders who needed a form of writing to record commercial data. The Minoan script in the form of short inscriptions occurs at a number of sites in central and eastern Crete, and became well known after the discovery of the famous "Phaestos Disc" made public in 1908. Later finds of Minoan inscriptions have demonstrated that there were two forms of Minoan script, designated as Linear A and Linear B. Tablets with inscriptions of Linear B were discovered on the Greek mainland in 1950 and 1952 at the site of Mycenae. In 1952, excavations at Pylos on the Greek mainland yielded some 350 additional tablets written in Minoan Linear B. From these finds and others, scholars have determined that Linear B was an archaic or *Achaean* form of Greek used 1,000 years before Plato. Translations of Linear B have added greatly to knowledge of Minoan culture. Linear A script is earlier than Linear B and probably in a different language. Linear A inscriptions are less common than B and have not as yet been translated. The Phaestos Disc itself is quite different from A and B and probably represents still another language, also as yet untranslated. Minoan writing thus demonstrates the mixed antecedents of Minoan culture.

Graphic seals were commonly used in Middle Minoan times and were cut with figures and occasional inscriptions made with Minoan characters. Gem-cutting of hard stone was also practiced. Indeed, most of the finer arts of the lapidary were known to middle Minoan artisans.

Middle Minoan pottery was distinctive in a number of definite forms. Polychrome-decorated vessels were made with walls of egg-shell thinness. At least some of the Middle Minoan pottery was manufactured on the potter's wheel. Most of the ceramic ware of this period shows great skill both in the form of the vessels and in the variety of the decoration. Curvilinear and naturalistic designs in polychrome paralleled many of the frescoes on the palace walls. Of the natural designs, those depicting the octopus or squid were probably the most popular, although other marine motifs were also common. Some pottery vessels were purposely stippled in a type of prickle ware. Others were crinkled on the surface, probably to imitate metal.

The most famous of the Middle Minoan pottery wares is that called *Kamares,* a type of pottery with polychrome decoration in a light-on-dark pattern. Middle Minoan pottery of a number of types was beautifully and gracefully shaped and tastefully ornamented. Most students of the history of art agree that the ceramic tradition of the high period of the Minoans was outstanding in the early world.

In Middle Minoan times, the tholos tomb built of cut blocks of stone formed in a beehive shape maintained its importance. Burials were also made in large jars. This form of interment was added to the other styles of burial already practiced from earlier Minoan times. In burial customs as well as in other cultural indications, Minoan practices clearly showed their eclectic origins.

Curiously enough, in the many frescoes painted on the palace walls, the Minoan artisans seldom gave any indication of their nautical activities. Fighting and bloodshed were never depicted and seldom suggested. Even the Minoan traders, who were for the most part undoubtedly pirates, were not recorded as such. There are, however, many indications of nautical and trading connections with other spots surrounding the shores of the eastern Mediterranean. Middle Minoan culture dominated the Cycladian of the same time. During these contacts, undoubtedly the Minoans incurred the enmity if not the envy of neighboring peoples. We may only guess which one of these first tried to overwhelm the island of Crete. In Middle Minoan II, about 1700 B.C., the palaces at Knossos and Phaestos were destroyed. Some invading peoples became strong enough to overwhelm the Minoan navy and sack the Cretan cities.

The invasion was not a permanent detriment to Minoan culture, however, and in the subsequent period of Middle Minoan III, the palaces were rebuilt and life went on more brilliantly than before. There was actually a renaissance or Golden Age of Minoan culture. After a brief period of brilliant culture, signs of degeneration and decay appeared. Perhaps the strength which had brought about the effervescent culture of mid-Minoan times had been sapped by the effort necessary to repel invaders, or the fighting could have been between the various Minoan centers themselves. About 1600 B.C. a violent earthquake rocked Crete, and trade with the Middle Kingdom of Egypt was cut off by the Hyksos or "Shepherd King" invasion. Late Minoan trade connections with Syria were also terminated by the conquests of the Hittites. Perhaps because of these difficulties, Minoan traders concentrated upon the mainland of Greece, where the Helladic culture was already established. From Middle Minoan III until the end of Minoan culture, the Greek mainland received an ever increasing amount of Minoan influence.

The Late Minoan period continued the old Cretan tradition but with definite signs of decay. In architecture, art, ceramics, and metalworking, the Late Minoan period was flashy and degenerate, but there were also some notable accomplishments. A new palace was built at Hagia Triada at this time. New additions and improvements were inaugurated at Knossos. Houses of a more complicated insular plan were erected. Public and private rooms were elaborately shaped and decorated, and the streets were paved. In Late Minoan II, Knossos apparently gained supremacy over other Cretan centers in what was virtually a Minoan kingdom.

Some of the finer arts reached their highest peak during this last period. Gem- and jewel-cutting reached an acme of perfection. Especially notable in the line of artistic accomplishment was certainly the Harvester Vase, a small goblet-like cup carved from a single piece of stone and depicting, in a frieze around its circumference, a procession of rolicking farmers. Such accomplishments as the Harvester Vase can scarcely be described as degenerate.

It was during Late Minoan times that the linear script became

A warrior of the Italic Bronze Age puts on his armor.

Etruscan bronze chariot or *Biga* (550–540 B.C.) from Monteleone.

Detail from the chariot on the opposite page.

The Roman Forum in its glory.

very widely spread, indicating that Cretan traders and perhaps also Cretan navies were active in Mediterranean waters. As Linear B is Greek, the implication is that traders from Greece were taking over more and more of the Cretan commerce. At this time also, Minoan raiding parties entered the several mouths of the Nile and plundered the Delta region of Egypt.

Pottery of the Late Minoan period was made in a number of styles. Some faïence ware was manufactured in imitation of Egyptian prototypes. Previous forms of Minoan ceramics with naturalistic decoration were carried on as before. Especially typical of Late Minoan III times was a type of pottery popular in late Minoan II. This ware, often called *Palace style,* was ornamented with designs which had become essentially conventionalized. The naturalism of previous Minoan inspiration gave way to rather stereotyped and stilted motifs. The Palace style is considered by many students as inferior to the artistic creations of earlier time.

Important in the Late Minoan period was the extension of Cretan culture to the Greek mainland and to other points in the Aegean area. While Minoan traders and pirates were absorbing ideas and wealth from many other spots in the eastern Mediterranean, these places in their turn were receiving Minoan culture. One that was to have great importance in later times was Mycenae, located near the southern tip of the Balkan Peninsula. As early as late Minoan I, Mycenae was a flourishing city which, although essentially of Helladic tradition, had already absorbed much Cretan culture. By 1500 B.C., Mycenae had outstripped even Knossos in power and importance.

It was probably one of these mainland cities, or a coalition of them, that destroyed the mother culture from which they had already derived so much. There is more than a suggestion that the Minoans had for many years levied tribute from the mainland cities under their jurisdiction. Possibly these satellite cities, having absorbed enough strength from the Minoan culture, turned upon it and destroyed it. In Late Minoan II the palaces at Phaestos and Hagia Triada were destroyed. Civil war ravaged Crete. Knossos, for a time, ruled supreme as the leader of Minoan civilization. Perhaps Late Minoan II, the time of this supremacy of Knossos, was also the time of King Minos of legendary fame. Under the absolute rule of Knossos, trade connections with the eastern Mediterranean, Egypt, and Greece reached a final peak of activity.

Then Knossos itself was destroyed by a force of unknown invaders. With the violent end of this brilliant center, the cultural leadership of the Aegean world passed over to Greece and especially to the one center, Mycenae.

The period of Late Minoan III was a faint flickering of the great flame that had been Minoan Crete.

While the Minoan sequence was unfolding on the island of Crete, a somewhat parallel development was taking place on the many islands of the Aegean, particularly in the Cyclades group. The Cycladic development closely paralleled events in Crete but with some outstanding differences. Cycladic beginnings were definitely inspired from Anatolia. As the Cyclades lie closer to the Anatolian coast, these connections were even more intimate than in the case of Crete. Cycladic pottery was of the Anatolian plain-ware tradition or burnished black on red. The Cycladic material has been divided on a basis of culture changes into a sequence similar to that of Minoan Crete. Phylakopi, which had its beginnings in early Cycladic III, was one of the most important towns in these islands.

The Cycladic metal age began early with the same general types of implements as those of Crete. Flat axes and daggers of copper were manufactured from metal found on the islands of Paros and Syphnos. Silver was also worked at an early date in the Cyclades.

Architecture, art, and even the Cycladic ceramic tradition were similar to the Minoan but less notable. Especially during Middle Minoan times the Cycladic cultural tradition was very close to that of Crete. Many pottery vessels and wall frescoes were ornamented with the same style which Minoan Crete made famous. Architectural traditions and burial customs were also similar.

Especially noteworthy in the Cycladic repertory of cultural objects were small figurines, often carved from marble. These were made in a rudimentary shape of the human figure, often so stylized as to show only the most fundamental outlines of neck, torso, and stubby limbs. These Cycladic idols were part of a cult, apparently common in that region, which stemmed from the Near East. The same type of idols were found over most of the Aegean area and in pre-Minoan Crete.

The great site of Hissarlik, or Troy, played an integral part in the development of the culture of the eastern Mediterranean as well as contributing to the culture of Europe. When Heinrich Schliemann first excavated the site and proved it to be the Troy of the *Iliad* and the *Odyssey,* he found the ancient town complicated by a series of cities piled one on the ruins of the other. Schliemann excavated down through these ruins in an enthusiastic but haphazard manner. He destroyed more evidence than he recovered. We may excuse Schliemann on the grounds that his excavations were done at an early period at the end of the nineteenth century when scientific digging had not been developed into its present careful form. Subsequent excavations at Troy, by Schliemann's assistant Wilhelm Dorpfeld and by the University of Cincinnati, have shown that this one site was the center of a high civilization representing several stages of culture in the succession of cities built on it.

The position of Troy was extremely important in the ancient world. It was located at the juncture of two continents and two seas. In this strategic position it commanded the flow of commerce in many directions and was in a position to absorb any influences and cultural traits that might pass through such a crossroads. Troy, at several stages of its career, undoubtedly had connections with ancient Crete. Trojan influences in their turn extended as far away as the Danube valley in Europe and possibly even farther. Because of the succession of Trojan cities at the same site, and more especially because of Trojan trade materials in other well-dated sites, the chronology of Troy is well substantiated. Trojan pottery forms and other cultural evidences are used as chronological indicators for surrounding regions. The Homeric legend which deals with the sack of one of the Trojan cities serves also as background evidence.

The first city of Troy was established around 2700 B.C. Even this earliest site was no simple Neolithic village; it was a fortified acropolis with ponderous walls obviously built to withstand pressure from any direction. In this form Troy very early served as a barrier to further movements of culture across the Hellespont from Anatolia to Europe.

The earliest settlement at Troy bore many resemblances to the Minoan culture on the island of Crete. There were trade contacts even in Early Minoan times. The site of Troy, because of its mainland position was, however, more closely in contact with the Anatolian hinterland. There was also less immunity from attack. The fortified nature of the Trojan cities is illustrative of their military history.

The second city or Troy II was built on the same site close to the year 2300 B.C. and endured for the next two centuries. It was also a fortified citadel with massive stone walls, and for convenience its span is divided into three periods. During the time of this second city, the site of Troy became even more important in the trading world of the eastern Mediterranean. The influences of Troy II made themselves felt in Thrace, Macedonia, on the Balkan peninsula, in southern Russia, and throughout the Aegean world.

One colonizing movement of Trojans from the second city extended into the coast lands of Macedonia and produced a variation known as the *Macedonian culture*. This early Macedonian culture had many characteristics which linked it to Troy, from which it was derived.

Riches in merchandise indicate that Troy II was a wealthy commercial center. Flat copper axes and daggers were common items of barter. Many weapons and tools of Troy II were made in true bronze. At this time, however, the secret of the alloying of copper and tin to make bronze had not yet passed on to Europe. Many items made of precious metals were found in Troy II. Diadems, spiral arm and leg ornaments, and pinheads of gold, silver, and electrum were typical of these opulent times. A great hoard of ceremonial battle-axes made of semiprecious stones from the third period of Troy II reflects influences from the battle-ax-using cultures of southern Russia.

Flat marble idols with a crude outline of the human figure suggest that the Trojans of the second city were also devotees of the Mother Goddess cult of the Aegean, since these idols followed the general Cycladic pattern wherever Mother Goddess worship reached a peak of fervor.

Of especial interest in Troy II is the appearance of the special type of building called the megaron. The megaron, as it appeared in Troy II, was a ceremonial or formalized type of house or hall rectangular in outline. It could be built of cut stone, timber, or both. The essential features were an interior hearth, usually flanked by four columns which supported the roof. On the façade of the megaron was an extended porch with one or two columns supporting the porch roof. These columns in front are described as *in antis,* with reference to their position between the antae or the extensions of the front walls. The roof of the megaron was usually gabled. This whole structure with its essential elements appeared in later times among a number of Greek cultures and areas to the north, and is found in its essentials as far north as Dimini and the Painted Pottery site of Erösd. It also became the basis of the later Greek temple.

The city of Troy II was destroyed by an invasion of nomad people from the steppes to the north. These barbaric newcomers swept over the wealthy city, breached the walls, and destroyed the town.

The city of Troy III was built about 2100 B.C. on the ruins of its more illustrious predecessors. Neither Troy III nor its successors Troy IV and Troy V were particularly notable. There is considerable evidence that the site of Troy was overawed at this time by the greater might and importance of the Minoan culture with its capital at Knossos. The destruction of Troy IV and V may indicate the vengeance of Minoan raiding parties protesting commercial rivalry or the payment of tribute to Troy for passage of their ships through the entrance to the Black Sea.

Troy VI was established around 1900 B.C. and almost immediately became a city of importance. This town has long been thought to be the city of the *Iliad*. However, Troy VI was destroyed about the middle of the fourteenth century before Christ. This is almost two hundred years too early for the Trojan War of Homer's great epic, for from the many chronological clues in the story of the fall of King Priam's city, the sack of Troy took place about 1183 B.C. This was the time of Troy VIIa, the city built on the ruins of Troy VI. Actually Troy VI was built by invaders called Minyans who had overrun Greece and most of the Aegean islands. The Minyans were perhaps a part of the Urnfield movement, for they cremated their dead and buried them in an Urnfield type of cemetery.

285

The city of Troy VI absorbed much of the greatness of the Minoan culture from its trade connections. Gradually the leadership of the Aegean world was passing from the hands of Knossos and the other Minoan cities into the domain of the Trojan merchants.

Coincidental with the rise of Troy VI there was a remarkable growth of certain mainland cities on the Peloponnesus. The culture represented by these cities is generally called *Mycenaean,* from the city of Mycenae, one of the foremost of these sites. Troy VI possessed a Mycenaean type of culture. Chronologically the Mycenaean times may be described as a Bronze Age. The weapons, tools, architecture, and general status of development of Troy VI closely paralleled that of the other Mycenaean cities. When the Greeks of Homer's thrilling tale sailed against the enemy city of Troy, they no doubt encountered a familiar culture. Both fought with the same weapons and were familiar with the same type of fortified cities.

Troy VI appears to be a city with the same Mycenaean culture as the Greek centers commemorated in Homer's immortal epic, but this particular town was destroyed before the Greeks, under Agamemnon's leadership, came to rescue the beautiful Helen. In spite of this discrepancy, the archaeological evidence of Troy VI corresponds very well with the literary information in Homer's writings.

Troy VIIa was built on the ruins of Troy VI after another incursion of armed invaders from southeastern Europe. But the latest building effort at the great site of Troy was only a faint echo of the importance which this spot had formerly enjoyed. In the centuries following the fall of Troy VI and Troy VII, the leadership of the Aegean world definitely passed to the mainland of the Balkan peninsula. It is difficult to recognize in the rather disappointing archaeological evidences of Troy VIIa, the mighty towers of Ilium which Homer described. Perhaps the Homeric legend of the siege of Troy still reflected the greatness of Troy VI. After Troy VIIa, other towns were built in this place, but never again was the site of Troy of real significance in Aegean events.

The trend of culture on the mainland of Greece which culminated in the Mycenaean is usually called the Helladic. This sequence has been divided into an Early, Middle, and Late Helladic, and each of these periods in turn is subdivided into three segments. The Late Helladic period is usually referred to as the Mycenaean.

The Early Helladic culture appears to have first been introduced at several sites in central Greece from the Aegean islands. Perhaps the most significant of the Early Helladic sites is that of Korakou near Corinth. Korakou is a stratified settlement with laminated layers of refuse from several epochs of human living which occurred at that place.

The pottery found at Korakou consisted of a dark, burnished ware, especially in askoid and spouted forms. This ceramic tradition was similar to that from the Cyclades.

In Early Helladic II another type of ware appeared, featuring red and black colors with burnished finishes. This ware was obviously influenced by the Vasiliki ware of Crete. The Early Helladic generally paralleled the Early Minoan III and Middle Minoan I. The beginning of the Helladic sequence was, then, somewhat later than the initiation of these events on the island of Crete.

Early Helladic III introduced a white-patterned ware. This type of pottery, likewise from the island of Crete, was also diffused to the Cyclades region. This white-patterned ware serves as a further check on chronology.

Early Helladic III spread as far as central Greece, but no farther. Pottery wares of Early Helladic III times replaced the typical Painted Pottery traditions in this region. The painted wares that had reached the Danube region and inaugurated the Painted Pottery influences there were derived from peoples earlier than the Helladic III. There were mixtures involving early Helladic III cultures and those of the Aegean. The Aegean peoples, however, remained essentially maritime and thus distinct from the Helladic.

The end of the Early Helladic was brought about by a series of incursions of new people presumably from the north. Most Early Helladic towns perished by fire and sword. The invaders brought with them the Greek language from their Aryan background, and they may thus lay claim to being the first Greeks. The newcomers overwhelmed the early Helladic culture and established a series of civilizations which are referred to as Middle Helladic. Technically, many scholars regard the coming of these invaders as the real beginning of the Classic period.

The new comers of the Middle Helladic built rectangular stone houses. Some of these approached the megaron type which had already appeared in Troy II. The typical form of interment of the middle Helladic people was a contracted burial in a stone cist. They utilized shaft-hole axes, knives, swords, and spearheads of bronze. The invaders were, then, obviously in possession of a well-developed Bronze Age culture.

The pottery of the Middle Helladic was typically a silver gray fabric with a rather soapy feel on the surface. This material was obviously made on the potter's wheel, foreign up to this time to the mainland of Greece. This gray ware is called Minyan ware or, more specifically, silver Minyan. In southern Greece near Korakou this pottery was imitated in local yellow clays which produced a type called gold Minyan.

Both the pottery forms and the gray color of the silver Minyan are similar to ceramic traditions from Troy. Trojan pottery had for some time previous to this featured these items. Because of the pottery, the new overlords of Greece are often called the Minyan Invaders. The Minyans did not exterminate the early Helladic population, but set themselves up as an aristocracy to rule over them.

In Middle Helladic times, the great sites of Tiryns and Mycenae were already flourishing. These cities, established in Early Helladic times, had been taken over by the Middle Helladic newcomers and made into impressive fortresses. By Middle Helladic II, a powerful dynasty was already established at Mycenae and burying its dead members there. At Orchomenos, another Middle Helladic city, there also was a settlement of great size with stone architecture and evidences of trade. Orchomenos was the center of a large agricultural area. Tiryns and Mycenae were military and trading centers with many maritime contacts. The culture of the latter two cities closely paralleled that of Troy VI. Obviously all were in close contact with many similar elements.

Minoan objects found in the graves of the early lords of the fortified sites of Tiryns and Mycenae undoubtedly were trade items or booty taken in raids on Crete. Cretan artists either came to Mycenae as slaves or were lured there by rich rewards promised by wealthy princes.

Because of the growing importance of these citadels, the Late Helladic period is referred to as the Mycenaean. During the My-cenaean period the major centers were the sites of Tiryns, Orcho-menos, Thebes, Troy, and, of course, Mycenae itself.

Mycenae, Tiryns, Troy, and Thebes were all walled cities. These centers were foci of powerful military dynasties that left roads and subsidiary fortresses over the surrounding countryside to mark the extent of their domain. The Homeric writings are rich with infor-mation on the arms, weapons, architecture, and customs of this time. The Trojan War recorded by Homer was apparently fought by forces having a Mycenaean type of culture, but the burial practices described in Homer's epic poem differ from the evidence of the exca-vations in Mycenaean centers. Nonetheless, archaeology has generally substantiated the literary descriptions of the Greek forces and the Trojan defenders.

Both Mycenae and Tiryns were examined by Heinrich Schlie-mann. At Mycenae, Schliemann discovered a walled citadel similar to Troy in its major aspects. Mycenaean builders used cyclopian or non-ashlar masonry to lay city walls of immense thickness. Galleries were left within the walls, and these ramparts were pierced by gates formed by means of corbeled arches rather than the true arch. The famous Lion Gate at Mycenae is topped by a triangular slab of stone with a lion carved in relief rearing up on either side of a pillar of the Cretan type.

Mycenae is usually remembered for the cemetery which Schlie-mann discovered in the so-called "grave circle." This circular area, outlined with large slabs of stone, was the burying place of Myce-naean kings and persons of importance from Middle Helladic times onward. The graves within the circle at Mycenae were shaft graves with multiple interments. The burials show a considerable sequence in time and variation in the richness of the mortuary deposits which accompanied them.

Graves numbered by Schliemann as IV and V of the grave circle at Mycenae were the richest. Accompanying the several bodies within these graves were gold plates, rhytons, gold masks, swords, pottery, and amber. This immense treasure was remarkable for both the richness of its materials and the excellence of workmanship. The gold plates were ornamented with geometric designs and with seminaturalistic motifs, some of them reminiscent of the Minoan. One rhyton was decorated with the complete scene of a siege embossed on its side. Justly famous is a pair of daggers whose bronze blades were inlaid by precious metals with scenes of warfare and the hunt. The gold masks from Mycenae represent interesting physical types with beards and mustachios and display metal-working techniques of a high order.

Recent excavations at Mycenae have revealed another grave circle outside the Lion Gate. This new cemetery also contains shaft graves with rich burial accompaniments.

Ostrich eggshell beads from North Africa and amber from the Baltic area indicate the wide trade connections of the Mycenaean merchant kings. The strongest influences at Mycenae, however, were Minoan; a single cup in the Mycenaean treasure was almost certainly of Minoan craftsmanship. Some of the material from Mycenae may actually represent loot taken by Mycenaean raiders from Knossos or other Minoan centers.

Minoan influence was also present at Tiryns and Thebes. Wall frescoes done in the Minoan manner show the Cretan sport of bull-baiting. Other wall murals, although more formal and stereotyped than Minoan examples, show many similar motifs.

The beehive tomb or tholos may have been originally a Cretan development, or it may have developed in Mycenae itself. The tholos became the outstanding mortuary structure in Mycenaean times. Several of these tombs, made with well-laid ashlar masonry, have been found near Mycenaean centers. Perhaps the best known of the Mycenaean beehive tombs is the one called the "Treasury of Atreus." It was not a treasure vault but a typical beehive tomb of the Mycenaean period. Such tombs as the Treasury of Atreus were constructed with an entranceway or dromos, a main circular chamber with a domed roof, and a small burial chamber to one side. Some of the more elaborate beehive tombs were embellished with bronze fittings and metal rosettes at the interstices of the stones. None of the beehive tombs, however, embodied the principle of the true arch. Regularly laid ashlars of masonry were chamfered in the interior to simulate a true arch, but the layers were horizontal and laminated.

One particular beehive tomb at the site of Vaphio near Sparta yielded two gold cups. The sides of these famous Vaphio cups were decorated with *repoussé* scenes. On one cup, wild bulls were worked with very successful movement and perspective. On the second Vapheio cup, tame bulls were shown in a pasture. The excellence of metal working as portrayed by the Vaphio cups was illustrative of the high tradition of these times.

An additional center of cultural importance among the Mediterranean islands was Malta, which was first affected by a migration, Asiatic in origin, around the turn of the third millennium before Christ. This movement of peoples to Malta was related to the Thessalian movement which brought the Neolithic way of life into northern Greece. Subsequent developments on the island were roughly parallel to those on the island of Crete and the Cyclades. The tholos or beehive type of architecture was early implanted here, possibly from the Greek mainland. On Malta a special development of this type of architecture resulted in the erection of several stone temple-like structures made up of units of round-end rooms. These apsidal plans may have affected the trend of Megalithic architecture as it appeared later in the western Mediterranean. Also at Malta are several hypogea, or underground catacomb-like buildings, apparently used for religious purposes.

The major trend of eastern Mediterranean cultural development climaxed in the Mycenaean period. Around the year 1000 B.C. the vitality of this development began to wane. From the north a movement called the Dorian invasion swept over the Mycenaean cities. The large fortified citadels typical of Mycenaean times were destroyed or abandoned. The population fled to minor centers or rural estates. This subsequent period of dispersal and decline is called the *Geometric*.

The term *geometric* is derived from the type of pottery which became popular in the centuries following the Mycenaean. The potter's wheel which had been used effectively in the middle Helladic was used to turn out large numbers of vases, jugs, and amphorae decorated with a variety of typical designs. Even this decoration of Geometric wares was largely done on the turning wheel, producing series of simple stripes. A few vague motifs of the earlier Minoan were continued. Even these, however, were made with a lack of skill and imagination which robbed them of artistic merit.

The Geometric period in Greece was marked by the use of iron weapons and implements. Iron swords, both the slashing type from the Mycenaean and the rapier of the Minoan, were in use during Geometric times. Bronze for ornaments and implements was still used. A wide assortment of bronze fibulae was used by Iron Age Greeks to fasten their flowing garments.

The full development of the Geometric period was distinguished by a special type of mortuary pottery named from the Dipylon cemetery near Athens. These pieces, some of them amphorae as much as five feet in height, were of brick-red fabric decorated on the upper portions with stylized geometric designs. The Dipylon vases were typically divided into registers according to Geometric custom. These registers were decorated with continuous bands of crudely portrayed figures, many participating in funeral rituals, ceremonial processions, or fights. Files of women mourners were portrayed with horses and chariots. In other registers, goats, birds, and other animals were shown in long, repetitive processions. Intervening areas were filled with circles, zigzags, swastikas, and rosettes.

The crude but interesting depictions of the Dipylon vases show men and women, weapons and warfare which were not typically Greek. They may be the indication of another intrusion of people into Greek lands. It has been suggested that the invasion of the Dorics may account for these differences in Dipylon art, but there are some difficulties in this simple explanation.

The Greek Iron Age or Geometric period showed a decided decline in architecture, art, and the other cultural traditions which had distinguished previous eras. The Geometric period is for this reason often called the Greek *Dark Ages,* but most of the Classic trend of culture was not completely lost. Out of the difficult and unco-ordinated period of the Geometric, there began to form, about the seventh century before Christ, the essentials of the high period of Greek culture. The Geometric period was not one of cultural development, but it provided the optimum mixture of ingredients necessary to produce the *Golden Age* of Greece. With the undercurrent of the Minoan culture still strong, the seventh century began to see the rise and development of the final culmination of Greek culture. Some authorities relate to the mixed racial and cultural background of the Grecian people a hybrid vigor not previously present.

Archaeologists often formalize the trend of Grecian events from the Mycenaean period to the formation of the true *Hellenic culture* by this succession of periods:

Mycenaean	1100–1000 B.C.
Proto-Geometric	1000–900 B.C.
Geometric	925–650 B.C.
Orientalizing	725–600 B.C.

The *Orientalizing period* again refers to pottery types and decoration. The forms of this era were smaller and different in shape, and motifs consisted typically of registers of griffins, lions, hunters, and other figures of Mesopotamia. Greece, at this time, developed constant intercourse with the Near East, especially the eastern Mediterranean.

During the Greek Geometric period, when the Mycenaean cities had disappeared as dominating political centers in the Mediterranean, a new eastern group—the Phoenicians—established a series of trading cities on the eastern coasts of the Mediterranean. The Phoenician traders broadened their contacts through their colony of Carthage in the middle Mediterranean. About this same time, the Etruscans also came out of the east and landed on the western coast of Italy, bringing with them an Oriental type of culture with many features typical of the Near East. This foreign culture merged with the European tradition already established in Italy.

Even through the unstable Geometric and Orientalizing periods, there was a certain virility, which manifested itself in colonization and expansion. At the same time the urbanization which had earlier begun in Greek lands marked the beginning of those great centers of Greek culture of two or three centuries later. Sicily was colonized by Greeks in 734 B.C. Other colonists, doubtless Dorian invaders from the north mixed with Mycenaean elements, moved westward to colonize the southern portion of Italy.

Archaeologists usually distinguish three definite periods in this progression. Early attempts at sculpture, architecture, and the other arts are termed *Archaic*. The Archaic period came to an end around 480 B.C. and reached maturity in the fifth century before Christ. The high point of Greek achievement is called the *Developed period,* the time of the great Athenian statesman, Pericles, and is often referred to as the *Periclean Age.* The periods of development of the brilliant Greek civilization centering in the mainland cities of Greece are distinguished as the *Hellenic culture.* The high point of Greek civilization was the product of the Hellenes, the Greek word for themselves. Hellenic is distinguished from the previous Helladic and the subsequent Hellenistic periods.

Frequent note has been made of the fact that the Hellenic culture reached an amazing climax of development in a very short time. This is true, but its many roots extended all the way from the Minoan on the island of Crete to the city of Troy and the Anatolian hinterland which lay behind the Troad. Even with the intervening Dark Ages of the Greek Geometric period, the rise of the Hellenic culture had begun as early as the Mycenaean period or even before. Indeed, by the fifth century B.C., the Greek peoples had achieved everything but political unity. Architecture, sculpture, ceramics, drama, and history developed to the ultimate, while fertile philosophical speculations laid the foundation for the great works of Plato and Aristotle in the following century.

The bulk of Europe during this period still continued an Iron Age barbarism. Real architecture was almost unknown, particularly in stone. The La Tène people of western Europe and the British Isles possessed a unique decorative style, but were far behind the Greeks in artistic achievement. The cultural contrast is likewise apparent in intellectual fields.

The political disunity which had prevented the Greeks from forming a single nation contributed to the end of the Hellenic period. Philip II of Macedon, as head of a small state in the north of Greece, had developed a lust for power and along with it a highly trained army with a co-ordinated method of fighting. In the decisive battle of Chaeroneia of 338 B.C., he conquered a disunited Greece and set himself up as leader of the Greek states in a crusade against their natural enemy, Persia. After the assassination of Philip of Macedon, his program for conquest passed to his son Alexander, later to be called Alexander the Great. This son, by his wars with the Persians and his extensive conquests in the Near East, spread Greek culture in that direction and initiated a new era. His untimely death in Babylon in 323 B.C. marks the beginning of the Hellenistic period.

Following the death of Alexander the Great, his empire was dismembered and divided among his followers. One of Alexander's generals, also a son of Philip of Macedon, was Antigonus, often called the One-Eyed. Antigonus took over that part of the empire which lay in Asia Minor, and his descendants later became the kings of Macedon.

The major portion of Alexander's conquests in the Near East was given to another of his generals, Seleucus Nicator, who founded a dynasty which bore his name. The Seleucids made their capital at Antioch on the Orontes River. Egypt became the separate domain of Ptolemy, another general of Alexander's. Ptolemy, which means "mighty in war," founded a dynasty which lasted until 30 B.C., and the Ptolemies ruled from their capital city of Alexandria on the Nile River. Although Alexander had conquered far to the east, his followers could not hold these distant conquests. The Ptolomies, the Seleucids, the Antigonids, and their successors in effect set up separate kingdoms which warred among themselves with individual political alliances and intrigues.

The Hellenistic period was also the time of the rise of Rome in the West and the spread of Roman imperialism in the Mediterranean basin.

Culturally, the Hellenistic period is marked by the diffusion of many aspects of Greek civilization to these new kingdoms. Greek culture in its pure Hellenic form, although it achieved its climax on the Greek mainland, had from earliest times many colony cities on the Anatolian coast. This area, called Ionia, had developed through Archaic and Transitional periods just as had the culture on the Greek mainland. Many of these cities, although overrun by the previous Persian regimes and diluted by large amounts of Oriental population and culture, nonetheless maintained their Greek character and thought of themselves as a part of the motherland across the Aegean.

With the wars of Alexander the Great, the center of Greek culture shifted from the Greek mainland to the cities of Egypt and Hither Asia. Egyptian cities, headed by Alexandria on the delta of the Nile, received large influxes of Greek peoples and culture. Egypt, which had enjoyed a cultural continuity extending over five thousand years, became Hellenized to a certain extent. Antioch, the capital of the Seleucids, steeped in a background of Semitic and Near Eastern culture, became essentially Greek. Greek buildings, Greek mosaics, Greek gods, and the writing and language which were the background of Hellenic culture became the outstanding features of the Hellenistic cities. Artisans, philosophers, dramatists, and mercenary soldiers were attracted to the brilliant courts which the Seleucids, the Ptolomies, and the other Hellenistic monarchs established. The great library at Alexandria became the chief repository of the knowledge of the times, followed closely by the library in the city of Pergamon on the Ionic coast.

Many Classical scholars have described the Hellenistic period as a time of decline. These purists have pointed out that Hellenistic architecture was more flowery and ornate than the simple, formal designs that were raised on the Acropolis at Athens in the fifth century b.c. Hellenistic sculpture and painting were also florid and cluttered. The superfluous style of much of the Hellenistic literature lacked artistic merit. Forms were stilted, and flattery of the current ruler or patron was considered more important than a basic philosophy. Most of the Hellenistic citizens regularly attended the famous chariot races in the great hippodrome at Antioch or enjoyed baudy and plebeian plays in the various theaters of the Hellenistic cities.

In spite of the many evidences of cultural decline in Hellenistic times, there was, nonetheless, a certain virility and vigor which characterized the period. Temples to the gods were larger and more audacious in design than the earlier, more refined Hellenic examples. Science and other intellectual studies progressed. There are many parallels between the Hellenistic civilizations and the culture of the United States. Both were transplanted. Both enjoyed a certain effervescent, but not always refined, progression. The Hellenistic culture, like the culture of the United States, became in its time the focal center of political events in its region.

During the course of Hellenistic events in the eastern Mediterranean, the rising power of Rome in the west became more and more involved in Hellenistic affairs. Squabbles between the various Hellenistic monarchs were often settled by the support or influence of Rome. The expansion of Roman power from Italy had already begun in the third century B.C. In the eastern Mediterranean, the Romans conquered one Hellenistic center after another, culminating in the annexation of Egypt.

Roman imperialism in the eastern Mediterranean, by conquest of the Hellenistic centers, added greatly to the Greek elements in Roman culture. The Greek artisans, writers, and scientists who had previously clustered around the Hellenistic monarchs and their courts naturally gravitated to Rome. But Roman culture had absorbed Greek elements long before Hellenistic times. Rome had not been the first to spread Classic culture, but with the rise of imperialism she carried it to the rest of Europe, where it was fused with the many traditions that had been developing in the body of Europe.

Rome, as a culture, did not spring directly from the same sources as did the Greek. The basic pattern for Roman culture was formulated in Italy in the late Bronze and early Iron Ages there. The Iron Age in Italy was propagated essentially by the brilliant Villanovan development augmented by influences from the iron-using centers in the Alpine regions farther to the north. The Bronze Age settlements of the Terremare also contributed to these later developments. Even the Bronze Age lake dwellers in the north and the Ligurian cave dwellers in northwestern Italy were to contribute cultures and populations to the formation of Roman culture.

Following the rise of the Mycenaean cultures in Greece around 1400 B.C., Grecian culture began to intrude increasingly upon the mainland of Italy. Greece colonized and expanded westward during the Geometric period and later, when merchants carrying their typical geometrically ornamented pottery pressed into southern Italy and Sicily. About the middle of the eighth century B.C., when Hellenic civilization was still in its Archaic stage of development in Greece, Greek colonists were established in southern Italy and eastern Sicily. In western Sicily, the Phoenicians were already settled, and several small towns and colonies backed by Carthage were able to withstand the pressure of the colonizing Greeks.

297

The oldest of the Greek colonies in western Italy is probably that of Cumae north of the Bay of Naples, founded by the Chalcidians from Euboea. This colonization was significant because it introduced a system of writing into Italy. Soon the whole southern portion of Italy from Cumae to Tarentum was occupied by Greek colonies, some of whom in their turn began to send out other colonies. The incoming Greeks fought off and partially Hellenized the indigenous settlers of the interior with whom they came in contact. By agricultural development and sea trade with their native land as well as with other centers in the Mediterranean, these Greek colonies became powerful and well established. The southern portion of Italy came to be called *Magna Graecia*.

An important element in the formulation of Roman culture was that of the Etruscans. The Etruscans have long been regarded as an Eastern people of an unknown Near Eastern origin who intruded into the Italian area. The date of the arrival of the Etruscans in Italy was possibly as early as the eleventh century, but according to other evidence could have been as late as the middle of the eighth century B.C. The Etruscan language was non-Indo-European and apparently related to the pre-Hellenic languages of Asia Minor. Originally the Etruscans inhabited portions of the Aegean area or the Anatolian coast as one of the pre-Hellenic, non-Indo-European-speaking peoples there. Many Etruscan cultural items reveal Oriental contacts. With the coming of the Dorian invasion many of the earlier Greek peoples were displaced. In their southern progress, the Dorians drove toward the islands of the Aegean, pushing other Greek peoples, the Aeolians and the Ionians, before them. These in turn pressed against the Tyrseni, or the Tursha, as the Egyptians called the Etruscans. Egyptian documents mention that the Tursha were among the "Peoples of the Sea" who attacked the Egyptian coast in the Nineteenth and Twentieth Dynasties. A double inscription found on the island of Lemnos written in Etruscan or a closely related language strengthens the supposition that the Etruscans came from that region.

The Etruscan newcomers landed on the western coasts of central Italy. The oldest Etruscan city in this area is probably that of Tarquinii, which became the focus of their further development. Subsequently they established twelve cities in this same region, organized into a confederation, and pushed slowly inland.

As the Etruscans landed in small groups, their conquest was necessarily slow. They brought with them, however, material arts and equipment superior to that of the indigenous Villanovans and the other people in the areas they covered. Although the Etruscan occupation of northern and western Italy was essentially a conquest, it was also a process of assimilation and fusion with indigenous Italic peoples. The Etruscans became a dominant class in those regions which they influenced, directing armies composed essentially of Italic soldiers. The Etruscans also brought with them finished architecture, engineering works, and organizational ability. Beginning in the seventh century before Christ, the Etruscans established an empire in Italy. Their cities were in trade contact with other Mediterranean centers, the cities of Greece, Sicily, the eastern Mediterranean, and Carthage. Inland, the Etruscans organized the country and improved the status of those living in areas over which they ruled.

The Etruscan empire extended beyond the Po River to the north and as far as the Greek settlements to the south. Beyond these confines, the Etruscans conquered and organized, touching the Greek colonies at Cumae and the rest of the Magna Graecia. These Etruscan conquests to the south had a profound effect upon the later development of the Roman rule in Italy.

The Etruscans formed an alliance with Carthage aimed against the Greeks who were still colonizing. A sea battle was fought with the combined fleets of Etruria and Carthage on the one hand and the Greek fleet of the Phocaeans on the other. Although the Phocaeans were successful in this contest, they suffered such serious losses that they retired, leaving the Etruscans and Carthaginians to continue their expansion.

During their consolidation of central Italy the Etruscans had taken over the territory of Rome. There were three traditional Etruscan kings of Rome, who were apparently a series of chiefs, rather than a continuous dynasty. The Etruscans, here as elsewhere, established a centralized government and well-integrated political state. Indeed, many scholars have with reason considered Roman culture as directly sprung from the Etruscans.

But Etruscan rule in Latium lasted only about a century and a half. Traditionally, a revolution beginning at Rome threw off the Etruscan yoke. Probably this revolution, which is chiefly based on legend and uncertain history, was part of a larger movement to overthrow the domination of the Etruscans in all of Italy. The Greeks, especially in Magna Graecia, resented the intrusion of the Etruscans. In a series of episodes and battles the Etruscans were expelled by the Greeks and several groups of indigenous peoples, including the Latins.

Although the power of the Etruscans had been broken in Latium, their occupation for a century and a half had left a decided mark. Farther north in Etruria, the cultural heritage of the Etruscans was even stronger and maintained itself until late Roman times. Although the Etruscans had never unified all of Italy into one empire, their conquests and their organization had nonetheless laid the foundation for Rome to do so. Rome, with a mixed heritage of Etruscan and Greek, began a series of conquests following the Etruscan model. Although Rome did not manage to unify all of Italy for more than two centuries, it was a process which had already been started.

The rise of Rome is largely a matter of recorded history. The Etruscans, disunited into city states, diminished in power and were finally overcome by Rome. Hellenism also, as carried by the many Greek colonies of Magna Graecia, began to decline. During the centuries prior to the fifth century B.C., Magna Graecia had enjoyed a peak of culture paralleling that in Greece itself. With the fourth century, however, the Greek colonies in Italy, harried by constant warfare with the tribes of the interior and conflict among themselves, entered a period of decline which ended in their eventual conquest by Rome.

A momentous event in Roman history was the Celtic invasion of Italy in the last of the fifth century B.C. These Celts, an offshoot of the Celts of western Europe, overcame the Etruscans and overran the Po valley in the north. Moving farther south, the Celtic armies approached Rome. They defeated the Romans and occupied the city itself. Finally, the Celts, or the Gauls as the Romans called them, were bought off by one thousand pounds of gold and induced to withdraw.

The Celts had brought across the Alps with them the La Tène culture. They settled down in northern Italy and their La Tène culture mingled with that of the more advanced Etruscans and the indigenous peoples who had already adopted a sedentary agricultural economy. In peninsular Italy the Gaulish invasions had no lasting effect, for the people did not permanently settle there. However, the terror which the Celts inspired had a unifying effect upon the Italian peoples. The Romans, through this contact, were for the first time in touch with La Tène culture and became cognizant of the region of Gaul beyond the Alps.

Adopting weapons and tactics from peoples who had shown their superiority, Rome reorganized her armies and revised equipment and military procedure. Through the fourth and third centuries B.C., Rome increased her area and power. After a long series of wars the Italian peninsula was consolidated and the last remnants of Magna Graecia and Etruria incorporated in a Roman union which was at first a confederacy rather than an empire. Carthage, the only real rival to Roman supremacy in the west, was finally defeated during the Punic Wars. In 202 B.C., P. Scipio, the Roman leader, completely routed the Carthaginians in the decisive battle of Zama, which completed Rome's domination of the west.

In the eastern Mediterranean also, Rome was extending her power. In a series of interventions in the wars between the Macedonian ruler Philip V, Antiochus III of Syria, the Ptolemies of Egypt, and Pergamon and Rhodes, the Romans in a little over a decade became the strongest political power in all of the regions remaining from the conquests of Alexander the Great. In 190 B.C., Rome defeated Antiochus of Syria at the Battle of Magnesia in Lydia. The suicide of Antony and Cleopatra in 30 B.C., brought the empire of the Ptolemies completely under Roman rule. The Roman armies and fleets in the conquest of the eastern Mediterranean posed as the liberators of Greece and the saviors of Hellenistic culture. In the western Mediterranean, after the defeat of Carthage, Roman culture became dominant. In the east, however, the Greek culture and language prevailed.

Rome, then, spread a culture which was a mixture of previous traditions. The Classical heritage of Greece was very strong and was increased after the Roman acquisition of the Hellenistic cities and territories. But Roman culture had from the first exhibited a decided Greek character. Hellenic, as well as Hellenistic, Grecian elements were a major ingredient in Roman achievement. Even the Etruscans from whom the Romans derived so much had been affected by Greek architecture and other cultural accomplishments in the Aegean homeland from which they came. From these sources Rome derived the Classic tradition which she carried to the rest of Europe.

Rome was also eclectic in other directions. The preceding Iron and Bronze Age peoples of Italy contributed to Roman beginnings. Even the Celts during their Italic invasion left some cultural heritage with the growing state of Rome. Roman culture borrowed and adopted from every group it encountered. For all of its polyglot beginnings, however, it was essentially a continuation of Classic Greek culture matured and changed by the Roman concept of Empire.

Cisalpine Gaul had been conquered by Rome before the Second Punic War, but had to be reconquered afterward. Here in northern Italy the Romans followed the Etruscans and continued policies which had been inaugurated by their predecessors. The conquest of Spain which Rome received as a heritage of the Punic Wars, as well as the control of the Gallic coast of the Mediterranean, paved the way for Caesar's triumphs farther north against the Celtic peoples of western Europe. The Roman legions that Caesar led against the Gauls brought the Classic culture of Rome in direct contact with the La Tène of western Europe. These two traditions, which had first come in contact when the Gauls invaded Italy, were brought together and blended. Roman invasions into Great Britain carried Classic culture there to join with the previous Iron Age cultures. Even in those areas where Roman military might did not prevail, Roman culture penetrated through trade and nonmilitary contact.

The curious paradox of Rome was in the direction of her efforts. Her real destiny lay in the west. In those regions were vast colonial areas to be developed, Gaulish peoples to be civilized, and new lands to be settled. But it was in the east that Rome attempted most of her conquests. Lured by the glitter and wealth of the Hellenistic world and beyond, Roman armies and energies were dissipated in power politics and endless commitments which were difficult to sustain.

Rome, like so many empires since her time, weakened her hold by attempting to grasp too much.

In western Europe the Classical heritage of Rome mingled with the La Tène culture in an uneven mixture. In southern regions and in Spain where Romanization was strongest, the fusion was complete. In northwestern Europe, and notably in those Germanic regions where the Roman legions had not conquered, the Roman culture penetrated more slowly and the La Tène tradition lingered. However, even in those troubled times when the political power of Rome was shrinking in western Europe, Classical culture with its architecture, laws, weapons, decoration, coinage, and even the Christian religion was becoming a part of European life.

The union of La Tène Europe with Roman culture formed the basis for Western Civilization. In the subsequent centuries of chaos following the collapse of Roman political power in the West in A.D. 476, these cultural ingredients, which had been so long developing, merged into one. The rise of the Merovingian monarchs was an example of this blend of barbaric Europe with the Classic culture of Rome. The Slavic invasion of Europe in the ninth and tenth centuries of the Christian era added new elements and did much to shape the map of Europe as we know it today. But Western Civilization, the pattern which was carried from Europe to North and South America, was the logical climax of a long series of events in Europe. Western Civilization had actually begun in the Palaeolithic period of Europe. Through the millenniums and centuries which followed, European prehistory had become European history. Western Civilization was a combination of both.

Suggested List
of Supplementary Reading

Aberg, N. *Bronzezeitliche und fruheisenzeitliche Chronologie.* 8 vols. Stockholm, 1930–35.

Academia Portuguesa da Historia. Anais, Vol. IV, Lisbon, 1941.

Banner, J. *Das Tisza-Maros-Körös-Gebiet.* Szeged, 1942.

Bittel, K. *Prähistorische Forschungen in Kleinasien.* Istanbul, 1934.

Böhm, Jaroslav. *Kronika Objeveného Věku.* Praha, 1941.

Broholm, H. C. *Danmarks Bronzealder.* 8 vols. Copenhagen, 1944–49.

Burkitt, M. C. *Prehistory.* Cambridge, 1925.

Buttler, W. *Der donauländische und westische kulturkreis der jüngeren Steinzeit.* Berlin, 1938.

Childe, V. G. *The Most Ancient East.* London, 1928.

———. *The Danube in Prehistory.* Oxford, 1929.

———. *New Light on the Most Ancient East.* London, 1935.

———. *The Prehistory of Scotland.* London, 1935.

————. *Prehistoric Communities of the British Isles.* Edinburgh, 1949.

————. *The Dawn of European Civilization.* London, 1950.

————. *Prehistoric Migrations.* Oslo, 1950.

Clark, Grahame. *The Mesolithic Settlement of Northern Europe.* Cambridge, Eng., 1936.

Cole, Sonia. *The Prehistory of East Africa.* London, 1954.

Coon, C. S. *The Races of Europe.* New York, 1939.

Darwin, Charles R. *Origin of Species.* 5th ed. New York, 1909.

Dechelette, J. *Manuel d'archéologie préhistorique, celtique et gallo-romaine.* 4 vols. Paris, 1908–14.

Emmons, William H., George A. Thiel, Clinton R. Stauffer, and Ira S. Allison. *Geology, Principles and Processes.* 4th ed. New York, 1955.

Evans, Arthur. *The Palace of Minos at Knossos.* 6 vols. London, 1921–28.

Garrod, D. A. E. *The Upper Palaeolithic Age in Britain.* Oxford, 1926.

Hall, H. R. *The Civilization of Greece in the Bronze Age.* London, 1928.

Hawkes, C. F. C. *The Prehistoric Foundations of Europe.* London, 1940.

Hawkes, Jacquetta and Christopher. *Prehistoric Britain.* London, 1949.

Kencken, H. O'N. *The Archaeology of Cornwall and Scilly.* London, 1932.

Heurtley, W. A. *Prehistoric Macedonia.* Cambridge, Eng., 1939.

Holste. *Die Bronzezeit in nordmainischen Hessen Vorgeschichtliche Forschungen, 12.* Berlin, 1939.

Hooton, E. A. *Why Men Behave Like Apes and Vice Versa.* Princeton, 1940.

Hubert, Henre. *Rise of the Celts.* New York, 1934.

Keith, Arthur. *The Antiquity of Man.* 2nd ed. London, 1925.

Kersten, K. *Sur älteren nordischen Bronzezeit.* Neumünster, 1936.

Kimmig, W. *Die Urnenfelderkultur in Baden.* (R.G.F. 14.) Berlin, 1940.

Kossinna, Gustav. *Die deutsche Vorgeschichte, eine hervorragend nationale Wissenschaft.* 3rd ed. Würzburg, 1921.

Kutzien, I. *The Körös Culture, (Dissertationes Pannonicae,* Vol. II, No. 23). Budapest, 1944.

Leakey, L.S.B. *The Stone Age Cultures of Kenya Colony.* Cambridge, Eng., 1931.

———. *Adams' Ancestors.* 4th ed. New York, 1953.

Le Gros Clark, W. E. *History of the Primates.* Chicago, 1957.

MacCurdy, George C. *The Coming of Man.* New York, 1935.

Mahr, A. *Das Vorgeshcichtliche Hallstatt.* Vienna, 1925.

Menghlin, O. *Weltgeschichte der Steinzeit.* Vienna, 1931.

Montelius, O. *"Die Chronologie der ältesten Bronzezeit in Nord-Deutschland und Skandenavien,"* from Archiv für Anthropologie, Vol. XXV–XXVI, 1899–1900.

Myres, J. L. *Who Were the Greeks.* Berkeley, 1938.

Obermaier, H. *Fossil Man in Spain.* New Haven, 1925.

Peake, H. *The Bronze Age and the Celtic World.* London, 1922.

Pendlebury, A. *The Archaeology of Crete.* London, 1939.

Penck, A., and E. Brüchner. *Die Alpen in Eiszeitalten.* Bds. I–III. Leipsig, 1909.

Pericot, L. *La Cueva del Parpalló.* Madrid, 1942.

Píč. *Čechy předhistorické.* Prague, 1899.

Randall-MacIver, D. *Villanovans and Early Etruscans.* Oxford, 1924.

Rust, A. *Das altsteinzeitliche Renntierjägerlager Meiendorf.* Neumünster, 1937.

———. *Die alt-aund mittelsteinzeitlichen Funde von Stellmoor.* Neumünster, 1943.

Schaeffer, C. F. A. *Stratigraphie comparée de l'Asie occidentale.* Oxford, 1948.

Schranil, J. *Vorgeschichte Böhmens und Mährens.* Berlin, 1928.

Stocky, Algin. *Bohème à l'âge de la pierre.* Prague, 1924.

———. *La Bohème prèhistorique.* Praha, 1929.

Szombathy, J. *Prähistorische Flachgräber bei Gemeinlebarn in Niederösterreich (Römisch-Germanische Forschungen 3).* Berlin, 1929.

Vassits, M. M. *Preistorijskaya Vinča.* 2 vols. Belgrade, 1932–36.

Wace and Thompson. *Prehistoric Thessaly.* Cambridge, Eng., 1912.

Index

Prehistoric Man in Europe

The freedom and simplicity of prehistoric art has suggested a format of the same character. The text is set on the Linotype in 11-point Granjon with 2 points of leading between the lines. In the chapter openings and on the title page, hand-set Alternate Gothic has been used to further the emphasis on simplicity. The decorative drawings on the title page and at chapter openings were derived from pre-historic cave paintings and stone carvings.

NORMAN : UNIVERSITY OF OKLAHOMA PRESS